FABRICATING THE ABSOLUTE FAKE

Fabricating the Absolute Fake

America in Contemporary Pop Culture

Jaap Kooijman

AMSTERDAM UNIVERSITY PRESS

Cover photo: 'Ice Cream Parlor', 2004 © Erwin Olaf
Cover: Neon, design and communications, Sabina Mannel, Amsterdam
Lay-out: Prografici, Goes

ISBN 9789053564929
E-ISBN 9789048506125
NUR 757

Table of Contents

Acknowledgments   7

Introduction
Fabricating the Absolute Fake   9

Chapter one
We Are the World: 21
America's Dominance in Global Pop Culture

Chapter two
The Oprahification of 9/11:   41
America as Imagined Community

Chapter three
The Desert of the Real: 67
America as Hyperreality

Chapter four
Americans We Never Were: 93
Dutch Pop Culture as Karaoke Americanism

Chapter five
The Dutch Dream: 119
Americanization, Pop Culture, and National Identity

Conclusion
Let's Make Things Better   141

Notes   147

Bibliography   163

Index   171

Acknowledgments

In his stand-up comedy show *Delirious* (HBO, 1983), Eddie Murphy does an amazing imitation of Stevie Wonder giving his acceptance speech after winning a Grammy Award. Stevie just cannot "shut the f*ck up" and is still saying "I want to thank…" when the credits of the televised Grammy Awards show are rolling. As a Dutch teenager, back in 1983, I loved Eddie Murphy and Stevie Wonder, not yet realizing that these American entertainers (and many others) helped to make "America" an integral part of my own culture. Now twenty-five years later, as I write these acknowledgments, the image of Eddie Murphy "doing Stevie at the Grammy's" keeps popping up in my mind.

I want to thank the students who participated in the courses that I have taught on this subject. Since 2001, I teach the MA courses *America in Global Media Culture* and *Images of America* at the Media & Culture Department of the University of Amsterdam. In 2003, I taught the graduate course *America in Media Abroad* at the Cinema Studies Department of New York University. In 2006, I taught the MA course *American Pop Culture as Hyperreality* at the American Studies Department of the University of Amsterdam. Discussing the subject with the students has been invaluable for the writing of this book.

I want to thank the organizers and the fellows of the two sessions of the Salzburg Seminar in American Studies that I attended: *The Politics of American Popular Culture: Here, There, and Everywhere* (October 2002) and *American Culture in the U.S. and Abroad* (September 2005). I want to thank Marty Gecek, Tilly de Groot, and the American Embassy in the Hague, the Netherlands, for making my participation possible. I want to thank Linda Berg-Cross, Jude Davies, Bart Eeckhout, Milena Katsarska, Carol Smith, and Reinhold Wagnleitner for continuing our discussions at other occasions, including the conferences of the European Association for American Studies.

I want to thank Kate Delaney and Ruud Janssens for commenting on parts of the manuscript that were published before in different form: "Bombs Bursting in Air: The Gulf War, 9/11, and the Super Bowl Performances of 'The Star-Spangled Banner' by Whitney Houston and Mariah Carey," in *Post-Cold War Europe, Post-Cold War America* (Amsterdam: VU University Press, 2004), edited by Ruud Janssens and Rob Kroes, and "Let's Make Things Better: Hyper-Americanness in Dutch Pop Culture," in *Over (T)here: Transatlantic Essays in Honor of Rob Kroes* (Amsterdam, VU University Press, 2005), edited by Kate Delaney and Ruud Janssens.

I want to thank my colleagues at the Amsterdam School for Cultural Analysis, the Media & Culture Department, and the American Studies Department of the University of Amsterdam for the inspiring intellectual environment. I want to thank Eloe Kingma for helping me to make research projects possible. I want to thank the members of *The 9/11 Effect* research group of the Amsterdam School for Cultural Analysis and the Institute for Culture and History, and in particular my fellow initiators Marieke de Goede, Joyce Goggin, and Margriet Schavemaker. I want to thank Joke Hermes, Jeroen de Kloet, Tarja Laine, Ruth Oldenziel, Maarten Reesink, Marja Roholl, and Jan Teurlings for commenting on parts of the manuscript. I want to thank Sudeep Dasgupta and Wanda Strauven for their feedback at crucial moments. I want to thank José van Dijck, Richard Dyer, Rob Kroes, Giselinde Kuipers, Anna McCarthy, and the anonymous reviewers for reading the entire manuscript.

I want to thank Thomas Elsaesser for letting me imitate his concept of karaoke Americanism and Chris Keulemans for letting me appropriate his concept of "the American I never was." I want to thank Erwin Olaf and his team for granting me permission to use the "Ice Cream Parlor" photograph on the book's cover. I want to thank Jeroen Sondervan, Christine Waslander, and the staff of Amsterdam University Press for turning the manuscript into a book. I want to thank Anniek Meinders for initiating this book project.

I want to thank some of my friends who actively kept me from writing, either in Amsterdam, Berlin, New York, or Minneapolis: Christopher Clark, Rob van Duijn, José Freire, Daniel Gerdes and Tesseltje de Lange, Richard Gonlag, Esther van der Hoeven, Theresa Kimm, Kenneth McRooy, Laura Minderhoud, Timon Moll, Donato Montanari, Francine Parling and John Stueland, Gus Reuchlin and Katinka Schreuder, Nelly Voorhuis and Sara van der Heide, my fellow players of the Amsterdam Tigers basketball team, and my fellow deejays of the Re-Disco-Very crew. I want to thank my (extended) family: my parents Aat Kooijman and Sonja Langeveld, my sister Annelies Kooijman, and my best friends Laura Copier and Maarten Vervaat.

I want to thank Stevie, Michael, Diana, Tina, Bruce, Ray, and all the other stars of USA for Africa for introducing me to "America" – and Eddie Murphy for making fun of them.

Jaap Kooijman
Amsterdam, June 2008

Fabricating the Absolute Fake

In 2006, Hasted Hunt Gallery in New York City hosted the exhibition *Rain* (2004), a series of six photographs by the Dutch photographer Erwin Olaf. Ken Johnson, art critic of *The New York Times*, described the photographs as "mysterious and touching," suggesting that the pictures present "scenes that Norman Rockwell's mordantly depressed cousin might have painted." Yet, Johnson singled out Olaf's photograph of a young Boy Scout with his dog in a 1950s ice cream parlor (which is also featured on the cover of this book) as an example in which "psychological resonance is sacrificed for the cheaper rewards of satiric faux-Rockwellism," adding that, if the photographer "intends a social or political commentary on American culture, it is unclear what he is trying to say."[1] In several interviews, Erwin Olaf has explained that he made the *Rain* series in response to the terrorist attacks of September 11, 2001. With his photographs, Olaf wants to return to an innocent pre-9/11 America, thereby making a political statement recognizing the importance of America as a symbol of the freedom of expression.[2] That the Dutch photographer chose to evoke the style of Norman Rockwell is fitting, as the painter is best known for his nostalgic and romanticized pictures of American everyday life, many of them published as covers of *The Saturday Evening Post*, and often has been recognized as "the most popular American artist of the twentieth century."[3] Moreover, Rockwell's depictions of President Franklin D. Roosevelt's Four Freedoms in 1943, including the freedom of expression, have become iconic representations of American idealism.

What strikes me in the ice cream parlor photograph is not only the return to an innocent America, but also its artificiality or fakeness, which Ken Johnson aptly identified as "faux-Rockwellism," although, unlike Johnson, I would not call it "satiric" but rather a form of pastiche.[4] Erwin Olaf "borrows" from Norman Rockwell by photographing in the same realist style as Rockwell's paint-

9

ings, bordering on kitsch, including the use of almost artificial pastel coloring, thereby mimicking the painter's trademark depiction of an idealistic America as well as bringing its artificiality to the foreground. By identifying the photograph's fakeness, I am not making a negative value judgment, but instead I recognize how Olaf successfully taps into the "artificial" character of American commercial pop culture, based on clichéd genre conventions, imitation, and continuously recycled images which tend to be viewed, particularly by Europeans, as signs of fakeness.[5] Identifying the fakeness of American commercial pop culture is not an act of dismissal but rather the recognition of one of its most attractive and seductive characteristics. This is also why I chose the title *Fabricating the Absolute Fake*, which is a quote from Umberto Eco who wrote that "the American imagination demands the real thing and, to attain it, must fabricate the absolute fake."[6] In Eco's definition, the absolute fake is a form of hyperreality in which a cultural artifact is perceived as an improved copy, more "real" than its original. Yet, whereas Eco only discusses American pop culture made in the USA as forms of hyperreality, I will also include non-American (and particularly Dutch) pop-cultural artifacts as absolute fakes, such as the photograph by Olaf, as they are often inspired by American pop culture. Such a perspective enables me to analyze specific cases of Americanization as forms of cultural appropriation, without reducing them to mere imitations of the American original.

The "America" that is depicted in the photographs by Erwin Olaf and other pop-cultural artifacts is not a representation of the nation-state USA but of an imagined America. Born in the Netherlands in 1959, Olaf never physically experienced the America of Norman Rockwell's era. Instead, he "returns" to an America that is based on the mass-mediated images of Hollywood cinema, television programs, advertisements, and pop music. The same can be said for me (born in the Netherlands in 1967), as I too grew up in a culture in which American pop culture is omnipresent through media. Such an imagined America is the topic of this book, which includes misconceptions of what "America is really like," as the globally mediated American pop culture presents an image of America that often leaves out the diversity of cultures in the USA. Moreover, my reading of America is undoubtedly a very subjective one, with the danger of "lump[ing] together 'non-Americans,' as if ... everyone outside the USA ... share[s] some common condition," or of assuming that "the perspective from western Europe can comfortably stand for the many different experiences of Americanization around the globe."[7] Instead of presenting one definite reading of how America is depicted in contemporary pop culture, *Fabricating the Absolute Fake* shows possible ways in which "America" can be interpreted, thereby developing effective tools to analyze pop-cultural

FABRICATING THE ABSOLUTE FAKE

artifacts as specific examples of cultural appropriation within a broader context of Americanization and globalization.

AMERICANIZATION AND GLOBALIZATION

Traditionally, the Americanization of European cultures has been perceived in two seemingly contradictory ways.[8] On the one hand, Americanization has been equated with American cultural imperialism. In this way, European consumers are seen as passive victims of a globally mediated American mass culture that threatens local and national cultures. On the other hand, Americanization has been equated with an act of liberation. Throughout the twentieth century, American popular culture (ranging from jazz and rock 'n' roll to Hollywood and hip-hop) has been appropriated by subcultures, often youth subcultures, which use American popular culture as a liberating form of expression. Rather than denouncing American popular culture as empty and shallow, youth subcultures welcomed the freshness which its emptiness and shallowness embodied. As Rob Kroes explains, "It was always a matter of younger generations rebelling against the entrenched cultural order and turning values upside down, embracing American forms of culture not for what they lacked but for what they offered in terms of vitality and energy."[9] As such, Europeans are seen as active consumers who appropriate American popular culture and its connotations to give shape to their rebellion within their own national cultures.

This distinction between passive cultural imperialism and active cultural appropriation follows the distinction between mass culture and popular culture – the first consisting of the mass-produced artifacts of the culture industry, a term coined by Max Horkheimer and Theodor Adorno, that keep consumers passively and uncritically entertained, the second consisting of the very same artifacts but then perceived as the "lowbrow" culture of the common people, in opposition to the "highbrow" culture of the elites, that functions as a potential source of social and political empowerment. Recognizing that American mass popular culture can work in both ways, and often does so simultaneously, I prefer to use the term American lightweight pop culture. I use "lightweight" instead of "lowbrow" not only to avoid the rather unproductive "highbrow" versus "lowbrow" distinction, but also to emphasize that its accessible character makes American pop culture so widely attractive. Lightweight pop culture tends to be so effective because its content is "light" (as opposed to "heavy" meaning "serious") and thus is easily taken for granted. Moreover, its lightness is meant to entertain, and, as Richard Dyer argues, entertainment should be taken seriously on its own merits: "The task is to identify the ideological im-

FABRICATING THE ABSOLUTE FAKE   11

plications – good or bad – of entertainment qualities themselves, rather than seeking to uncover hidden ideological meanings behind and separable from the façade of entertainment."[10] Instead of presenting farfetched interpretations of pop-cultural artifacts, ascribing more meaning to them than they actually contain or produce, I analyze the ideological implications of these pop-cultural artifacts within the larger context of an imagined America. I use "pop" rather than "popular" culture to emphasize that its cultural artifacts are commercially mass-produced and mass-mediated, intended to make a profit (in contrast to popular culture, which also includes "underground" subcultures and folklore), as well as to make an association with the Warhol-esque pop aesthetic – pop art's use of the language of advertising and the continuous recycling of commercial images.

The passive cultural imperialism versus active cultural appropriation divide also runs parallel to the distinction made in the globalization debate between George Ritzer's concept of "grobalization," resulting in global homogeneity, and Roland Robertson's concept of "glocalization," resulting in global heterogeneity.[11] Ritzer argues that the American-style capitalist expansion of multinationals has turned the world into one global consumer market, in which the very same products are being consumed in very similar surroundings around the globe – thus passive consumption and global homogeneity. Robertson, on the contrary, argues that these global consumer products are not consumed passively, but instead are being actively appropriated and translated into local contexts and idioms, leading to hybrid forms that may have been inspired by American global mass culture, but that also reflect the experiences of local cultures – thus active consumption and global heterogeneity. Again seemingly contradictory, these two different perspectives do not exclude but reinforce each other. The strength of global yet American-style capitalism is its ability to incorporate diversity within mass production and mass consumption, and to do so in forms that are widely attractive to a broad range of consumers around the world. Through media such as film and television, in the language and style of mass advertising, a global pop culture is formed that is not so much intended to produce a mini-version of American pop culture, but rather tries, as Stuart Hall states, "to recognize and absorb those [local] differences within the larger, overarching framework of what is essentially an American conception of the world."[12]

In this way, Americanization can include both passive and active consumption of American pop culture, enabling the two perspectives that the receiving culture either tends to become passively and gradually more American, or rather actively appropriates American pop culture, translating the American influx into a local or national context. In addition to these two perspectives

FABRICATING THE ABSOLUTE FAKE

on Americanization, there is a third option: the omnipresence of American pop culture that is neither an explicit and direct result of passive American cultural imperialism nor a liberating subcultural act of appropriation. Writing about possible responses to the importation of "foreign films" (without defining these as Hollywood or American), Andrew Higson recognizes three different results: first, "an anxious concern about the effects of cultural imperialism, a concern that the local culture will be infected, even destroyed by the foreign invader," second, "the introduction of exotic elements may well have a liberating or democratizing effect on the local culture, expanding the cultural repertoire," and third, "the foreign commodity will not be treated as exotic by the local audience, but will be interpreted according to an 'indigenous' frame of reference; that is, it will be metaphorically translated into a local idiom."[13] In the latter case, the foreignness of the imported culture is taken for granted or is no longer recognized. Higson's description fits the perception of Americanization as an act of active (yet not necessarily liberating) appropriation in which the local or national culture is not being Americanized, but the American influx becomes localized or nationalized; or when Rob Kroes talks about the Netherlands, Americanization is actually Dutchification.[14] However convincing this perspective on Americanization may be, it continues to make a rigid distinction between what is "foreign" (read American) and what is "local" or "national" (read Dutch). The real challenge in the study of Americanization is to find a way to recognize the active appropriation of American pop culture without falling back on essentialist notions of what is American and, in the case of the Netherlands, what is Dutch. Rather than a foreign commodity, American pop culture has become an intrinsic part of global pop culture, a continuous presence that often is no longer experienced as completely foreign.

That Andrew Higson does not refer explicitly to Hollywood and American pop culture is rather surprising, at least when applied to a western European country such as the Netherlands, as the "foreign commodities" that are subjected to these three different responses tend to be either American or perceived as being originally American. Even if a pop-cultural artifact has not actually been produced in the USA, it can still be recognized as being American. For example, the reality television programs *Expedition Robinson* (also known as *Survivor*) and *Big Brother*, both of which became major commercial successes internationally, originally came from, respectively, Sweden and the Netherlands. However, as far as I can tell, there is nowhere in the world where either of these shows are considered to be a Swedish or Dutch "invasion" of local pop culture; instead, if perceived as a foreign commodity at all, these programs are seen as being American. In these examples, the line between Americanization and globalization has become blurred, suggesting that the language of American pop culture – both the literal use of American English as well as audiovisual language in the form of Hollywood and American television genre conventions – functions as a global lingua franca.[15]

Moreover, American pop culture produced in the USA is not a fixed entity, but is itself subject to processes that often tend to be perceived internationally as forms of Americanization. As the McDonaldization thesis of George Ritzer shows, the process of the rationalization of pop-cultural consumption (eating fast food at McDonald's and Burger King, vacationing at Disney World, going to the movies at multiplexes, shopping at mega-malls, drinking coffee at Starbucks) is not only altering – or threatening, as Ritzer convincingly argues – non-American local cultures, but American local cultures as well.[16] A similar point has been made about Disneyfication or Disneyization, which Alan Bryman defines as "the process by which *the principles* of the Disney theme parks are coming to dominate more and more sectors of American society as well as the rest of the world."[17] In other words, not only non-Americans but Americans as well are subjected to processes of globalization, McDonaldization, and Disneyfication, which are not synonymous to Americanization, but do share many of its characteristics and are often recognized as such. Although not the same, these processes are interrelated and tend to reinforce each other.

Finally, processes of Americanization and globalization encompass more than merely the worldwide consumption of American pop-cultural products, as they also include the production of "American" pop culture outside of the USA. When the "foreign commodity" is no longer recognized as "foreign" but has been appropriated and translated into local or national contexts (yet still can be associated with "America"), then the question if something "American" is actually produced in the USA loses its relevance. The production of "American" pop culture outside of the USA (or more specifically, as far as this study is concerned, in the Netherlands) reveals important problems of definition. If the distinction between what is experienced as American or as local has become blurred, how can one recognize specific pop-cultural artifacts within explicit national or local contexts as examples of Americanization? Moreover, such identifications may differ among different cultural groups within the local society or among different generations (in the Netherlands blue jeans tend to be perceived by older generations as a sign of "America," whereas to younger generations such a connotation no longer seems to hold). In other words, whether or not a specific pop-cultural artifact is an example of Americanization is in the eye of the beholder, often based on subjective associations which cannot be "objectively proven" without falling back upon essentialist notions of what constitutes Americanness. Rather than making definite yet unproductive claims about which elements of a national or local pop culture are Americanized, I will analyze pop-cultural artifacts produced both within the USA and outside (in the Netherlands) that I assume can be perceived as examples of Americanization, to show how such a perspective opens up ways to explore how forms of Americanization can work.

ANALYZING THE OBJECT WITHIN A BOMBARDMENT OF SIGNS

Fabricating the Absolute Fake is made up of two parts, each consisting of text-based close readings of specific case studies. Each chapter takes one specific case study and theoretical concept as its starting point, and subsequently makes a connection to other case studies through association. Part one examines American pop-cultural artifacts that are produced in the USA but that are globally mediated, including in the Netherlands. The first chapter discusses the pop song and music video "We Are the World" (1985) by USA for Africa as an example of Americanization and globalization, specifically focusing on the global dominance of American pop culture through the language of advertising. In the second chapter, I use Benedict Anderson's concept of imagined community to make a distinction between the nation-state USA and an imagined America that became most explicitly visible on American television after the terrorist attacks of September 11, 2001. I discuss specific episodes of television programs that commented on 9/11 immediately after the attacks, based on three case studies: the daily talk show *The Oprah Winfrey Show* and two drama series, *The West Wing* and *Ally McBeal*. The third chapter connects the "America" of post-9/11 television to the depiction of "America" in connection to the first and the second Gulf Wars by both television and Hollywood cinema. Based on the concepts of myth by Roland Barthes and hyperreality by Jean Baudrillard, I analyze four televised performances of the American national anthem at the annual Super Bowl by, respectively, Whitney Houston in 1991, Mariah Carey in 2002, the Dixie Chicks in 2003, and Beyoncé Knowles in 2004. Subsequently, two of the few Hollywood films explicitly dealing with the first Gulf War are analyzed: *Three Kings* (David O. Russell, 1999) and *Jarhead* (Sam Mendes, 2005). Together, these three chapters show how an imagined America can be recognized, an America which remains intertwined with the nation-state USA yet which does enable the separation of American idealism from the actual politics of the USA. In addition, although these pop songs, television shows, and Hollywood movies are made in the USA, they are also mediated around the world, thereby helping to shape the way non-Americans view "America."

Part two of *Fabricating the Absolute Fake* examines pop-cultural artifacts that are produced and (in most cases) only consumed in the Netherlands, and which clearly have been inspired by American pop culture. Building on Umberto Eco's notion of the absolute fake as hyperreality, I analyze these pop-cultural artifacts as examples of hyper-Americanness to identify their imitative character, being copies of the American original. However, to avoid limiting the discussion to the question whether or not the Dutch copies are successful imitations, I use two additional concepts. From the multi-media project by Chris Keulemans, I borrow the term "the American I never was" to specify the ambiguous position of those living outside of the geographical borders of the nation-state USA yet within a culture in which American pop culture is omnipresent.[18] I apply the concept of karaoke Americanism, coined by Thomas Elsaesser, to perceive Dutch pop-cultural artifacts not merely as imitations of the American original, but as cases of active cultural appropriation, or, citing Elsaesser, "that doubly coded space of identity as overlap and deferral, as compliment and camouflage."[19] In chapter four, I apply these two concepts to four different case studies of Dutch celebrities who all can be perceived as "Americans they never were" performing karaoke Americanism, although each in a different way: singer Lee Towers, celebrity couple Adam Curry and Patricia Paay, former soap actress Katja Schuurman, and rapper Ali B. In chapter five, I explore how Dutch pop culture can function within an explicitly political context. Similar to the way American pop culture has commented on the first and second Gulf Wars and 9/11, Dutch pop culture, often inspired by the American example, has commented on 9/11 and the assassinations of the controversial politician Pim Fortuyn in 2002 and filmmaker Theo van Gogh in 2004. In this final chapter, I analyze pop songs and music videos by Dutch pop singers and rappers, ranging from tributes to Pim Fortuyn to rap songs about Dutch multicultural society, the special "Dutch Dream" issue of the glossy magazine *LINDA*, and Dutch hit movies like *Shouf Shouf Habibi!* (2004, Albert ter Heerdt), which all use the genre conventions of American pop culture to comment on the post-9/11 political debate about national identity and multiculturalism. My choice to focus exclusively on contemporary Dutch pop culture does not imply that the Netherlands is significantly different from other countries in its appropriation of American pop culture (although comparative studies undoubtedly will find cultural differences). Instead, the focus on Dutch pop culture is based on my own subject position as "the American I never was," a Dutchman who has grown up in a culture that is permeated with American pop culture, using the Netherlands as just one specific example that can make a contribution to theories of Americanization.

At first glance, it may seem that the case studies have been chosen quite arbitrarily. Pop culture covers a wide range of different cultural artifacts, and picking one case study over the other appears to be a random act. But the choice not to strictly define a body of study objects is made deliberately. Pop culture consists of, to use Jean Baudrillard's words, a bombardment of signs, which continuously refer to each other.[20] By picking these case studies seemingly at random, I mimic the way pop culture works: finding the intertextual connections between different pop-cultural artifacts through random association. Obviously, in practice, the choice of case studies has been far less arbitrary. All case studies are connected to the notion of an imagined America and all are commercial pop-cultural artifacts that implicitly or explicitly comment on political realities, such as the first and second Gulf Wars and 9/11 in the American examples and the assassinations of Pim Fortuyn and Theo van Gogh in the Dutch examples. The advantage of such an approach is that the pop-cultural artifact is analyzed in a manner similar to how it is used, namely as an object to be consumed in an intertextual relation with other pop-cultural artifacts, nothing more and nothing less. Moreover, citing Mieke Bal, the focus on the object and its intertextuality "enrich both interpretation and theory," allowing "theory [to] change from a rigid master discourse into a live cultural object in its own right."[21] The disadvantage, however, is that the analysis of the pop-cultural artifact, like the object itself, tends to remain literally on the surface, whereby its historical and economic contexts are easily ignored. Its superficiality (here meaning not going beyond the surface rather than a value judgment) makes the study of pop culture ambiguous, as one tends to underestimate its ideological implications because one takes the objects for granted – after all, they are "only entertainment" – or instead overestimate the ideological implications by reading more into the objects than the realm of entertainment really allows for.[22]

To grasp the superficiality of both American pop culture and its imitative counterparts in other countries, the theoretical concept of hyperreality as defined by Umberto Eco and Jean Baudrillard proves helpful – although the two European philosophers each provide different definitions. Both Eco and Baudrillard have identified American pop culture as a form of hyperreality while traveling through the USA, yet whereas Eco defines the hyperreality of America as consisting of artificial copies of authentic originals (hence the absolute fake), Baudrillard sees America as the ultimate simulacrum, no longer an artificial copy of an authentic original but an endless chain of copies referring to each other.[23] The question whether or not Eco and Baudrillard are correct in identifying America as being a form of hyperreality is in itself irrelevant. However, the perspective of hyperreality opens up ways to analyze an imagined America, both within as well as beyond the geographical borders of the nation-state USA, and particularly the ways in which such an imagined America is globally mediated and emulated. Moreover, the two European philosophers and their charismatic theories have themselves become part of American pop culture, which was recognized in the obituary for Jean Baudrillard on the Pop-Matters website. The celebrity status of Baudrillard has resulted in the perception that "his theory [is] more pop – more spectacle than substance," thereby forgetting that Baudrillard indeed made pop matter: "If this 'real' of popular culture has become the real of the everyday American, then mining the shiny and salacious surfaces of American media becomes more fascinating and eerily relevant."[24]

In addition to hyperreality as defined by Eco and Baudrillard, *Fabricating the Absolute Fake* builds on important studies of pop culture, Americanization, and the relation between Hollywood and Europe. As mentioned before, Richard Dyer's *Only Entertainment* shows the significance of recognizing the relevance of pop culture based on its own merits, thereby neither taking it for granted as sheer entertainment nor overemphasizing its political impact. In *If You Seen One, You've Seen the Mall*, Rob Kroes convincingly challenges the cultural imperialism thesis by arguing that Americanization should be perceived as a form of active cultural appropriation, showing that in the Netherlands the influx of American pop culture did not make the Dutch more American, but that "American models had been Dutchified," a line of argument that has been taken up by Richard Pells in his book *Not Like Us*, on "how Europeans have loved, hated, and transformed American culture."[25] Yet, these studies predominantly focus on the European reception of American pop culture, whereas *Fabricating the Absolute Fake* also analyzes "American" pop culture actually produced in the Netherlands. The book also builds on *European Cinema: Face to Face with Hollywood* by Thomas Elsaesser, who effectively goes beyond the conventional binary oppositions that mark the America-Europe divide, showing that the seemingly antagonistic oppositions between Hollywood and European cinemas do not contradict but complement each other. Moreover, Elsaesser challenges the oft-made claim that Hollywood presents a universal rather than an explicitly American conception of values such as freedom and democracy by recognizing Hollywood as "an engine of global hegemony."[26] With *Fabricating the Absolute Fake*, I expand Elsaesser's argument beyond cinema into the broader realm of the globally mediated American pop culture.

CONCLUSION: THE UNBEARABLE LIGHTNESS OF POP CULTURE

When analyzing commercial pop culture, one almost automatically comes to be perceived as being an exponent of the phenomenon that is being studied. In

2004, I was invited to speak at a symposium on how the Dutch media reported on the then-current American presidential elections. In my talk, I suggested that the media representation of the candidates George W. Bush and John Kerry could be compared to the television talent show *American Idol*, as there are great similarities in the way the candidates are being judged on their televised media performances. Like the *American Idol* contestants, the presidential candidates are continuously tested to see whether or not they succeed in presenting the illusion of being their "authentic" selves, reminiscent of Umberto Eco's words that to "speak of things that one wants to connote as real, these things must seem real," resulting in the absolute fake.[27] I was not claiming that these two media events are the same. Obviously, the winner of the American presidential elections has a far more serious impact on the world's political realities than America's next pop idol. Nevertheless, showing the way these two events use similar media strategies helps to understand how pop culture has become intertwined with our everyday experience of the political. At the end of the day, the host of the symposium publicly thanked me for providing the entertainment, adding that my presentation gave the audience some breathing room, a welcome interruption of the dense and serious discussion of the American political system. Certainly well-intended, the compliment reveals how easily we continue to take the ideological implications of pop culture for granted as being "only entertainment."

I received a similar response to my essay about the performances of the American national anthem at the annual Super Bowl by Whitney Houston in 1991 and Mariah Carey in 2002, which I interpreted as supporting the American war effort during the first Gulf War and the War on Terror, respectively.[28] Published in the edited collection *Post-Cold War Europe, Post-Cold War America*, the essay fits the book's overall pessimistic view on the unilateralist foreign policy of the USA since 9/11. Yet in his review of the book in the academic journal *American Studies International*, Bernard Mergen comes to a quite different conclusion: "Whether the highly stylized rituals of the Super Bowl really reveal anything about the construction of American national identity remains, of course, an open question, but Kooijman's essay brings a welcome lightness to an otherwise grim topic."[29] Again, analyzing pop culture is equated with its object, judged to be just as light. From the journalistic end of the spectrum, however, came an opposite opinion. Commenting on my essay on karaoke Americanism, written for the Dutch weekly magazine *De Groene Amsterdammer* as a short prepublication of *Fabricating the Absolute Fake*, journalist Paul Arnoldussen called the essay "exceptionally pretentious," suggesting that the lightweight character of the discussed pop culture was taken way too seriously.[30] Doomed to be either too lightweight or exceptionally pretentious, the academic analysis of pop culture turns out to just as ambiguous as pop culture itself. *Fabricating the Absolute Fake* acknowledges such ambiguity as an essential characteristic of pop culture, and of American pop culture in particular. To grasp the global dominance of American pop culture and the process of Americanization, pop culture needs to be analyzed in all its "light-weightiness," thereby recognizing both its seductive manipulation as well as the significance of its triviality.

Chapter One

We Are the World:

America's Dominance in Global Pop Culture

Of all the American pop-cultural products that are being consumed around the world, ranging from Hollywood films and Coca-Cola to television soap operas and hip-hop, the 1985 pop song "We Are the World" by USA for Africa is one of the most blatant examples of America's dominance in global pop culture. A relatively simple charity pop song recorded by a group of American stars named the United Support of Artists (USA) can make such abstract notions as Americanization and globalization concrete. "There are people dying," sings Stevie Wonder, without a doubt genuinely concerned about the starving Ethiopians in Africa. However, the American stars are there to provide relief with optimism and good cheer. "We Are the World" is not merely a charity pop record to raise western awareness of the Ethiopian famine and to collect money for aid, but is most of all a showcase of American superstars who function as ideological ambassadors of American values such as freedom and democracy within a free market economy, using a language that is strikingly similar to the rhetoric of Pepsi and Coca-Cola commercials. In this way, "We Are the World" can be perceived as part of "an engine of global hegemony," presenting these American national values of democracy, freedom, and open exchange of goods and services as universal.[1]

The complexities of Americanization and globalization obviously cannot be covered completely by merely focusing on a singular pop song, notably one that was recorded and released more than twenty years ago. Nevertheless, "We Are the World" does show how processes of Americanization and globalization work through pop culture, in this case wrapping a potentially provocative message about dying people in Africa in sheer pleasure. I clearly remember my personal experience of enjoying the song as a teenager, back in 1985. Although I was not particularly thrilled by the music (as a pop song, "We Are the World" seems rather contrived and tepid, easily reduced to elevator music), I was enthralled by the combined star power of all those great American pop stars coming together to sing a song and save the world. The music video added to this pleasure, showing the stars performing together in the recording studio so unselfishly, all patiently waiting their turn to sing their lines. My teenage experience is similar to the one of Greil Marcus's daughter, who, at that time, explained to her father how "We Are the World" gave her and her teenage friends so much pleasure: "The music washes over you and makes you feel good – and it's a game too, trying to identify each singer then checking against the video."[2] The metaphor of American pop culture as a wave that "washes over you and makes you feel good" is an oft-used one, not only applied to pop music like "We Are the World," but also to the escapist quality of Hollywood cinema and television, to the childlike innocence as embodied by Disney, and to the refreshing taste of Coca-Cola.

As a product of the global pop music industry with its multinational forms of distribution and communication technologies, "We Are the World" fits within a discourse of globalization that emphasizes homogeneity and universalism. In the assumed free global market, borders are disappearing and identities become hybrid, as "we" are all consumers buying the same products. Yet, in addition to its universal and global character, "We Are the World" is also part of an image of "America" which is broadcast around the world. I will discuss "We Are the World" as an example of Americanization and globalization, without suggesting that my analysis demonstrates the only possible way in which these processes can work. Instead, I want to show, by a subjective reading of one specific case study, how the combination of pleasure, pop stardom, and the commercial rhetoric of mass advertising ends up promoting an American conception of the world, thereby presenting the values of democracy, individual freedom, and choice through consumerism as seemingly universal and global ones.

The World as One Great Big American Family

Produced by Quincy Jones and written by pop stars Michael Jackson and Lionel Richie, "We Are the World" is the American follow-up to the British Band Aid charity hit single "Do They Know It's Christmas? (Feed the World)," released in December 1984 to raise money to fight the famine in Ethiopia. On January 28, 1985, right after the taping of the annual American Music Awards, a wide range of American pop stars, including Stevie Wonder, Bruce Springsteen, Tina Turner, Cyndi Lauper, Bob Dylan, Willie Nelson, Billy Joel, Diana Ross, and Ray Charles, joined Jackson and Richie at the Los Angeles A&M Recording

Studios to spread a semi-religious message of human universalism. "We are all a part of God's great big family," sings Turner, followed by Joel who adds, "and the truth, you know, love is all we need." With the exception of Wonder's line about people dying, there is no explicit reference to the political reality of African famine and poverty, let alone to its causes or possible solutions. Also, no images of the African famine are included in the music video, only the smiling faces of the American pop stars recording their message in the studio, singing about the promise of a better future, as "we" are all God's children sharing one world as a family.

Band Aid's "Do They Know It's Christmas?" differs from USA for Africa's "We Are the World" in two significant ways. First, in its lyrics, written by Band Aid's initiator Bob Geldof (music by Midge Ure, produced by Trevor Horn), "Do They Know It's Christmas?" makes a strong distinction between "us" celebrating Christmas in "our world of plenty," while "they" in "a world outside your window" are starving, suggesting that "we" should be grateful that the African tragedy is happening to "them" rather than to "us." As a result, the lyrics seem to invite a cynical interpretation, particularly when U2's Bono cries out "well tonight, thank God it's them instead of you," followed by Paul Young's call to raise "our" glasses for "everyone," including for "them, underneath that burning sun." In this way, the message of "Do They Know It's Christmas?" seems more realistic – aware of the geopolitical reality that divides the world in rich and poor sections – than USA for Africa's one world human universalism. Although the seriousness of Band Aid's message is undermined by the music video, which shows the white male singers and musicians frolicking around in the recording studio, the difference between the two songs remains telling: Band Aid's almost cynical recognition of the discrepancy between "us" and "them," thereby emphasizing global inequality, versus USA for Africa's rather naïve celebration of "we" as part of one world, propagating the notion that "we" are all the same.

Second, although women and non-white men are featured in the chorus, all solos of "Do They Know It's Christmas?" are sung by white men: Paul Young, Boy George, Wham!'s George Michael, Duran Duran's Simon Le Bon, Sting, Spandau Ballet's Tony Hadley, and U2's Bono. The women, consisting of the white girl group Bananarama and the black (American) singer Jody Watley, and the men of color, consisting of three members of the black (American) band Kool & the Gang, do not appear until more than halfway through the song, which is emphasized by the music video, showing their arrival at the studio right after the white men have finished recording their solos. USA for Africa, on the contrary, is a true celebration of American multiculturalism. Old and young, male and female, black and white, all are included with their specific musical genres, ranging from soul, country, and gospel, to folk, pop, and rock. "We Are the World" combines these different genres quite nicely by pairing off African-American rocker Tina Turner with white piano player Billy Joel, white folksinger Paul Simon with white country star Kenny Rogers, white working-class hero Bruce Springsteen with African-American Motown star Stevie Wonder, and African-American soul singer Dionne Warwick with white country legend Willie Nelson. USA for Africa fits the conventional multicultural image of "America" as a mirror of the world, where people of all nations come together as one to pursue their common American Dream. That this group of diverse yet united artists is named the United Support of Artists is telling, as the name obviously refers to the nation-state USA.

To overemphasize the differences between Band Aid's "Do They Know It's Christmas?" and USA for Africa's "We Are the World" is tempting, as it reinforces conventional distinctions between Europe and America, including, in this case, European art/authorship versus American entertainment and European realism versus American optimism. The seemingly unrehearsed recording of the Band Aid music video gives the impression that the British white male pop singers just happened to show up in the studio to help out their buddy Bob Geldof with his initiative to "do something good" for Africa. The USA for Africa music video, on the contrary, is a slick and professional Hollywood production, recorded at the center of American entertainment and featuring America's greatest pop stars. This distinction is also reflected by the lyrics of the pop songs. As stated above, "Do They Know It's Christmas?" is a rather bleak and cynical depiction of the geopolitical state of affairs that, according to the promotional media coverage during the single's initial release, was Bob Geldof's (arguably simple yet genuine) personal view of the situation. In stark contrast to Band Aid's message, "We Are the World" is an optimistic fantasy of a multicultural world that promises a happy ending to an African tragedy, which is emphasized by the fact that USA for Africa is the product of a collective effort, uniting a group of multiethnic artists, rather than the project of one white male rock singer.

Yet ultimately, the similarities between Band Aid's "Do They Know It's Christmas?" and USA for Africa's "We Are the World" are far more striking than the differences. Both pop songs use well-known pop stars to present a melodic and rather plain message about famine and poverty in Africa in an attempt to raise awareness and money. Both songs make explicit references to God, which, particularly in the case of "Do They Know It's Christmas?," are clearly based on Christianity. Most importantly, both singles are consumer products, turning the act of giving to charity into another form of consumption. The Band Aid and USA for Africa music videos, both solely consisting of pop star images, function as commercials to sell the charity singles, using the surplus value of celebrity (perhaps even more than the musical talent of the pop stars) to attract a wide global audience. Recognizing not only the differences but also the similarities is significant for two reasons. First, as Thomas Elsaesser argues, the distinction between Europe and America in global pop production is used to maintain the status quo and keep the non-western world out of the equation. Writing about the distinction between Hollywood and European cinema, Elsaesser states, "this usually binary relation of buried antagonisms and resentment actually functions not only as a two-way-traffic, but acts as an asymmetrical dynamic of exchange, whose purpose it is to stabilize the system by making both sides benefit from each other, paradoxically by making-believe that their regular and ritual stand-offs are based on incompatible antagonisms."[3] Applied to the global music industry that produced Band Aid and USA for Africa, this means that only looking at the distinctions between the European and the American charity single tends to mystify the way the two singles are interrelated as part of the same music industry. Second, rather than being opposites, "We Are the World" can be seen as a commercially improved version of "Do They Know It's Christmas?," better equipped to reach a worldwide audience. Although both charity singles became global hit songs, the slick and professional production, its optimistic and cheerful message of human universalism, and the presence of American superstars, made USA for Africa's "We Are the World" the generic archetype, setting the standard for other charity singles to follow.

After the success of Band Aid and USA for Africa, artists from different countries around the world recorded their own charity singles to raise money for Ethiopia, including, to name just a few, the Canadian Northern Lights with "Tears Are Not Enough," the German Band für Ethiopia with "Nackt Im Wind" ("Naked in the Wind"), the Belgian "Leven Zonder Honger" ("Life without Hunger"), the French Chanteurs Sans Frontières with "Ethiopie," the Finnish Apua! Orkersteri with "Maksamme Velkaa" ("We Are Paying the Debt"), the Dutch "Samen" ("Together"), the Yugoslavian Yu Rock Misija with "Za Milion Godina" ("For a Million Years"), the Australian Australia Too with "The Garden," and the Latin American Hermanos with "Cantaré Cantarás" ("I Will Sing, You Will Sing"). While there are national and regional variations between these different songs, with language being the most obvious one, their generic similarity reveals a global homogeneity, suggesting that the audiovisual conventions of Band Aid and USA for Africa have become dominant in this new global pop genre. As Simon Frith notes, these multinational charity singles share a "global pop sound," consisting of "an unobtrusive but determined rock beat, soul-inflected sincere vocals, and a balladic chorus line to pluck the heart strings."[4] The dominance of USA for Africa (and, to a lesser extent, Band Aid) is thus partially based on its being the global generic archetype that is being imitated on national and regional levels, resulting in both global homogeneity (the songs and music videos all sound and look the same) and global heterogeneity (all songs and music videos contain specific national and regional characteristics).[5] However, these global-sounding charity singles, national and regional variations on USA for Africa, do not reach beyond their geographical boundaries, because, in addition to language barriers, their appeal is predominantly based on the use of local rather than global pop stars. "We Are the World" (and, again to a lesser extent, "Do They Know It's Christmas?"), on the contrary, can reach a worldwide audience, suggesting that USA for Africa has become dominant on a global level not only by providing a generic example as a lingua franca, but also by effectively transcending its national boundaries, using its global pop stars to present a universal message.

THE POP STAR MYTH AND THE AMERICAN DREAM

As argued before, the strength of USA for Africa's "We Are the World" is based on its combined star power, presenting an image of American multiculturalism by featuring multiethnic pop stars ranging from music legends such as Ray Charles and Bob Dylan to (at that time) young pop singers such as James Ingram and Huey Lewis. However, two American stars stand out, both vocally on the record as well as visually in the music video: Michael Jackson and Bruce Springsteen. In 1985, Jackson and Springsteen were both at the commercial and popular peak of their singing careers. Michael Jackson's *Thriller*, released in December 1982, had just become the bestselling album of all time, whereas the music videos of the album's hit singles, "Billie Jean," "Beat It," and "Thriller," broke the racial barrier of the then-newly established MTV music television channel.[6] In addition, his 1983 performance of the moonwalk on American national television, broadcast worldwide, skyrocketed Jackson into global mega-stardom.[7] Not yet tainted by the controversies that destroyed his career in later years (as will be discussed in chapter three), Michael Jackson became the living example that, by the 1980s, African-Americans could also make their American Dream come true. Around the same time, in June 1984, Bruce Springsteen released his bestselling album *Born in the USA*, featuring seven hit singles, including "Dancing in the Dark," "Born in the USA," "Glory Days," and "I'm on Fire." While already a critically acclaimed recording artist since the mid-1970s, the commercial success of *Born in the USA* turned Springsteen into a global rock star. His image, music, and popularity fit the renewed investment in white American working-class masculinity, that, in the early 1980s, became embodied by, among others, President Ronald Reagan, Arnold Schwarzenegger, and Rambo, the latter being the Hollywood action hero played by Sylvester Stallone.[8] In significantly different ways, the star images of Michael Jackson and Bruce Springsteen both present an image of America, which came together in the USA for Africa charity single and music video. However, before analyzing the way in which these two star images embody an imagined America, I first will discuss how stars can be analyzed as star texts.

Since the publication of Richard Dyer's *Stars* (1979) and *Heavenly Bodies* (1986), the study of stars has become an essential part of film, television, and media studies.[9] As Dyer and others have shown, stars function in various and sometimes contradictory ways. Stars are the products of the culture industry, a marketing tool to sell films, television shows, pop songs, and, in extension, soft drinks, fashion, and other consumer products to a large market. The star image, however, is constructed by both its industrial production as well as its reception and consumption. The construction of the star image can be read as a star text, containing meanings that are not only produced by the actual performances on screen, record, and stage, but also by promotional material, interviews, critical reception, gossip about their private lives in the tabloid press, and fan cultures, including fanzines and websites. As a commodity of production and consumption, the star image contains a wide range of meanings, which can include conflicting values and fantasies. Stars are constructed as being both ordinary, enabling fans to identity with them, and extraordinary, enabling fans to admire them. Although stars are the products of the culture industry (as the reality television program *Pop Idol* or *American Idol*, known in the Netherlands as *Idols*, makes perfectly clear), they need to have an intrinsic individual talent – a star is born, not made – or at least maintain the suggestion that they are naturally talented. The notion that stars used to be ordinary individuals, preferably from a less-privileged social background, with an extraordinary talent just waiting to be discovered, is defined by Richard Dyer as the star myth, one which can be read back in countless star biographies, ranging from Marilyn Monroe and Elvis Presley to Michael Jackson and Madonna. Dyer explicitly connects this star myth to the American Dream, another myth of meritocracy which is based on the belief that individual success is attainable for anyone, regardless of social background or constraints, as long as one is talented and works hard to achieve his or her goal.[10]

With its exclusive focus on pop stars, most of them successful examples of the American Dream, USA for Africa's "We Are the World" evokes the rhetoric of the star myth, thereby implying that its message of human universalism is based on active individual agency rather than a passive subjection to social and political circumstances. "There's a choice we're making," as the stars exclaim, suggesting that even a collective effort is essentially an individual choice. While the presence of American pop stars assured that the charity pop single would reach a wide and global audience, effectively using the stars as marketing tool, their presence also signified individualism and self-reliance, presenting an American interpretation of meritocracy as a universal value. This double function of American stardom is made clear by the opening of the "We Are the World" music video, consisting of an animated globe showing the USA, followed by the signatures of the featured celebrities. These signatures not only convey the capital value of pop stardom (signatures of stars are valuable commodities in their own right), but also stress the individual commitment of each pop star. In this way, the pop stars become ambassadors of American ideology, representing with their star image a globally mediated example of the American star myth. This does not mean, however, that there is no room for ambiguity. Particularly the star images of Michael Jackson and Bruce Springsteen show that the representation of America and its values can be contradictory, yet reaffirming at the same time.

As the most successful pop artist of that time and as co-composer of "We Are the World," Michael Jackson already stood out among his fellow stars. Both the song and the music video, however, reinforce his special position. While Lionel Richie, his co-composer, sings the opening line, Jackson is the first to sing the song's chorus – by himself. Throughout the music video, all stars who sing solo lines are filmed in close-up, the camera moving horizontally from the face of one pop star to another. When Michael Jackson sings his lines, however, the camera's horizontal movement is temporarily interrupted, as Jackson is introduced by a tilt shot, with the camera moving vertically from the bottom (a close-up of his feet) to the top (a close-up of his face), similar to the conventional way in which the protagonists of classic Hollywood westerns are introduced. As the camera moves over Jackson's body, the trademark elements of his star image are highlighted: his Bass Weejun shoes and the white sequined socks, the matching single white sequined glove, the black and golden jacket, and his carefully made-up face. Almost reduced to an iconic figure, Michael Jackson can easily be recognized as the greatest pop star. "People will know it's me as soon as they see the socks," he allegedly exclaimed. "Try taking footage of Bruce Springsteen's socks and see if anyone knows who they belong to."[11] As the behind-the-scenes documentary reveals, both the vocals as well as the visuals of Michael Jackson's segment were recorded separately, a fact which reinforces his special position within USA for Africa.[12] Right after Jackson's introduction, the camera returns to its horizontal movement with a close-up of Diana Ross, who sings two solo lines before being joined by Jackson. Singing together "it's true, we'll make a better day, just you and me," Jackson and Ross appear in split screen, emphasizing the similarities in both their vocals and facial features.

That "We Are the World" explicitly connects Michael Jackson to Diana Ross is not a coincidence. Back in 1969, as part of the marketing strategy of their record label Motown, Ross was announced to be the one who had discovered the young Michael Jackson and his brothers, the Jackson 5. The special connection between Jackson and Ross continued to develop, as they were joined in the public's mind through the myth that Jackson "really" wanted to become Diana Ross, allegedly altering his face by cosmetic surgery to make himself look more like her.[13] As lead singer of the popular girl group the Supremes in the 1960s and glamorous solo pop star in the 1970s, Diana Ross became an American success story by making a crossover into white American mainstream culture and thereby defying the racial barriers that kept African-American artists from broad popular acceptance.[14] As several scholars have pointed out, Michael Jackson took Ross's crossover strategy a step further by not just making a crossover into white mainstream culture, but by becoming the greatest American pop star of his times, showing that, in spite of racial boundaries, an African-American man could become a major American mainstream pop star.[15] During the mid-1980s, the powerful image of Michael Jackson and Diana Ross together was synonymous with black achievement. "Diana and Michael: They are the undisputed king and queen of entertainment," announced the African-American magazine *Ebony* in November 1983, proudly featuring a picture of the two stars on its cover.[16]

The second USA for Africa singer that stands out is American rock star Bruce Springsteen. While Jackson is the first to sing the song's chorus as solo, Springsteen is the second. Producer Quincy Jones had asked Springsteen to sing his solo as if he was "a cheerleader of the chorus," notes David Breskin, who, as reporter of *Life* magazine, attended the recording session. "Springsteen sticks his sheet music in his back jeans pocket. His voice is rough, pained, reduced to the essence – perfect for this part."[17] Breskin's description – "rough, pained, reduced to the essence" – fits the oft-made comment that Bruce Springsteen adds a rock sensibility to "We Are the World," thereby providing a sense of authenticity often associated with rock music to the alleged artificiality of pop. Following the bubbly vocals of Al Jarreau, Springsteen literally breaks into the song, both vocally and visually, by stepping into the frame from the background, singing "we are the world, we are the children" with a raspy voice, his head tilted backwards, and his eyes closed. Once the high-pitched pop vocals of Kenny Loggins take over, the rock moment has passed, only to return again at nearly the end of the song. For almost a minute of the song's seven minutes, Springsteen's solo recording of the chorus is pasted together with Stevie Wonder's, resulting in a duet, with their voices alternating and echoing each other's lines. The clear distinction between the raspy rock voice of Springsteen and Wonder's soulful vocals is repeated in the visual, as they are presented in split screen. While the split screen of Michael Jackson and Diana Ross emphasizes the similarities between the two singers, the split screen of Bruce Springsteen and Stevie Wonder places Springsteen's white rock in juxtaposition to Wonder's black soul. Moreover, the face of Springsteen is presented in extreme close-up, filling the left side of the screen with whiteness, thereby suggesting that Springsteen not only represents the rock sensibility, but also white American culture in general. As a result, the rigid distinction between whiteness and blackness seems to symbolize the united effort of USA for Africa, showing that white and black can work together to achieve a common goal.

Here the difference between the star images of Michael Jackson and Bruce Springsteen comes to the foreground. In the academic literature, Jackson tends to be perceived as a performer who challenges the boundaries of race, gender, and sexuality.[18] Kobena Mercer, for example, argues that "neither child nor adult, nor clearly either black or white, and with an androgynous image that is neither masculine nor feminine, Jackson's star image is a 'social hieroglyph' as Marx said of the commodity form, which demands, yet defies, decoding."[19] The star image of Bruce Springsteen, on the contrary, tends to be perceived as reinforcing the boundaries of race, gender, and sexuality. Comparing him to Ronald Reagan and Rambo, Bryan Garman suggests that "the apparently working-class Springsteen was for many Americans a white hard-body hero whose masculinity confirmed the values of patriarchy and patriotism, the work ethic and rugged individualism, and who clearly demarcated the boundaries between men and women, black and white, heterosexual and homosexual."[20] Applied to "We Are the World," Jackson embodies the crossover American Dream, presenting America as a land where individuals can make their dreams come true regardless of their social, racial, or gendered backgrounds, while Springsteen embodies a nostalgic America, based on traditional values, or, as Gareth Palmer has stated, "Springsteen's America is a conservative land where the [white male] heroes struggle to understand the limits of their horizons but can see little beyond them."[21]

Whether Bruce Springsteen's embodiment of a nostalgic America should be perceived as a sign of patriotism or instead as a criticism of the nation-state USA has been a topic of heated debate among fans, rock journalists, and academic scholars, revealing the ambiguity of his star image. Particularly his album *Born in the USA* could be misinterpreted as a tribute to the nation-state USA. Although most lyrics of the album's songs are critical of the social, economic, and political situation in 1980s America, *Born in the USA* presents Bruce

Springsteen as a relic of Americana, using the red-white-and-blue signs of the American flag, blue jeans, baseball, and the hometown to evoke a nostalgic image of those "glory days" in small-town America. The album's promotional photographs show him posing in front of an enormous American flag (reminiscent of the famous image of General Patton), wearing the "uniform" of the white working-class male: tight-fitting blue jeans and white T-shirt, showing off his muscular biceps. The *Born in the USA* album cover features a close-up of his backside in blue jeans, with a red baseball cap nonchalantly dangling from his right back pocket. This imagery of Americana, including the American flag as backdrop, was repeated in the live performances of Springsteen's *Born in the USA* world tour of 1984-1985.[22] The album's title song, "Born in the USA," contains a similar ambiguity. While the song's verses tell the grim story of an unemployed Vietnam veteran, the chorus consists of a patriotic chant of the song's title, raising the question of how the song should be interpreted. "Was the song part of a patriotic revival or a tale of working-class betrayal? A symptom of Reagan's America or antidote to it? Protest song or national anthem?"[23] As is often the case with up-tempo rock songs, the music tends to overpower the lyrics. That many youngsters (including myself as teenager back in 1984) perceived "Born in the USA" as a celebration of America rather than a critical commentary is therefore not surprising.[24]

One year before the recording of USA for Africa's "We Are the World," the star images of both Michael Jackson and Bruce Springsteen were appropriated by the administration of President Ronald Reagan. On May 14, 1984, Jackson visited the White House to receive an award as part of the National Campaign Against Teenage Drunk Driving, which used the music of his hit song "Beat It" in one of its public service announcements. The highly publicized ceremony consisted of President Reagan honoring "one of the most talented, most popular, and most exciting superstars in the music world today," praising Jackson's "years of hard work, energy, tireless dedication, and a wealth of talent that keeps on growing," and concluding that his "success is an American dream come true."[25] That he was invited to attend a racially "neutral" occasion rather than a specific African-American cause (as is often the case with other African-American artists who are invited to the White House) shows that Michael Jackson had come to symbolize a multicultural America and that his star myth transcended racial categories. Four months later, on September 19, President Reagan referred to Bruce Springsteen at a Reagan-Bush presidential elections campaign rally in New Jersey: "America's future rests in a thousand dreams inside your hearts. It rests in the message of hope in songs of a man so many young Americans admire – New Jersey's own, Bruce Springsteen. And helping you make those dreams come true is what this job of mine is all about."[26]

Unlike Jackson, Bruce Springsteen did not appreciate the presidential endorsement and he publicly distanced himself from the Reagan administration and its conservative policy of Reaganomics. Yet, in spite of his critical stance, Springsteen's ambiguous star image could nonetheless easily be incorporated within President Reagan's patriotic rhetoric.

Although they embody different Americas, both Michael Jackson and Bruce Springsteen could be turned into symbols of the American Dream, as Reagan's speeches reveal. One can argue that Reagan's political rhetoric consists of hollow words, based on clichés such as "making your dreams come true," one which the president used on both occasions. The rhetoric works, however, because Jackson and Springsteen did make their own dreams come true by becoming superstars, thereby reinforcing the star myth and the American Dream. In that sense, the way the Reagan administration uses the star images of Jackson and Springsteen does not differ from the way USA for Africa uses them. Moreover, the shared optimism based on these myths of meritocracy, together with a shared belief in the promise of a better future, suggests that President Reagan's political rhetoric is actually quite similar to USA for Africa's message of human universalism. That such American rhetoric also befitted the language of global mass advertising will be discussed below.

THE PEPSI AND COCA-COLONIZATION OF THE WORLD

Twenty years after USA for Africa, one of its prominent singers made a startling revelation that quickly spread across the internet. "I remember most of us who were there didn't like the song, but nobody would say so," Billy Joel told *Rolling Stone* magazine. "I think Cyndi Lauper leaned over to me and said, 'It sounds like a Pepsi commercial.' And I didn't disagree."[27] Perhaps Cyndi Lauper did make such a comparison, but Joel also might have read Greil Marcus's frequently cited essay "Number One with a Bullet," originally published in *Artforum* (May 1985). In his essay, Marcus not only argues that "We Are the World" celebrates American pop celebrity instead of addressing the political reality of the African famine, but he also shows that the charity pop single, intentionally or not, is intertwined with the global marketing of American corporations. As Marcus points out, at the time "We Are the World" was being composed, its two songwriters, Michael Jackson and Lionel Richie, were both starring in their own Pepsi commercials: the one of Jackson premiered during the annual television broadcast of the Grammy Awards in 1984 and the one of Richie at the same event a year later. Coincidentally, "We Are the World" does sound like a Pepsi commercial, particularly the oft-repeated line "there's a choice we're making," which echoes the 1980s trademarked Pepsi slogan "The Choice of a New Generation." The choice that USA for Africa makes thus may not be a commitment to fight famine in Africa, but rather a preference for Pepsi over its main competitor Coca-Cola. As Marcus writes:

> As pop music, "We Are the World" says less about Ethiopia than it does about Pepsi – and the true result will likely be less that certain Ethiopian individuals will live, or anyway live a little bit longer than they otherwise would have, than that Pepsi will get the catchphrase of its advertising campaign sung for free by Ray Charles, Stevie Wonder, Bruce Spring-steen, and the rest. But that is only the short-term, subliminal way of looking at it. In the long-view, real-life way of looking at it, in terms of pop geopolitical economics, those Ethiopians who survive may end up not merely alive, but drinking Pepsi instead of Coke.[28]

Marcus's observation becomes even more poignant by the fact that initially the line was "there's a chance we're taking" instead of "there's a choice we're making." As the behind-the-scenes documentary *We Are the World: The Story Behind the Song* shows, the line was changed during the recording of the demo version. Producer Quincy Jones suggested the change: "One thing we don't want to do, especially with this group, is look like we're patting ourselves on our back. So it's really, 'There's a *choice* we're *making*.'"[29] In an ironic twist of fate, the producer's attempt to make the stars of USA for Africa appear less self-indulgent resulted in the endorsement of an American soft drink instead.

Without downplaying the significance of Marcus's observation, the focus on how "We Are the World" seems to promote Pepsi rather than Coca-Cola ignores the fact that, within a global market, both brands signify an imagined America, in uncannily similar ways. Whether "We Are the World" is a commercial for Pepsi or for Coca-Cola is actually irrelevant, as the song shares the American-dominated consumer discourse of both. In its rhetorical and emotional content, for example, USA for Africa's "We Are the World" is quite similar to the popular 1971 "Hilltop" Coca-Cola commercial. This famous commercial features a multiethnic group of smiling youngsters on an Italian hillside, lip-synching to the words of "I'd Like to Teach the World to Sing," a hit song by the New Seekers.[30] Like USA for Africa, the commercial promotes a human universalism by suggesting that the world can be taught "to sing in perfect harmony," only to be followed by "I'd like to buy the world a Coke and keep it company." Moreover, "We Are the World" and "I'd Like to Teach the World to Sing" share the American value of individualism within a free market economy, as both emphasize the importance of individual agency and also promote human universalism through the act of consumption. The only difference seems to be in the explicitness of the message. While, as Greil Marcus has shown, "We Are the World" can only implicitly suggest that Pepsi can make the world a better place, the message of the "Hilltop" Coca-Cola commercial is straightforward: "Coke is what the world wants today."

That the connection between "We Are the World" and the "Hilltop" Coca-Cola commercial is not just an arbitrary association made by myself is shown by the fact that these two pop-cultural artifacts often tend to be confused. A quick internet search produces three random yet relevant examples of the way "We Are the World" is connected to the "Hilltop" Coca-Cola commercial. First, when in 1997 Jane Fonda's husband Ted Turner, founder and former president of the Cable News Network (CNN), announced to CNN's Larry King that he was planning to donate one billion dollars to the United Nations, he motivated his decision by stating: "I love that Coca-Cola commercial where they all, the kids got on the mountaintop and sang, 'We are the World.' I like that."[31] Second, the Australian academic Paul Duncum starts his article on globalization with the statement that "Coca-Cola advertisements with young people from various nations singing 'We are the World' highlight the sense that we are now all interdependent."[32] Third, describing the global aspirations of the 2004 Olympic Games, *National Review* sports columnist Geoffrey Norman exclaimed that "We can all drink a Coca-Cola (or is it a Pepsi?) and sing 'We are the world; we are the people.'"[33] These three completely different examples not only show that USA for Africa's message of human universalism has become indistinguishable from the commercial rhetoric of American-style yet globally mediated soft-drink advertising (promoting both Pepsi and Coca-Cola), but also suggest that its American character has indeed come to be perceived as universal, shared across the globe.

"We Are the World" has been compared to Coca-Cola commercials in the academic literature as well. In her book *Primitive Art in Civilized Places*, cultural anthropologist Sally Price argues that the rhetoric of Coca-Cola and "We Are the World" expresses an intrinsically western perspective on globalization. As Price shows, Coca-Cola commercials present "a many-shaded sea of faces, all smiling, and united by their human warmth and shared appreciation of the good things in life, including Coke," which is an expression of multicultural and – seemingly – universal happiness that turns out to be remarkably similar to the "brotherly smiles" and "phenotypic diversity" of "We Are the World."[34] The act of presenting such an American-style happy multiculturalism (or "multiculturalism lite") as a universally shared global value is aptly captured by the term Coca-Colonization, a phrase which was initially coined during the 1950s French Coca-Cola debates, used to denounce the growing

FABRICATING THE ABSOLUTE FAKE

import of American consumer goods that allegedly threatened French national culture.[35] Coca-Colonization not only implies that the process of Americanization is indeed a form of cultural imperialism resulting in a homogeneous global pop culture, but also (and more importantly) that such a process is based on a paternalistic discourse which tends to reduce its global subjects to a state of childlike innocence and pleasure. We are not just the world but, as the chorus of USA for Africa tells us, also its children, who cannot help but love that refreshing taste of Coca-Cola, while saving the world by buying a cheerful pop tune performed by our favorite superstars. I deliberately define "us" – consumers of this Coca-Cola and "We Are the World" rhetoric – as its global subjects, as the not (yet) consuming Ethiopians obviously are not (yet) included within its commercial ideal of human universalism, or, as Sally Price rightfully observes, "The 'equality' accorded to non-Westerners … is not a natural reflection of human equivalence, but rather the result of Western benevolence," of which USA for Africa's "We Are the World" is a telling example.[36]

By labeling the multicultural rhetoric of Coca-Cola and "We Are the World" as an example of Coca-Colonization, I echo the perspective of Americanization as passive cultural imperialism, suggesting that American pop-cultural consumer products that are marketed as universal embodiments of American values like freedom and democracy are passively perceived and consumed as such. Yet, to stay with the example of Coca-Cola, several scholars correctly have pointed out that Coca-Cola does not contain the same symbolic value for all people around the world, but instead is actively appropriated within national and local contexts, its possible meanings changing from place to place and over time.[37] Coca-Cola often is creolized, resulting in hybrid forms, mixed both figuratively (with local myths and superstitions) and literally (with local drinks like rum or beer). Writing from a historical Cold War perspective, Richard Pells addresses the difference between the way Coca-Cola was introduced and received in western Europe, immediately after World War II, and in eastern Europe, after the collapse of communism in 1989. In many western European countries, Coca-Cola was introduced along with the American military presence, symbolizing both the seductiveness of American pop culture as well as the American cultural and economic dominance. In eastern Europe, on the contrary, Coca-Cola tended to be seen as the symbol of western capitalism and economic progress, a welcome alternative to the inefficiency of the Soviet-dominated economies.[38] Recently, the symbolic value of Coca-Cola as the emblem of the capitalist triumph over communism seems to be decreasing in some eastern European countries, or at least that is suggested by the renewed popularity of imitation Coca-Cola brands such as Polo-Cofta in Poland and Kofola in the Czech Republic, both former communist soft drinks that are now marketed as trendy nostalgia.[39] A more explicitly anti-American political challenge to Coca-Colonization has been the highly publicized introduction of the "counter-cola" soft drink Mecca-Cola in 2002, a clear case of trying to beat the enemy at his own game, as the Arabic imitation of Coca-Cola not only copies the actual soft drink, but also its global marketing strategies to promote Mecca-Cola's explicit message of anti-capitalist and pro-Palestinian resistance through the act of consumption.[40]

While the significance of the creolization and active appropriation of pop culture on national and local levels should not be underestimated, as the above examples make perfectly clear, the powerful rhetoric of American pop-cultural products such as Coca-Cola and USA for Africa's "We Are the World" on a global level should not be ignored either. The fact that Coca-Cola and similar American consumer products can (and have been) perceived differently around the world, obtaining symbolic values which its manufacturers never intended or considered, does not alter the striking resemblance in the way these products are globally marketed, heavily invested with American values and ideology. Writing about the western European perception of Coca-Cola, Richard Pells has suggested that the ideological implications of the soft drink should not be taken too seriously: "Still, the acceptance of Coca-Cola did not mean that Europeans were becoming more 'Americanized' or that they had abandoned beer and wine. Coke, after all, was a soft drink, not a foreign ideology. One could swallow it without giving up one's cultural loyalties or sense of national identity."[41]

Undoubtedly unintended, with this statement Pells reveals two reasons that can explain the rhetorical strength of Coca-Cola and, in extension, USA for Africa's "We Are the World." First, Coca-Cola effectively functions as a carrier of American values and ideology because it is "just a soft drink," like "We Are the World" is "just a charity pop song" (and Hollywood "just an entertaining movie"). I am not suggesting that these pop-cultural artifacts contain hidden ideologies or disseminate subliminal messages; quite on the contrary, both Coca-Cola and "We Are the World" show that their ideological content is rather obvious. However, that pop-cultural artifacts are being produced, marketed, and consumed as pleasurable experiences just makes it more easy to take their ideological content for granted. Second, Coca-Cola effectively functions as a carrier of American values and ideology because it is not presented as "a foreign ideology" (as Pells rightly notes), and indeed does not replace "cultural loyalties or sense[s] of national identity." Instead, and again like "We Are the World," Coca-Cola presents its "foreign" ideology as a universal one, promoting an American interpretation of values like freedom, democracy, and individual agency, all within a free market economy, as the shared values of

FABRICATING THE ABSOLUTE FAKE

global multiculturalism and human universalism. Ironically, the notion that "we" are not subjecting ourselves passively to the American values promoted by Coca-Cola, Pepsi, and "We Are the World," but instead actively appropriate these pop-cultural products, reinforces rather than undermines the global dominance of the American ideology of freedom and individual agency, as merely the suggestion that "there's a choice we're making" befits its American rhetoric.

USA FOR AMERICA

On April 23, 1985, at a ceremony honoring the American Peace Corps, President Ronald Reagan proudly announced: "Today, every few minutes on the radio, you can hear the stars of rock, soul, and country music who came together as 'USA for Africa,' singing the chorus of 'We Are the World,' America's recent number-one song hit. Every time a record is sold, more money is raised for African famine relief."[42] Reagan failed to mention that "We Are the World" also was an international bestseller, topping the pop charts in many countries outside of the USA. Three weeks earlier, on April 5, Good Friday (emphasizing the song's being a predominantly Christian act of benevolence), USA for Africa had been launched as a worldwide media event, when "We Are the World" premiered simultaneously on more than 5,000 radio stations around the globe. Reagan also failed to mention that "every few minutes on the radio" the world was subjected to an American ideology, promoting freedom, democracy, and individualism, although the American president undoubtedly supported its message, hence his reference to "We Are the World" at a ceremony honoring the American Peace Corps. In addition, by mentioning both the song's omnipresence in the media as well as its commercial success, Reagan revealed that the USA for Africa hit single is most of all a bestselling consumer product, showing that within the capitalist free market economy, even the act of charity can be marketed and sold.

Now more than twenty years after Band Aid, USA for Africa, and Live Aid (the live concert organized by Band Aid's Bob Geldof, broadcast globally on July 13, 1985), not much has changed in the geopolitical situation. Even if the profits of these events have provided some relief to the Ethiopian population back in 1985, no structural solutions have been found to fight – let alone end – famine in Africa.[43] In 2005, Bob Geldof organized Live 8, another worldwide pop concert bringing together superstars to raise western awareness of global inequality. In the meantime, "We Are the World" has become a pop classic which continues to be played on the radio and on music television. During the spring of 2006, when I was writing this chapter, I unexpectedly encountered "We Are the World" in different places around Europe, including as background music to my workout at the Gold's Gym in Berlin, at my office at the University of Amsterdam where the song (played on the radio of the construction workers outside) came blasting through the window, and at the airport of Larnaca, Cyprus, where I arrived to attend the European Association for American Studies conference. Listening to the song in these different contexts made me realize that its original message about Africa has disappeared. "We Are the World" has been reduced to a golden oldie, one of those relentlessly repeated classic pop songs that evoke feelings of nostalgia to the times when they were hits. However, its message of global multiculturalism and human universalism is still present, even though its constant repetition has made "We Are the World" even more clichéd than it was back in 1985.

That ultimately USA for Africa is not about Africa but instead celebrates "America" – both the nation-state USA as well as an imagined America – as the embodiment of multiculturalism and human universalism was made obvious on January 17, 1993, when "We Are the World" was performed as the grand finale of the American Reunion concert, in honor of the first inauguration of President Bill Clinton. Produced by USA for Africa's Quincy Jones, the concert starred Ray Charles singing "America the Beautiful," Diana Ross singing "God Bless America," Aretha Franklin singing "Someday We'll All Be Free" and "Respect," and Kathleen Battle singing "We Shall Overcome," the anthem of the civil rights movement. Performed in front of the monumental Lincoln Memorial (a site which not only symbolizes the nation-state USA, but the civil rights movement as well), the concert was a celebration of a multicultural America, as was underlined by the prominent presence of African-American singers and the choice of repertoire.[44] In the same spirit, Diana Ross subsequently led an all-star choir in the singing of "We Are the World." With only a few of the original pop stars present (including Kenny Rogers, James Ingram, and Stevie Wonder), the USA for Africa singers were joined by, among others, Debbie Gibson, Kathleen Battle, Aretha Franklin, Ashford & Simpson, and Michael Bolton. Emphasizing the song's multiculturalism, a few lines were sung in Spanish. Whereas Bruce Springsteen was conspicuously absent, Michael Jackson made a grand entrance at the same moment as in the music video, this time accompanied by a children's choir. At the end of the song, Diana Ross welcomed President Clinton and his family on stage to sing along with the stars: "We are the world, we are the children."

At first glance, the inclusion of USA for Africa's "We Are the World" in the celebration of President Bill Clinton's inauguration seems commonsensical. Being the first president of the baby boom generation, Clinton already was associated with American "youth" pop culture, an image which not only had been promoted by him playing the saxophone on *The Arsenio Hall Show*, but also by the theme song of his presidential campaign: Fleetwood Mac's "Don't Stop [Thinking about Tomorrow]." Moreover, after twelve years of Republican conservative politics, the election of the Democratic President Clinton suggested a revival of liberalism and an optimistic future – a multicultural promise reminiscent of "We Are the World" that was captured by Maya Angelou when she read her poem "On the Pulse of the Morning" at the inauguration ceremony. On second thought, however, the inclusion of USA for Africa in an official celebration of a new American president, televised worldwide, is at least problematic. Not only has Africa disappeared from the picture, but, performed within this context, "We Are the World" becomes a patriotic national anthem that promotes imperialism. Hypothetically, if sung to honor any other grand nation (China, France, Germany, Russia), celebrating its leadership by proudly exclaiming that "they" are the world, such a performance could easily be perceived as – potentially dangerous – propaganda. The fact that the song could be performed at President Clinton's inauguration without causing any major concern internationally suggests that USA for Africa's "We Are the World" indeed has come to be accepted globally as being "universal." While the song's performance at the inauguration does celebrate Americanness, its explicit nationalist character is mystified by its implicit universalism.

Conclusion: An American Conception of the World

Even after two decades, USA for Africa's "We Are the World" continues to provide an illustrative example of how Americanization can function on a global level. Rather than transforming the world into another USA, thereby replacing national, local, and regional cultures, American pop culture presents itself, using the commercial rhetoric of advertising, as being universal, while being (to cite Stuart Hall) "essentially an American conception of the world."[45] Whether the global omnipresence of American pop culture is passively consumed, actively appropriated, or even not recognized as being American at all, does not alter the way American pop culture promotes its American conception of the world as an assumed self-evident ideal of human universalism. To recognize its American character remains significant not so much to prove its Americanness, but instead to challenge its claim of being universal, as the human universalism presented by American pop-cultural artifacts such as Coca-Cola and "We Are the World" tends to depoliticize global politics by reducing social economic and political issues (like famine and poverty in Africa) to a personal matter of individual choice. As I have suggested, USA for Africa's "We Are the World" does so in three ways. First, in contrast to Band Aid's "Do They Know It's Christmas?," USA for Africa presents a happy world of global multiculturalism, in which "we" are all equal and united by diversity, rather than being divided by global inequality. Second, by its exclusive focus on American superstars, USA for Africa invests its ideal of global human universalism with the star myth and the American Dream, both based on a belief in meritocracy which promotes individual agency and self-reliance. Third, USA for Africa's message of global multiculturalism and human universalism is presented using the commercial rhetoric of mass advertising, similar to Pepsi and especially Coca-Cola commercials, thereby not only turning the act of benevolence into an act of consumption, but also suggesting that world citizenship can be reduced to global consumerism within a free market economy. Here I should emphasize that "We Are the World" does present a conception rather than a construction of the world, one which can be contested, resisted, or interpreted differently. Its power, however, rests in its being a highly entertaining, star-studded, and pleasurable pop song, which has been broadcast repeatedly around the globe and which fits within a broader American-style commercial discourse that tends to dominate in the processes of Americanization and globalization.

The double bind of Americanness and self-acclaimed universalism makes USA for Africa's "We Are the World" exemplary of the American dominance in global pop culture. American pop culture has the capacity to be produced, sold, and consumed as being universal, assumed to represent the human experience in general without being culturally specific or bound by national geography, even when, and often especially when, its Americanness is made explicit. Referring to Hollywood cinema, Thomas Elsaesser has called this capacity "an engine of global hegemony," claiming not only that Hollywood successfully presents the American conceptions of freedom, democracy, and a free market economy as universal values, but also that these values "have, until the end of the last century, been widely endorsed and aspired to by people who neither share territorial proximity with the United States nor language, faith, customs, or a common history."[46] As I have suggested with this chapter, the same can be said about American pop culture at large. USA for Africa's "We Are the World" is of course merely a small part of this engine of global hegemony, but as long as we uncritically sing along with the cheery pop tune every time it's played on the radio, eventually we may find "our" world reduced to its American commercial conception.

CHAPTER TWO:

The Oprahification of 9/11:

America as Imagined Community

On September 11 and 12, 2001, for the first time in its fifteen-year' run, *The Oprah Winfrey Show* was cancelled. The talk show resumed its daily broadcast on September 13 with an episode aptly entitled "America under Attack," which was repeated the next day. The cancellation of *Oprah!* (as the talk show is most commonly referred to) fit the state of confusion that American television found itself in right after the terrorist attacks. On the one hand, 9/11 was a television event. From the moment the first plane hit the Twin Towers, millions of viewers around the world stayed glued to their television sets to capture the latest news and to relive the moment again and again. Yet, on the other hand, the flow of American television had been interrupted, as its regular programming was replaced by nonstop commercial-free news coverage and other "appropriate" content. As Lynn Spigel has shown, American television needed just a little time to regain its balance between public service and commercial interest, quickly returning to the programming that "channeled the nation back to normalcy – or at least to the normal flows of television and commercial culture."[1] Within two weeks after 9/11, *Oprah!* too returned to normalcy, with an episode of "Oprah's Book Club" (24 September 2001) and, four days later, an episode on "What Parents Should Know about Ecstasy" (28 September 2001).

In this chapter, I will discuss how *The Oprah Winfrey Show* presented the aftermath of 9/11 and the pending war in Iraq in its episodes. In addition, I will analyze two special episodes of the drama series *The West Wing* and *Ally McBeal*, which both explicitly comment on 9/11. These television shows are significant, as they all contribute to the American public debate and present "America" as an imagined community (to use Benedict Anderson's concept). Although belonging to different genres, namely the daytime talk show and the fictional drama series, they share the quality of presenting a more personalized and dramatized account of 9/11, in contrast to the (arguably) factual accounts by the conventional news programs. While often considered "only entertainment" by many, these television shows enable viewers at home to make sense of 9/11 by making a connection to their own daily lives. In addition, the shows are watched by millions of viewers outside of the USA. *Oprah!* is broadcast daily in 132 countries around the world, making Oprah Winfrey arguably one of the most influential Americans in global media culture.[2] The popular drama series *The West Wing* and *Ally McBeal* are not only broadcast on international television, they are also commercially available, and bestsellers, on DVD in many countries. In this way, these television shows help to shape the way non-Americans view "America" as both a nation-state and an imagined community, specifically by representing how the USA deals with the tragedy of 9/11, the War on Terror, and the war in Iraq.[3]

AMERICA AS IMAGINED COMMUNITY

To make a distinction between the nation-state USA on the one hand and an imagined America on the other, Benedict Anderson's concept of imagined community proves to be helpful. Anderson defines the nation as "an imagined political community – and imagined as both inherently limited and sovereign."[4] Since the citizens of a nation cannot know each other individually, an imagined community is created through shared notions of nationhood and belonging, using different media (in Anderson's historical case study of what would become Indonesia, newspapers and novels) to construct a collective national identity. The imagined community is limited to exclude those beyond the boundaries of the nation and to distinguish one nation from others. The nation is imagined as a sovereign state to enable a shared identity among free citizens, rather than among subjects to a divine ruler. Most importantly, the nation is "imagined as a *community*, because, regardless of the actual inequality and exploitation that may prevail in each, the nation is always conceived as a deep, horizontal comradeship."[5] As a result, the collective national identity not only transcends identities based on class, race, gender, religion, and sexuality, but also conceals the inequality of power that exists between these different identities.

Thomas Elsaesser has rightfully argued that, in media studies, Anderson's concept of imagined community has been applied too easily, providing a quick answer to a set of complex and historically specific questions.[6] Anderson spoke of the creation of a future nation-state in colonial times, constructed by printed media such as newspapers and novels. In media studies, the concept of

FABRICATING THE ABSOLUTE FAKE

imagined community is most often applied to well-developed nation-states, in modern and postmodern times, focusing on film and television, which are audiovisual media that function quite differently than the printed media. To assume unquestionably that film and television construct – or maintain the construction of – the nation-state is at least problematic. As Elsaesser questions: "Do cinema and television help foster identities and feelings of belonging, or are they merely parasitic on existing values and attitudes, even undercutting them by playing with their visual and verbal representations, as suggested by postmodern pastiche?"[7] In other words, rather than constructing the nation-state, film and television are part of an audiovisual media culture which continuously appropriates and reinvents, while at the same time reinforcing and undermining, preexisting notions of belonging to a national identity. This point becomes even more pertinent when applied to the nation-state USA as an imagined community, as the mediated representations of America are recycled and reinterpreted on a global level, by both Americans as well as non-Americans. If "America" is based on allegedly universal values, as the previous chapter suggests, who actually belongs to this American imagined community? Are non-Americans part of "America" as well?

Rather than to the nation-state USA, Anderson's concept of imagined community should be applied to an America that goes beyond the geographical boundaries of the nation-state, one that is not so much constructed by, but most of all continuously reinvented through, audiovisual representations in pop culture, specifically Hollywood film and television. It is not in spite of, but because this reinvention of America is based on recycled and even clichéd representations, that the concept of imagined community becomes an effective tool to analyze these representations. These preexisting values, connotations, and images of an imagined America came explicitly to the foreground after the terrorist attacks of September 11, 2001. Not the nation-state USA but "America" was under attack, prompting, among others, Jean-Marie Colombani, editor-in-chief of the French newspaper *Le Monde*, to boldly declare that "*nous sommes tous américains*" (we are all Americans).[8] The terrorist attacks and their aftermath became marked by the term "9/11," which attained, as Dana Heller points out in her introduction to *The Selling of 9/11*, "the cultural function of a trademark, one that symbolizes a new kind of national identification – or national branding awareness."[9] However, unlike Heller suggests, the identification with "America" that came to be marked by "9/11" was actually not that new, but rather based on a rhetoric of American exceptionalism that is easily recognized, by Americans and non-Americans alike. "9/11" as trademark presents an America reduced to clichéd representations in audiovisual media culture, often referring to assumed self-evident notions and values such as Manifest Destiny and the American Dream, and also to familiar artifacts of pop culture, such as Irvin Berlin's "God Bless America" and Norman Rockwell's iconic paintings that visualize President Franklin D. Roosevelt's Four Freedoms.[10] Tellingly, Berlin's "God Bless America" was the most frequently performed song immediately after 9/11, including by both Republican and Democratic members of the American Congress who, the very next day, sang the alternative national anthem on the steps of the Capital building (televised around the world), and, on September 21, 2001, by Canadian-born singer Celine Dion as part of the star-studded *America: A Tribute to the Heroes* telethon, and, also on September 21, 2001, by African-American pop diva Diana Ross at the first Mets baseball game played in New York City since 9/11. The preference for "God Bless America" over "The Star-Spangled Banner," the official national anthem, suggests that not so much the nation-state USA but "America" was perceived to be under attack and in need of defending by rearticulating the values of freedom and democracy that "America" self-evidently embodied.

American pop culture responded to 9/11 in two distinctively different, yet related ways. On the one hand, American pop culture took on the tough patriotic stance of the "Angry American" who was going to teach those terrorists a lesson, a masculine rhetoric strongly present on the Fox News Network and arguably initiated by President George W. Bush when he described the American response to the terrorist attacks as if it were a Hollywood western, starring the USA as John Wayne: "[The terrorists] will try to hide, they will try to avoid the United States and our allies – but we're not going to let them. They run to the hills; they find holes to get in. And we will do whatever it takes to smoke them out and get them running, and we'll get them."[11] Popular country songs such as Toby Keith's "Courtesy of the Red, White, and Blue" echo Bush's cowboy rhetoric, warning the terrorists that "You'll be sorry that you messed with the US of A / 'Cause we'll put a boot in your ass / It's the American way," which prompted William Hart to note that many 9/11 country songs use "the threat of forcible sodomy as the nation's preferred method of payback."[12] That such a sexualized and gendered (not to mention homophobic) threat was expressed not only in country songs has been observed by Jasbir Puar and Amit Rai: "Posters that appeared in midtown Manhattan only days after the attacks show a turbaned caricature of [Osama] bin Laden being anally penetrated by the Empire State building. The legend beneath reads, 'The Empire Strikes Back' or 'So you like skyscrapers, huh, bitch?'"[13] The expression of a possible American military retaliation in the language of American pop culture, whether exclaimed by the president, country singers, or anonymous street posters, reveals that there remains a connection between the nation-state USA and an imagined America inspired by Hollywood and television.

On the other hand, however, American pop culture also took on an almost naïve stance of innocence, expressed by President Bush in his televised address to the American Congress: "Americans are asking, why do they hate us?"[14] This innocent stance is possible, as the "us" does not so much refer to the USA as an imperialist nation-state active in international politics, but to America as the Land of Freedom and Opportunity – thus not the nation-state USA but America as imagined community. In other words, the question that "Americans are asking" is based on a strong belief in American ideology: "[If America symbolizes individual freedom and democracy, which supposedly are universal values shared globally,] why do they hate us?" Subsequently, rather than questioning American ideology, American pop culture ended up reinforcing this ideological image of America. One significant example, also given by Lynn Spigel, is the twice-postponed broadcast of the annual Emmy Awards of November 4, 2001. Hosted by the most famous lesbian of American television, Ellen Degeneres (who quipped, "What would bug the Taliban more than seeing a gay woman in a suit surrounded by Jews?"), its opening sequence showed the iconic images of "America," including the American flag and the Statue of Liberty, with a soft female voiceover announcing: "Tonight television speaks to a global audience as we show the world images of an annual celebration. Our presence here tonight does more than honor an industry, it honors freedoms that set us apart as a nation and a people."[15] Here the double bind of Americanness and self-acclaimed universalism becomes visible. While the annual Emmy Awards is an event organized by the American television industry to promote its own programs and stars, a global audience is assumed, which is then subjected to a conception of "freedom" (not only embodied by the American iconography, but also by Ellen Degeneres as a gay woman and by the television programs honored) that is perceived as being universal yet, at the same time, exceptionally American, "set[ting] us apart as a nation and a people."

By suggesting that American pop culture celebrates an imagined America instead of the nation-state USA, I do not imply that the nation-state is completely absent. On the contrary, the nation-state USA and "America" are intertwined, as the opening sequence of the Emmy Awards made perfectly clear. An explicit distinction between the nation-state USA and an imagined America, however, does enable an understanding of the perspective that the assumed universal yet exceptionally American values of freedom and democracy remain recognized as being self-evident, regardless of the lack of freedom and democracy that may exist as a result of the political and military actions by the nation-state USA. In this way, the almost innocent belief in American ideology can maintain its strength, among both Americans and non-Americans, in spite of being challenged by such controversial politics as the Patriot Act, the War on

Terror, Guantánamo Bay, and the war in Iraq. "America was targeted for attack because we're the brightest beacon for freedom and opportunity in the world," exclaimed President George Bush in his first post-9/11 address to the nation, televised live on September 11, adding, "And no one will keep that light from shining."[16] As will be shown, these words could just as easily have been pronounced by Oprah Winfrey or by one of the characters on the 9/11 episodes of *The West Wing* and *Ally McBeal*, revealing that the rhetoric of America as imagined community reaches beyond the political realm into the globally mediated American pop culture.

9/11 ON THE OPRAH WINFREY SHOW

During the first two weeks after 9/11, almost all of the episodes of *The Oprah Winfrey Show* focused on the terrorist attacks and the way American citizens should respond to such a tragedy: "America under Attack: Where Do We Stand Now?" (17 September 2001), "How to Talk to Children about America under Attack" (18 September 2001), "Dr. Phil Helps Grieving Americans, Part 1 and 2" (19 and 25 September 2001), "Tribute to Loved Ones Lost" (20 September 2001), "Music to Heal Our Hearts," starring Sam Harris singing "You'll Never Walk Alone" (21 September 2001), "What Really Matters Now?" (26 September 2001), and "Americans Take Action" (27 September 2001). In the months that followed, *The Oprah Winfrey Show* continued to devote regular attention to 9/11 and its aftermath, specifically showing how American viewers should cope with the threat of terrorism within their daily lives, educating the American viewers about Islam within an international context, providing a forum for both experts and viewers to discuss international politics, and, most significantly, restoring the faith in an imagined America and its ideals of freedom and democracy.

In her excellent essay on American television after 9/11, Lynn Spigel has criticized the way *The Oprah Winfrey Show* tends to personalize and dramatize 9/11 as an event that needs therapeutic counseling rather than an understanding of international politics. Spigel specifically focuses on an episode which features a pregnant widow whose husband died in the September 11 attacks and who has not only lost her husband but her voice as well. According to Spigel, "the program implicitly asks viewers to identify with this woman as the moral and innocent victim of *chance*," and thus "any casual agent (or any sense that her suffering is actually the result of complex political histories) is reduced to the 'twist of fate' narrative fortunes of the daytime soap."[17] Although *The Oprah Winfrey Show* indeed depoliticizes 9/11 by turning it into an individual personal experience, thereby oversimplifying the social-political context, the talk show does emphasize personal agency, suggesting that its guests and viewers are not innocent victims of their circumstances, but are capable of changing if they choose to do so. In this specific episode, the voiceless widow is advised by *The Oprah Winfrey Show*'s regular therapist Dr. Phil (in his infamous quick fix psychology style) to take back control over her own life. Similarly, in all 9/11 episodes, the viewers are challenged to "see what you can do at home" to make sense of the terrorist attacks, thereby actively turning the political into the personal. To describe such a process, Jane Shattuc borrows from the mainstream press the term "Oprahification," which originally was used to denounce American television's sensationalism. As Shattuc explains, talk shows such as *The Oprah Winfrey Show* not only connect the private to the public sphere by including the perspectives of ordinary people in the public debate (which traditionally tends to be dominated by certified and mostly male experts), but also "translate politics into the everyday experience of the political."[18]

This process of Oprahification, a characteristic of the talk show genre in general, can be viewed as having both a positive and a negative impact on the public debate on television. Positively, Oprahification has resulted in a more open and diverse debate, enabling voices to be heard that before were often excluded, including those of women, ethnic minorities, and gays and lesbians.[19] Yet negatively, Oprahification has often resulted in oversimplification, trivialization, and sensationalism, as serious issues tend to be reduced to confessions of personal scandal and sexual lifestyle meant to entertain rather than to inform the public. Both this positive and negative side of Oprahification run parallel to the Americanization debate. The talk show, often considered to be originally an American television genre, presents characteristics that traditionally are associated with American commercial television in contrast to European public service television. In such a comparison, American television is perceived as popular entertainment, while European television is considered to be part of the bourgeois public sphere. European television, historically rooted in public broadcasting, addresses its viewers as citizens ("audience-as-public") who need to be informed to enable a public debate based on rational argumentation, resulting in political consensus. Commercial American television, on the contrary, addresses its viewers as consumers ("audience-as-market") who need to be kept entertained, thereby placing a strong emphasis on emotional argumentation and personal choice, resulting in sensationalist conflict.[20] Several scholars, including Ien Ang, Graham Murdock, and Laurie Ouellette, have rightfully argued that such a distinction is much too rigid, as there are many examples, both in the USA and in Europe, which show that the two traditions are present in the media cultures on both sides of the Atlantic. Moreover, the distinction tends to become strongly gendered, reinforcing the rationality of the public sphere as masculine and the emotionality of the private sphere as feminine. However problematic, recognizing this distinction remains significant, if only to show how it is being challenged by *The Oprah Winfrey Show*, which actually merges the two traditions.

On *The Oprah Winfrey Show*, and particularly the 9/11 episodes, Oprah Winfrey often explicitly addresses her viewers as citizens who have a right to be informed in order to decide for themselves about important political and social issues. Noteworthy, and perhaps rather surprisingly, in spite of her large global audience (which actually might outnumber her American one), Winfrey tends to identify her viewers as *American* citizens, whose undeniable rights are identified as being fundamentally American as well. In addition, *The Oprah Winfrey Show* provides ordinary Americans with a forum to discuss current affairs, not only as featured guests, but also through audience participation and discussion boards made available on the show's website. However, *The Oprah Winfrey Show* is also a heavily sponsored program, targeting its viewers as consumers constituting a large market for a wide variety of commodities to be sold, ranging from fashion, film, and pop music, to furniture, food, and literature. Products that are featured on *Oprah!* (including Oprah as a trade-marked commodity herself) often become instant bestsellers, a commercial impact which became highly visible with the success of Oprah's Book Club.[21] Moreover, the effective combination of American citizenship with consumerism is heavily invested with American ideology. Oprah Winfrey herself, as a formerly overweight African-American woman who became one of the most powerful individuals in the American media industry, embodies an American success story, whose star myth (Oprah's American Dream) is reinforced by each episode of her talk show. As Eva Illouz has shown, Oprah Winfrey uses her life biography, including her personal history of sexual abuse, poverty, racism, and being overweight, to make a connection with her audience and to help them to make the political personal.[22] In addition to using Winfrey's star myth, *The Oprah Winfrey Show* regularly employs American celebrities, who appear on the show to promote themselves and their recent products by revealing a glimpse of their personal lives, suggesting that they too are just ordinary people, encountering the same problems as the *Oprah!* viewers do.[23] This use of the star myth is not limited to the celebrities of the entertainment industry. During the presidential elections of 2000, both the Democratic candidate Al Gore and the Republican candidate George W. Bush visited *Oprah!* (respectively, 11 and 19 September 2000). Although the interviews include "serious" political topics, most attention is paid to the "person" behind the candidate. Al Gore recalled how the priorities in his life shifted drastically after his young-

FABRICATING THE ABSOLUTE FAKE

est son had been seriously injured in a car accident, whereas George Bush, in turn, discussed his ongoing battle with alcoholism, revealing that he decided to quit drinking while he was jogging. In this way, while reaffirming the mythical American Dream, *The Oprah Winfrey Show* combines citizenship with consumerism, politics with entertainment, and public issues with private affairs, all in one commercially profitable television show.

Although more severe than most of the talk show's regular topics, 9/11 does fit easily within the format of *The Oprah Winfrey Show*. Similar to the way *Oprah!* approaches other traumatic experiences, 9/11 is treated first as an issue which can be dealt with pragmatically. Practical questions are addressed, such as "How to Control Your Fears" (18 and 25 October 2001), "When Will You Fly Again?" and "Will You Fly This Holiday Season?" (12 October and 16 November 2001), "What Does High Alert Mean?" (2 November 2001), and "Living with Terrorism" (9 November 2001), the latter episode consisting of pre-taped interviews with women living in Northern Ireland and Israel. In the twice-broadcast episode "America under Attack" (13 and 14 September 2001), Dr. Phil tells the audience that "it is not a weakness to hurt and feel and cry," and that giving blood and displaying the American flag might help to cope with the pain. "We do need to give ourselves permission to grieve." The episode "How to Talk to Children about America under Attack" (18 September 2001) features First Lady Laura Bush as guest, who explains that 9/11 has made her realize that "the people we love, [and] our country" are the most important. Answering Oprah Winfrey's question if the president is still able to sleep at night, Laura Bush answers: "Yes, we're both sleeping. ... He's so proud of America. ... We've never been so unified. It strengthens him and it strengthens me when we see how people are handling it all over the country." Like Dr. Phil, Laura Bush emphasizes the therapeutic quality of loving each other and honoring America, as she suggests that, to deal with the fear and anxiety brought on by 9/11, American children can "write letters to their own firefighters and policemen in their neighborhood to thank them in honor of those that were lost." By transforming possible feelings of fear, anger, anxiety, and grief into acts of explicit American patriotism, *The Oprah Winfrey Show* translates 9/11 into a personal yet collective experience of the political, albeit with little room for political dissent.

In addition, *The Oprah Winfrey Show* provides its viewers with background information on international affairs, specifically on the history of Afghanistan and Islam, in the episodes "Is War the Only Answer?" (1 October 2001), "Islam 101" (5 October 2001), and "Inside the Taliban" (11 October 2001). Although the role of the USA as nation-state is mentioned, most notably the "billions of dollars in weapons supplied by the United States" to Afghanistan in its war with the Soviet Union, the emphasis is placed on the distinction between Muslim fundamentalism and the peaceful character of Islam. That the 9/11 terrorists do not represent the majority of Muslims, either worldwide or within the USA, is the talk show's most repeated message. In the episode "Where Do We Stand Now?" (17 September 2001), Oprah Winfrey's question "Why do they hate us?" is answered by Judith Miller, a reporter of *The New York Times* specialized in the Middle East: "I find that most Middle Easterners admire and envy America. There is only a small minority that hates us and resent us for our power and what they perceive as our arrogance." The episode "Islam 101" (5 October 2001) features portraits of two "normal and modern" American Muslim women, Manal and Noreen, who explain that their practice of Islam, including wearing the hijab veil, is an example of the American freedoms of religion and choice, rather than an example of religious oppression. "We're just leading our lives, practicing our faith, doing everything else that normal America does." Different than in the later episodes that question whether on not the USA should invade Iraq (which will be discussed further on in this chapter), there is little room for dissenting voices, as the talk show's focus is primarily on promoting unity and human universalism, suggesting that, in spite of religious and cultural differences, ultimately all people are the same. Thus, although *Oprah!* touches upon the political reality of American foreign policy, the talk show does so uncritically by presenting America as the embodiment of freedom and democracy, thereby justifying rather than questioning the dominant role the USA plays in international politics.

Again, the double bind of Americanness and self-acclaimed universalism comes to the foreground. In an essay written before (but published after) 9/11, Eva Illouz argues that *The Oprah Winfrey Show* exports an American conception of suffering around the world, one which "is individual, is located in the private sphere, has a psychic character and concerns the self." By making a distinction between "imported suffering" (images of anonymous non-western suffering as shown on the western news) and "exported suffering" (narratives of suffering by individuals as presented on the globally mediated American talk shows), Illouz suggests that "the first is a daily and perhaps by now routinized reminder of the inequality in the distribution of collective resources across the globe, [whereas] the second is more democratic in that it includes all and invites all of us [both Americans and non-Americans] to join in the community of sufferers."[24] In other words, American suffering is individualized and personalized in such a way that it becomes widely (even globally) accessible as a universal human experience. This notion is made visible by the 9/11 episodes of *The Oprah Winfrey Show*, which present 9/11 not only as a tragedy that happened specifically to the USA, but also as a collective traumatic suffering that can be shared universally, across national and cultural boundaries. The *Oprah!* episodes "Music to Heal Our Hearts" (21 September 2001), "Dr. Phil on Deciding What's Important Now" (9 October 2001), and "Photos That Define Us" (5 November 2001) use artistic expressions, such as poetry, gospel music, photography, and prayers, as inspirational sources for collective healing. Even "Martha Stewart's Comforts of Home" (8 November 2001), featuring the latest trends in home decoration, is presented as part of this 9/11 healing process, suggesting that "staying home is offering a new sense of comfort." By focusing on the belief that the love for one's family and home is a globally shared ideal, *The Oprah Winfrey Show* suggests that cultural differences can be overcome by celebrating a universal multiculturalism, thereby mystifying the social-economic realities of international politics. Moreover, these episodes fit the general way American pop culture tends to universalize explicitly American experiences, as I have discussed in the previous chapter.

The intertwinement of 9/11 with American pop culture (of which *The Oprah Winfrey Show* itself is also part) became clear when movie star John Travolta visited *Oprah!* (29 October 2001) to promote his latest film *Domestic Disturbance* (Harold Becker, 2001). After recounting his recent visit to 9/11's Ground Zero to provide moral support to the firefighters, John Travolta shares with the audience his thoughts on 9/11: "I believe in the human spirit, and I believe collectively that we are now stronger. America is the strongest country in the world. ... Terrorism is supposed to scare us and feel weak, and we're not that. We're a tough group." Pronounced by a global movie star who embodies Hollywood heroism, Travolta's statement includes both universalism ("the human spirit") and American patriotism ("America is the strongest country in the world"). In this way, similar to the Hollywood hero, John Travolta can capture a global audience with American patriotism, making "us" a collective by presenting explicit Americanness as an alleged universality.

This perspective of American exceptionalism as universal ideal is reinforced by the way *The Oprah Winfrey Show* repeats the conventional depiction of an imagined America as the Beacon of Freedom and Opportunity, which provides a safe haven for refugees coming from all around the world. The episode "Why I Came to America" (31 October 2001) features pre-taped interviews with former and recent immigrants who describe how they found "freedom" in America after they escaped from oppressive regimes, including Nazi Germany, the Cambodian Khmer Rouge, and the Taliban of Afghanistan. The "before America" segments are shown in black-and-white, with gloomy music as soundtrack. However, when the immigrants begin talking about their arrival in the USA, the screen returns to color, while the camera zooms in and the soundtrack plays upbeat music, clearly an attempt to invoke the clichéd metaphor of light triumphing over darkness. The episode's main guest is Mawi Asgedom, who, as a young child, immigrated to the USA with his family. A pre-taped video segment describes the family's "escape" from "their war-torn country of Ethiopia after spending years in a refugee camp and trekking through the brutal deserts of Africa." As Winfrey's voiceover states: "Mawi has taken full advantage of what America has to offer. … [He] received a scholarship to Harvard and was chosen by his class to give the commencement speech at graduation." Although, in the pre-taped segment, Asgedom mentions the racism and inhospitality that he and his family encountered in the USA, in the following studio interview, Winfrey exclusively focuses on him being an American success story. Asgedom confirms Winfrey's view by exclaiming: "Where else but America can someone have no money, not know the language, grow up, work hard, respect other people, and end up getting a scholarship to go to college? That's only possible in America. That's the American Dream that people have been dreaming about for years." In the thread "What kinds of opportunities does America offer that might not be found elsewhere?" on the Oprah.com message board, this claim of American exceptionalism prompted some disagreement. Canadian viewers point out that in Canada immigrants also live in a free society and that they too can make their dreams come true. One viewer, being herself an immigrant from Ethiopia living in the USA, explains that Mawi Asgedom is the exception, not the rule. Most Ethiopian immigrants work in low-paid jobs, do not have the chance to go to college (let alone Harvard), and encounter structural racism in their daily lives. Such dissenting voices, however, are not included in the talk show's broadcast, because they do not fit within *Oprah!*'s presentation of America as the Beacon of Freedom and Opportunity.

By using Mawi Asgedom's American success story, thereby emphasizing the values of meritocracy such as individual agency and self-reliance, *The Oprah Winfrey Show* not only claims that freedom is exceptionally American, but also uncritically assumes that the American conception of these values is universally shared. Subsequently, the talk show explicitly connects the American Dream to 9/11, albeit in a subtle way. One of the pre-taped interviews features Thida Mam, a refugee from Cambodia who, as Winfrey's voiceover tells us, "walked hundreds of miles to reach freedom in the United States." Freedom is often taken for granted, Thida Mam explains, except by those who do not live in freedom, adding: "After September 11, we, as Americans, need to protect [our American freedom] because there is no other America to go to." One could, of course, easily dismiss *The Oprah Winfrey Show* as another example of hollow American rhetoric, as it continuously repeats outworn clichés of America mixed with the therapeutic jargon of self-help psychology. Such a perspective, however, would ignore how *The Oprah Winfrey Show* effectively makes individual stories of the American Dream visible. Not only Oprah Winfrey herself but also her featured guests (both celebrities and ordinary Americans) again and again are presented as living examples that the American conception of meritocracy, including its values of freedom, individualism, and self-reliance, is attainable and also – allegedly – universally shared. That such a message is not limited to the talk show genre is shown by two special 9/11 episodes of the television series *The West Wing* and *Ally McBeal*, as will be discussed below.

9/11 ON THE WEST WING

While *The Oprah Winfrey Show* immediately could incorporate the September 11 attacks within its regular talk show format, fictional television programs faced the dilemma of whether or not to include 9/11 within their narratives. Particularly crime series such as *Law & Order* (NBC, 1990-present), *NYDP Blue* (ABC, 1993-2005), and *Third Watch* (NBC, 1999-2005), which are all set in New York City and feature New York police officers as main characters, could not ignore 9/11 without losing their credibility as realistic television drama. *Law & Order* waited twenty-three episodes before referring to 9/11 in its episodes "Patriot" (12:24, 22 May 2002) and "American Jihad" (13:1, 2 October 2002). *NYDP Blue* added two scenes mentioning September 11 in its first post-9/11 episode "Lie Like a Rug" (9:175, 6 November 2001), using the aftermath of 9/11 to provide an explanation for the high stress level among New York police officers. *Third Watch* responded by replacing its new season opener with a special nonfiction episode entitled "In Their Own Words" (3:45, 15 October 2001), featuring real-life New York police officers, firefighters, and paramedics telling about their experiences, and by renaming the season's first episode "September Tenth" (3:46, 22 October 2001). The subsequent episode, entitled "After Time" (3:47, 29 October 2001), takes place ten days after 9/11 and focuses on the ambiguous feelings of the New York rescue workers about their newly acquired status as heroes, while they continue to search for missing casualties in "the pile" (Ground Zero). With its next episode "The Relay" (3:48, 12 November 2001), *Third Watch* returned to normalcy, dealing with the case of a young woman's suicide.

The popular drama series *The West Wing* (NBC, 1999-2006) faced the same dilemma. Set in the White House of the fictional President Jed Bartlet (Martin Sheen), *The West Wing* has been praised for providing a realistic view on the American presidency, in spite of its romanticized dramatization.[25] The series was created by Aaron Sorkin, who before had written the romantic comedy *The American President* (Rob Reiner, 1995), starring Michael Douglas as the widowed President Andrew Shepherd who falls in love with the environmental lobbyist Sydney Wade (Annette Bening). Like President Shepherd, Jed Bartlet is a liberal Democrat of high moral standard, initially functioning as an attractive alternative to President Bill Clinton, whose morality had come to be questioned due to the Monica Lewinsky scandal. After the controversial election of President George W. Bush in 2000, *The West Wing* could be viewed as a fictional shadow administration, presenting a "what if the Democrats were in the White House" scenario. Although never referring to actual real-life events, the series features fictional yet realistic events, thus challenging the television audience to question whether or not President Bush would act the same as President Bartlet in similar circumstances, and vice versa. To sustain its political realism, *The West Wing* could not ignore the dramatic reality of 9/11 and its aftermath.

Just like *Third Watch*, the new season opener of *The West Wing*, episode "Manchester 1" (3:1, 10 October 2001), was postponed and replaced by a special 9/11 episode, entitled "Isaac and Ishmael" (3 October 2001). On *The West Wing* promotional website, NBC announced that the episode would deal "with some of the questions and issues currently facing the world in the wake of the recent terrorist attacks on the United States" and, as NBC's entertainment president Jeff Zucker suggested, even would be "helping the dialogue in this country and continuing the healing process."[26] Written by Aaron Sorkin and shot in only ten days, the episode presents a fictional security alert at the Bartlet White House. Similar to the way 9/11 interrupted the regular flow of American television, the fictional security alert does not fit the regular timeline of the series. As one of the actors explains in its opening sequence, the episode is a "storytelling aberration," breaking with the narrative of the series to address the significance of 9/11, without having to include the actual event within its storytelling. That "Isaac and Ishmael" is not a regular *The West Wing* episode but a single "play" dealing with the aftermath of 9/11 is made explicit immediately. The usual opening sequence is replaced by close-ups of the main characters, filmed against a black backdrop, who alternate in explaining the episode's special purpose. The episode is to pay tribute to "New York's finest and bravest," the actors explain, adding that its profits will be donated to New York Firefighters' 9/11 Disaster Relief Fund and the New York Police and Fire Widows' and Children's Benefit Fund. However, the actors reassure the viewers that, with the next episode, the series will return to its conventional storylines: "We're in show business. We'll get back to tending our egos in short order." Subsequently, the introduction becomes a teaser for the coming season, as the actors provide a glimpse of some of the upcoming exciting developments, ending with the revelation by Janel Moloney that her character Donna will finally get a boyfriend.

The "Isaac and Ishmael" episode consists of two separate storylines, which both implicitly refer to 9/11. The first one focuses on a group of high school students who have been selected to visit the White House. When staff member Josh Lyman (Bradley Whitford) is welcoming them in the lobby, a security guard exclaims: "Station One. Code Black. Crash." Not knowing what exactly is going on, Josh tells the students that "something's happened." At that moment, the episode is interrupted by its first commercial break, announcing the telephone numbers of the Twin Towers Fund and the American Red Cross. What actually did happen never becomes clear, yet the call for donations connects the "crash" to 9/11. After the commercial break, Josh moves the students to the White House cafeteria, where they remain the entire episode, being lectured to by the show's main characters, including President Bartlet and the First Lady, on terrorism, Muslim fundamentalism, and freedom and democracy, the latter being explicitly presented as American values. The second storyline concerns the White House employee Rakim Ali (played by Ajay Naidu, an American actor of Hindu South Asian ethnic background), who happens to have the same name as a possible suspect of terrorism. Rakim Ali is first shown sitting at the open window of his office, smoking a cigarette, when suddenly white security officers burst into the room. Ali has become a security risk, warranting an interrogation by Leo McGarry (John Spencer), the White House chief of staff. Set in a dramatically dark-lit office, McGarry grills Ali about his past and his ethnic identity, prompting Ali to question such a hostile treatment. "I don't think you understand the seriousness of what's happening right now," exclaims McGarry, to which Ali responds, "I don't think *you* do," immediately followed by another commercial break. Obviously, "what's happening right now" refers not only to the fictional interrogation, but also to 9/11 and its political aftermath, including, as Ali's response suggests, the actual practice of racial profiling whereby Arab Americans (of assumed Muslim background) automatically become suspect of being potential terrorists.

By turning the White House cafeteria into a classroom, the episode's main setting, the episode becomes a lecture on terrorism and Islam, trying to answer the question which the high school students (and, in extension, the American public) are asking: "Why does everyone want to kill us?" Not everyone does, explains Josh: "Islamic extremist is to Islam as KKK is to Christianity. … It's the Klan gone medieval and global. It couldn't have less to do with Islamic men and women of faith of whom there are millions and millions." Another White House staff member, Toby Ziegler (Richard Schiff), adds that the people in Afghanistan are also innocent victims of Muslim fundamentalism, thereby quoting the well-known e-mail by the Afghan American Tamim Ansary, which was published on the Salon.com website and featured on the

Oprah! episode "Is War the Only Answer?" (1 October 2001): "When you think of Afghanistan, think of Poland, when you think of Taliban, think of the Nazis, when you think of the citizens of Afghanistan, think of Jews in concentration camps."[27] Like the 9/11 episodes of *The Oprah Winfrey Show*, the "Isaac and Ishmael" episode emphasizes that Muslim terrorists do not represent the majority of Muslims. However, and again similar to *Oprah!*, the episode does so by celebrating the values of freedom and democracy that "America" embodies. As the White House staff members tell the students, "[America] is a plural society. That means we accept more than one idea. It offends them." At the end of the episode, Josh repeats the message: "Remember pluralism. You want to get these people? I mean, you really want to reach in and kill them where they live? Keep accepting more than one idea. It makes them absolutely crazy." Instead of opening up the debate, the pluralism argument polarizes the debate by making a rigid distinction between "us" and "them," using, as Lynn Spigel rightly points out, "historical pedagogy to solidify national unity *against* the 'enemy' rather than to encourage any real engagement with Islam, the ethics of U.S. international policy, or the consequences of the then-pending U.S. bomb strikes."[28] Thus, the lesson that the "Isaac and Ishmael" episode teaches is not one of questioning the role of the nation-state USA in international politics, but instead one of reaffirming America as an exceptional embodiment of freedom and democracy.

The second storyline works in a similar way, as the racial profiling of Rakim Ali is recognized yet never criticized. Ali makes the issue of racial profiling explicit by noting that "it is not uncommon for Arab Americans to be the first suspected when that sort of thing happens," to which Leo McGarry responds with sarcasm: "I can't imagine why. No, I'm trying to figure out why anytime there's terrorist activity, people always assume it's Arabs. I'm racking my brain." After Ali expresses his discomfort with the situation, McGarry adds: "Well, that's the price you pay." Not until the end of the episode, after information of the Secret Service indicates that Rakim Ali is not a possible terrorist, McGarry finishes his sentence by stating, "That's the price you pay for having the same physical features as criminals." One could perceive McCarry's statement as a criticism of racial profiling, suggesting that wrong has been done to Ali. It was this storyline that prompted *Washington Post* television critic Tom Shales to state that "even in this moment of pain, trauma, heartbreak, destruction, assault and victimization, Hollywood liberals can still find some excuse to make America look guilty."[29] Yet, by using the excuse that Rakim Ali has "the same physical features as criminals" the episode does not criticize the practice of racial profiling in itself, but rather suggests that, with the threat of terrorism, racial profiling is a necessary evil of which Ali, regretfully yet understandably, has become a victim.

In their essay "Monster, Terrorist, Fag," Jasbir Puar and Amit Rai argue that the American media turn American viewers into docile patriots by presenting the "enemy" as a dangerous Other, by reinforcing racial and ethnic stereotypes, and by connecting the "terrorist" to conventional imagery of the monster and sexual deviancy. Their analysis of the "Isaac and Ishmael" episode confirms their overall argument, particularly in how the settings of the two storylines form a "double-framed reality," thereby placing the normative American in juxtaposition to the deviant Other:

> On the one side, brightly lit and close to the heart (invoking the home and the family), is the classroom, a racially and gender-plural space. ... A space where the president as Father enters and says that what we need right now are heroes; where the first lady as Mother tells the precocious and sometimes troublesome youngsters a kind of bedtime story of two once and future brothers, Isaac (the Jews) and Ishmael (the Arabs). ... On the other side of the frame, a dimly lit room, an enclosed, monitored space, managed entirely by white men, at the center of which is a racially and sexually ambiguous figure, a subject who at one and the same time is a possible monster and a person to be corrected. ... A subject whose greatest moment, it seems, comes when, after being terrorized at gunpoint, racially profiled, and insulted, he goes back to work.[30]

The White House cafeteria, functioning as a classroom, is the place where American values of freedom and democracy are taught, presented as a space of enlightenment where pluralism (allegedly or perhaps ideally) provides room for different opinions and political positions. The office where the interrogation takes place, on the contrary, is a dark space where the foreign and deviant threat is isolated, monitored, controlled, and thus excluded from the pluralism promoted in the "enlightened" classroom. In this way, the opposition between "us" and "them" (American versus foreign), between normative and deviant, is reinforced, again expressed through the imagery of lightness triumphing over darkness, that clichéd metaphor so common in American 9/11 rhetoric.

Puar and Rai's notion of the docile patriot is similar to Lauren Berlant's concept of "infantile citizenship," which Lynn Spigel uses to critique the repeated "Why does everyone wants to kill us?" question posed on *The West Wing* (and other American television shows, including *Oprah!*), allowing "adult viewers comfortably to confront the horrors and guilt of war by donning the cloak of childhood innocence."[31] Although the "Isaac and Ishmael" episode of *The West Wing* seemingly attempts to present a nuanced perspective on terrorism, Muslim fundamentalism, and the practice of racial profiling, the show ends up presenting freedom and democracy as exceptionally American values, with little room to reflect critically upon the nation-state USA and its role in international politics. As a result, the viewers of *The West Wing* are invited to accept these American values as being self-evident and uncontested, quite similar to the viewers of *The Oprah Winfrey Show*. As my analysis of its 9/11 episode will show, the same can be said about the viewers of the *Ally McBeal* drama series.

9/11 ON ALLY MCBEAL

The drama series *Ally McBeal* (Fox, 1997-2002) stars Calista Flockhart as the thirty-something post-feminist lawyer whose main goal consists of combining her successful professional career with a fulfilling love life. On first sight, the series appears to be groundbreaking, addressing controversial social-political issues such as sexual harassment, interracial dating, and euthanasia. The series also uses unconventional special effects, cameo appearances by celebrities, and innovative adaptation of pop music to create an atmosphere that embodies the ambiguities of postmodern life. Yet, in the end, *Ally McBeal* proves to be rather conventional, often reducing politics to personal dilemmas and individual life-style choices. Moreover, as several scholars have suggested, *Ally McBeal* tends to reconfirm rather than challenge existing gender and racial stereotypes.[32] It is therefore not surprising that the image of America as presented in its 9/11 episode ends up being quite conventional as well.

Initially entitled "Christmas: Now More Than Ever" (5:7, 10 December 2001), the *Ally McBeal* 9/11 episode was broadcast by the Fox network three months after the September 11 attacks. Although none of the episode's three storylines explicitly addresses 9/11, they do share the theme of healing and the restoration of hope and faith. Its substitute title "Nine One One," used in the television guides and on the show's website, makes the connection to 9/11 clear. According to Fox, the special episode touched so many Americans that, due to popular demand, it was rebroadcast on Christmas Eve 2001. The "Nine One One" episode differs from other *Ally McBeal* episodes, as its main focus is on the collective national experience rather than the personal experiences of the show's main characters. Even when compared to the previous *Ally McBeal* Christmas episodes, which all tend to be more reflective and spiritual than the regular ones, the "Nine One One" episode is different in the way the individual identities of the characters are overshadowed by a strong sense of collectivity. Although the question of how to maintain faith in a time of adversity is presented as a personal dilemma, the answer – the need to restore hope in all that is good – turns out to be a collective one.

Like most *Ally McBeal* episodes, "Nine One One" consists of three separate but related storylines. The first storyline deals with the preparation for the annual office Christmas party, a recurring event in the *Ally McBeal* Christmas episodes. Different than in the previous years, however, none of the law firm employees seems eager to celebrate. While no particular reason is given as to why the Christmas spirit is lacking, employee Corretta (Regina Hall) tries to convince her boss Richard Fish (Greg Germann) that the office Christmas party should not be cancelled, "as we all need one." This feeling of desperation is widely shared, as becomes clear in a scene set in the office's unisex bathroom. Dressed in an elf costume, John Cage (Peter MacNicol) tells Richard Fish that each year he rents an elf costume, as the Santa Claus costumes tend to be all rented out. Yet this year, all the Santa Claus costumes have remained in the store, suggesting that the entire city lacks in Christmas spirit. "The world seems so desperate," John concludes. "We've all flat-lined."

The lack of Christmas spirit is even more prominent in the second storyline, dealing with Minister Harrison Wyatt (Tom Berenger) who, after his wife Suzanne has been brutally murdered, has lost his faith in God and, subsequently, is fired by his church. "God no longer believes in us, or if he does, he simply no longer cares." Ally becomes more personally involved when she realizes that the minister's son Malcolm (Josh Groban), the boy with the angelic voice who, since the death of his mother, can no longer sing, is the same boy she accompanied to his high school prom only a few months earlier (4:23, 21 May 2001). As she reminds Malcolm, "tragedies happen to good people." In other words, Suzanne is not merely an innocent victim, but a symbol of the "good" in opposition to the "evil" she encountered. That Suzanne also represents "America" as an innocent victim of the recent terrorist attacks is suggested by Malcolm's subsequent question: "Why did she have to be shot in the neck, bleed to death on the sidewalk?" The image presented by Malcolm recalls the image of the planes flying into the Twin Towers: America is taken by surprise and shot in the neck. This interpretation becomes less farfetched when minister Wyatt makes the connection explicit, telling both Ally and Malcolm how his wife reacted after the attack: "After she was shot, she was lying there on the sidewalk and she looked up at the man who just mortally wounded her and she asked him to dial 911… Nine One One. She looked at the man who just shot her and somehow she sees enough good in him that she believes… That's Suzanne." The reference to the American national emergency telephone number 911, and its emphasized repetition in particular, shows that the attack on Suzanne represents the attack on America. After reminding them of the "good" that Suzanne symbolizes, Ally convinces both Minister Wyatt and Malcolm that instead of giving up faith, they should honor Suzanne's soul by continuing to believe that she ("good") will always prevail. If not, as the minister admits, "evil will have won." Thus, the minister returns to his church to lead the congregation during the Christmas Eve midnight sermon, where his son Malcolm will sing again.

The third storyline, dealing with the case of the citizens of the small-town Jackman versus their mayor, makes the connection to 9/11 even more obvious. The mayor has prohibited the citizens of Jackman from holding their annual Christmas parade, because the local factory that produces Christmas decorations has burned down, thereby killing six firefighters. The case directly addresses the dilemma of how to continue holding traditional parades of celebration in the wake of a tragedy of such collective importance. "People just are not in the mood for Christmas this year," the mayor states, thereby emphasizing the overall lack of Christmas spirit. "This is not the time to be throwing parades, I'm sorry. It's disrespectful for a town to be celebrating in the streets. … Out of respect for our economy and the loss of those lives, I think we should be allowed to mourn out of common courtesy-ism." The arguments used in this fictional *Ally McBeal* case echo the arguments made in the public debate about the New York Columbus Day Parade of October 2001. Eventually, the New York parade was presented as a tribute to the 9/11 victims and the rescue workers, with a single fire truck representing both the New York Fire Department and the New York Police Department. The mayor's argument is countered by John Cage, who presents a melodramatic yet (arguably) compelling closing argument. Similar to Ally's plea to continue believing in "good" over "evil," John argues that "this is no year to be skipping Christmas," as giving up Christmas would equal giving up faith. As he pleads: "The people of Jackman, they have been knocked to the ground. When that happens, we get back up. It's who we are. That factory, Jackman's economy was built on hope and optimism and it needs to be rebuilt with those same ingredients. As to the human loss, as profound as it very much is, it is no honor to the fallen for the surviving to stay down." The implication that Jackman stands for "America" is suggested by John's shift of using the third person plural to the first person plural. The people of Jackman ("they") have become the American collective ("we"). Moreover, as he continues, John nationalizes the "we" as being the American people by presenting Christmas as a national holiday:

> Now we are not asking for the right to be out on the streets, slurping margaritas, singing "Que Sera Sera." We just want to go on and sometimes to do that it helps to celebrate. Good will toward men, peace on earth, and joy. A lot of things Christmas stands for in this country. Of course everybody hurts for those firefighters. They are heroes and they

represent the best of what we are. But I think that instead going dark, let's let the light shine in their honor. ... As a people, this community has an emotional need now that they've never... It's not a year to be skipping Christmas.

The melodramatic character is emphasized by the soundtrack (which swells when John starts talking about the firefighters), the clichéd use of the light triumphing over darkness metaphor, and the tear that runs down John's face during his plea's climax. In addition, the reference to the firefighters as heroes places the plea within the hero worship of the New York Fire Department and the New York Police Department, which has become an intrinsic part of the American national 9/11 remembrance rhetoric.

The final scene brings the three storylines together. The scene begins in the church, with the midnight sermon by Minister Wyatt, whose faith has been restored. Moreover, Ally has convinced Malcolm to sing at his father's sermon. Malcolm, standing behind the catheter and dressed in a red choir gown, sings "To Where You Are" (a rather melodramatic pop song written and produced by Richard Marx) while raising his eyes upwards.[33] This gesture leaves it open to interpretation whether Malcolm is singing to his murdered mother or to God in heaven. A close-up of a tear running down the face of Ally, who is sitting in the audience, emphasizes the melodramatic character of the song. The performance is presented in the style of a music video, as shots of Malcolm singing are intercut with shots of the Jackman Christmas parade and shots (in slow-motion) of the office Christmas party. Similar to the real-life New York Columbus Day Parade, the Jackman parade turns out to be a vigil in the honor of the deceased firefighters, rather than a celebratory Christmas parade. Uniformed policemen march together with citizens, including John Cage, holding burning candles. The mayor of Jackman wipes away a tear as he watches the parade passing by. The overall view is colored by the red-white-and-blue flashes from the lights of a police car and a fire truck. A small boy dressed as Rudolf the Red-Nosed Reindeer carries the helmet of a deceased firefighter, while the boy's red nose is blinking like a flashing light. Intercut with shots of the Christmas sermon and the vigil in honor of the fallen firefighters, accompanied by Malcolm's spiritual song, the slow-motion shots of the office Christmas party also become reflective, suggesting that celebrating good tidings can go together with remembering tragedy. Eventually, in all three storylines, faith is restored, coming to the conclusion that, in the wake of 9/11, Christmas needs to be celebrated, though not as a season to be jolly, but as a time to reflect and remember.

In the episode's final shot, right before the "*Ally McBeal* was sponsored by Martini" closing message, Ally places flowers on Suzanne's grave where, at the beginning of the episode, she first had met Minister Wyatt. This time, however, the tombstone is shot from the back, suggesting that the grave stands for all 9/11 victims. In this way, Ally's gesture – and in extension, the entire "Nine One One" episode – can be perceived as a tribute to the victims of the September 11 attacks, making the episode similar to the "Isaac and Ishmael" episode of *The West Wing*. Although not explicitly addressing the terrorist attacks of September 11, they both respond to the aftermath of 9/11, questioning how the American people should cope with tragedy. However, *The West Wing* explicitly addresses international politics, while *Ally McBeal* merely implicitly refers to the political reality of 9/11, excluding the issues of terrorism, Muslim fundamentalism, and anti-Americanism. Instead, *Ally McBeal* presents a national collective identity of being American based on fictional stories of personal and local tragedy, one which takes its Christian character for granted (Christmas is celebrated as both a national and religious holiday), using a melodramatic and therapeutic narrative of restoring faith and hope. In this way, similar to *The Oprah Winfrey Show*, *Ally McBeal* translates the political into a personal experience of the political, yet one that mystifies issues of international politics in favor of celebrating that eventually good – read American idealism – will triumph over evil.

IRAQ ON THE OPRAH WINFREY SHOW

During the year following 9/11, *The Oprah Winfrey Show* continued to pay attention to the aftermath of the terrorist attacks with episodes focusing on personal experiences, such as "Lauren Manning's World Trade Center Survival Story" (11 March 2002), and episodes remembering the victims of 9/11, such as "A Tribute to the Mothers of September 11" (10 May 2002) and "A Tribute to the Fathers of September 11" (14 May 2002). However, *The Oprah Winfrey Show* also addressed the political debate, specifically during the end of 2002 and the beginning of 2003, questioning whether or not the USA should invade Iraq, including episodes such as "Is War the Only Answer?" (22 October 2002), "Should the U.S. Attack Iraq?" (6 February 2003), "What You Should Know About Iraq" (6 March 2003), and "Anti-Americanism: Why Do So Many Dislike the U.S.?" (18 March 2003). These episodes received an ambiguous response, as proponents of the war effort have criticized Oprah Winfrey for promoting "non-patriotic" and "anti-Bush" views on national television, while the opponents criticized her for using *Oprah!* to "market the war" to a mass audience, conform to the "propaganda" of the Bush administration.[34] Once the

FABRICATING THE ABSOLUTE FAKE

USA had invaded Iraq, Winfrey did follow-up shows, such as "Reporters on the Front Lines in Iraq" (27 March 2003) and "War Stories" (15 April 2003).

Similar to the 9/11 episodes, the Iraq episodes fit within the regular format of *The Oprah Winfrey Show*. Winfrey talks with both experts and the studio audience about the necessity of an American attack on Iraq, the political position of the USA in the world, and the personal consequences for Americans in the military and their families back home. Expert studio guests include Daniel Benjamin, co-author of *The Age of Sacred Terror* (22 October 2002), Fawaz Gerges, author of *America and Political Islam* (6 and 18 March 2003), and Kenneth Pollack, author of *The Threatening Storm: The Case for Invading Iraq* (22 October 2002 and 6 March 2003), all of whom appear on *Oprah!* not only to inform the audience about their expertise and political standpoints, but also to promote their books. In addition, *The Oprah Winfrey Show* features pre-taped segments featuring well-known opinion makers and politicians, ranging from documentary maker Michael Moore explaining how American military actions in the past have resulted in a growing anti-Americanism around the world (18 March 2003) to Condoleezza Rice, introduced by Oprah Winfrey as "our cool, collected national security advisor," who justifies an American invasion of Iraq by stating that the USA is "helping to free the Iraqi people" (15 April 2003).

Conventionally, the public debate on war and foreign policy tends to be dominated by (often male) experts who use technical and military jargon. *The Oprah Winfrey Show* breaks with this mode by including both male and female laymen within the debate. The invited experts are encouraged by Winfrey to translate the debate into terms that can be understood by the average viewer at home. Moreover, as the implied viewers of *The Oprah Winfrey Show* are female (more specifically, as Winfrey often points out in her show, housewives and mothers), other voices are included within the traditionally masculine debate on warfare. In other words, by including the "housewife" in the discussion, the distinction between the masculine public and feminine private sphere is bridged. By combining political and personal arguments, *Oprah!* shows the potential for a broader and inclusive debate. A wide range of arguments are voiced by the audience members, both approving and opposing the war in Iraq, using both "rational" and "emotional" arguments, ranging from "we are only involved in Iraq because of the oil and the economic interests of big business" to "I don't want my son to go to war." The debate continues in the "After the Show" segment, which is not broadcast but can be viewed on the Oprah.com website, where viewers are invited to send in comments.

The episode "Is War the Only Answer?" (22 October 2002) is telling in the way in which gender plays a significant role in changing the political into a personal experience of the political. The aforementioned Daniel Benjamin and Kenneth Pollack are present as experts in the studio. Both see the war (then still pending) in Iraq as a necessary evil. Saddam Hussein needs to be disarmed to guarantee American national security. While Benjamin and Pollack are being interviewed in the studio, their comments are alternated by pre-taped interviews with two female experts, Helen Caldicott and Jody Williams, who, unlike Benjamin and Pollack, oppose the war. Caldicott fears that a war in Iraq will lead to nuclear war; Williams warns that "pre-emptive self-defense" will set a dangerous precedent. Different than the studio interviews, the pre-taped segments are melodramatically edited through the use of close-ups, Winfrey's voiceover, added images of warfare, and a swelling soundtrack. Whether or not intentionally, the juxtaposition of the male studio experts and the female pre-taped experts suggests a gender divide between male proponents and female opponents of the war, which is emphasized by the melodramatical editing of the "feminine" argument (although both female experts use the conventional masculine jargon to question the necessity of war). This gender divide is challenged by the pre-taped – and again melodramatically edited – interview that follows. Peggy Noonan, journalist of *The Wall Street Journal*, former speechwriter of President Ronald Reagan and consultant to *The West Wing* television drama series, emphasizes the distinction between a male and female perspective on warfare. In principle, as Noonan tells the *Oprah!* audience, women are against war, as they pass on life. However, women are also caring and want to protect their children. At the moment when "children are being threatened" (thus not something abstract like "national security"), women "naturally" will support the war. As Noonan continues:

> Is war the only answer? I am not completely convinced at this point that it is in America's interest to move the war to Iraq and remove Saddam Hussein. As a mother, you do not want your kids to go to war, and you don't want your kids to live in wartime. You want your kids to live in peace. ... My big question is: Do we have to go to war now to make ourselves safe? Is moving on Iraq going to make the world safer? War is brutal. It is full of waste. It is full of cruelty. Inevitably, children and civilians are harmed. But it is not the worst thing. Sometimes wars have to be fought to protect people, and to protect the world. Not protecting the world is the worst thing.

With her argument, Peggy Noonan personalizes the debate by addressing the audience as mothers, playing on their assumed emotions of "maternal instinct" in stark contrast to the "rational" arguments by the other (both male and female) experts. Noonan cleverly appropriates the anti-war stance to eventually present a pro-war position, justified not by the conventional masculine jargon of warfare but by evoking the image of a mother protecting her children.

As shown by the contradictory reactions of both the proponents and the opponents of the war in Iraq, accusing Oprah Winfrey of either opposing or promoting the war effort, the Iraq episodes of *The Oprah Winfrey Show* can be perceived in different ways. On the one hand, the talk show has broadened the public debate by including both supporting and opposing arguments, made by both experts and ordinary audience members. Moreover, *Oprah!* has enabled the inclusion of personal "emotional" arguments that tend to be excluded from the political "rational" debate, thereby bridging the gap between the public and the private sphere. On the other hand, by turning the political into a personal experience of the political, *The Oprah Winfrey Show* seems to suggest that political positions are predominantly an individual and personal choice, thereby mystifying the way *Oprah!* structures the debate through its choice of guests and the way their contributions are edited, as is shown by the segment with Peggy Noonan. In addition, the emphasis on individual and personal choice tends to hide other social-economic and political interests, including (but not limited to) Oprah Winfrey's own economic interest as a commercial television maker.

CONCLUSION: THE OPRAHIFICATION OF AMERICA

On September 20, 2002, one year after 9/11, global megastar Bono of the Irish rock group U2 visited *The Oprah Winfrey Show* to tell the American public (and in extension, the global audience) about famine, poverty, and AIDS in Africa. How, Oprah asks, does this relate to the average American woman at home, who worries about her own family? "What does this have to do with her life?" "Wow," Bono answers: "See, there's the country of America, that you have to defend, but there's also the ideal of America. America is more than just a country. It's an ideal, okay ... an ideal that's supposed to be contagious." "I love that," Oprah responds, "I wanna cry right now. I do, I love that." Although unmentioned by Bono, he is paraphrasing his good friend Wim Wenders, the German filmmaker, who once wrote: "AMERICA, always means two things: a country, geographically, the USA, and a concept of this country, its ideal."[35] That it takes an Irish rock star echoing the words of a German filmmaker on a talk show hosted by America's most popular television personality to make such a distinction explicit reinforces the notion that America as imagined community transcends the geographical boundaries of the nation-state USA. Bono's reference to American idealism in his fight against African poverty harks back to the rhetoric of "We Are the World" as discussed in the first chapter. Yet, it also connects to 9/11 and its aftermath, to television shows like *The Oprah Winfrey Show*, *The West Wing*, and *Ally McBeal*, which use the same rhetoric to make sense of 9/11, thereby mystifying the role of the nation-state USA in international politics in favor of celebrating the alleged universal yet – equally alleged – exceptionally American values of freedom and democracy which "America" as "contagious ideal" embodies.

Commenting on the large number of American fictional television shows which have included 9/11 in their narratives, ranging from, in addition to the shows mentioned in this chapter, *The Education of Max Bickford* (CBS, 2001-2002) and *Boston Public* (FOX, 2000-2004) to *7th Heaven* (CBS, 1996-2007) and *American Family* (FOX, 2002-2004), Amanda Lotz claims that "the plurality of series enacting these stories and the audience size of any of these series makes analysis of one '9/11 episode' incomplete in seeking to address how 'television' explored these events and their aftermath."[36] True enough, with my analysis of the 9/11 episodes of *The Oprah Winfrey Show*, *The West Wing*, and *Ally McBeal*, I have not intended to present one singular way in which American television has dealt with 9/11, nor do I suggest that the viewers, both American and non-American, all share the same perspective after watching these television shows. Not all American viewers will be hailed successfully into the position of "docile patriot" or "infantile citizen" and not all non-American viewers will be seduced by the uncritical portrayal of America as the Beacon of Freedom and Democracy. Moreover, as Lynn Spigel has pointed out, there are other television shows and other media that provide counter-narratives, presenting a more critical perspective on the role of the nation-state USA.[37] The significance of the 9/11 episodes analyzed in this chapter can be found in the way all of them take the acceptance of American idealism for granted, each of them assuming that viewers will uncritically recognize these American values as being self-evident and universal. By celebrating the values that an imagined America embodies, these television shows can ignore the actual politics of the nation-state USA.

The political power of such an uncritical perspective has been recognized by the Bush administration. When, at a press conference on October 11, 2001, President George W. Bush again was confronted with the "Why do they hate us?" question, his answer assumed the docile patriotism and infantile citizenship which the 9/11 episodes of the analyzed television shows generate: "How do I respond when I see that in some Islamic countries there is vitriolic hatred for America? I'll tell you how I respond: I'm amazed. I'm amazed that there is such misunderstanding of what our country is about, that people would hate us. I am, I am – like most Americans, I just can't believe it. Because I know how good we are, and we've got to do a better job of making our case."[38]

FABRICATING THE ABSOLUTE FAKE

CHAPTER THREE:

The Desert of the Real:

America as Hyperreality

On November 22, 1990, during the first Gulf War, President George H.W. Bush gave a pep talk to the American soldiers stationed near Dhahran, Saudi Arabia. "Now, look, look, we know that the days can get pretty long out here, and you'll be glad to know that if it goes on too long we have a secret weapon in reserve," Bush joked. "If push comes to shove, we're going to get Roseanne Barr to go to Iraq and sing the national anthem. Baghdad Betty, eat your heart out."[1] Bush was referring to the controversial performance of the American national anthem by comedian and television sitcom star Roseanne Barr. On July 25, 1990, in between two games of the San Diego Padres baseball team, she had sung an extremely off-key a cappella rendition of "The Star-Spangled Banner." Adding insult to the injury, she also grabbed her crotch and spat on the ground. Many viewers were not amused. Roseanne Barr was booed by the audience, strongly criticized by the press, and denounced by Bush, who called her performance "disgraceful."[2] President Bush's true secret weapon, however, proved to be not Roseanne Barr, but African-American pop diva Whitney Houston, whose rousing rendition of "The Star-Spangled Banner" at the 1991 Super Bowl became a symbol of American unity and patriotism. Broadcast live on television by ABC on January 27, 1991, only ten days after the official beginning of Operation Desert Storm, Houston's performance turned the Super Bowl into a pep rally to cheer on the American army in its war against Iraq.

Both President Bush's reference to Roseanne Barr and the Super Bowl performance by Whitney Houston show how American pop culture has become intertwined with American politics. In this chapter, I will look at explicit moments of such intertwinement. First, I will discuss the Super Bowl performances of the American national anthem by Whitney Houston in 1991 during the first Gulf War, by Mariah Carey in 2002 during the American invasion of Afghanistan after 9/11, by the Dixie Chicks in 2003 during the pending

American invasion of Iraq, and by Beyoncé Knowles in 2004, nine months after President George W. Bush had announced the invasion of Iraq to be a "Mission Accomplished." Second, I will look at the role of American pop culture in two of the few Hollywood films that deal with the first Gulf War: *Three Kings* (David O. Russell, 1999) and *Jarhead* (Sam Mendes, 2005), the latter based on the bestselling memoirs by first Gulf War veteran Anthony Swofford. Before analyzing these pop-cultural artifacts, I will introduce the concept of myth, as defined by Roland Barthes, and the concept of hyperreality, as defined by Jean Baudrillard, both of which are helpful in understanding how American pop culture not only enables the popular translation of American military actions, but simultaneously invites a justification of the American political position, even if some of these expressions (like *Three Kings*) may appear to be critical of the nation-state USA. Although the televised Super Bowl performances and the Hollywood movies *Three Kings* and *Jarhead* belong to different genres, they all effectively combine American politics and pop culture by applying the connotations of an imagined America to explain and often justify the politics of the American nation-state. Moreover, as these television and film performances by American pop and movie stars are globally mediated, they not only present a national self-image to American viewers, but an ideological image of America to an international audience as well.

BARTHESIAN MYTH AND BAUDRILLARDIAN HYPERREALITY

In his essay "Myth Today" (originally published in 1957), Roland Barthes uses a 1955 *Paris Match* cover depicting a young black soldier as an example of how myth is constructed. To analyze its construction, Barthes recognizes two levels of signification: denotation and connotation. On the level of denotation, the primary level of signification, the cover shows a young black soldier saluting the French flag, the latter not present but implied through the cover's use of the national tricolor red, white, and blue. On the level of connotation, the secondary level of signification, the magazine cover offers a positive image of French imperialism and patriotism. Placed within the historical context of the then recent defeat in Vietnam and the raging war in Algeria, the depiction of a black soldier implies that French imperialism is justified and widely supported, including by the non-white population of the French empire. More important, the myth that French imperialism is positive is presented as self-evident and uncontested. As Barthes explains: "Myth does not deny things, on the contrary, its function is to talk about them; simply, it purifies them, it makes them innocent, it gives them a natural and eternal justification, it gives them a clarity which is not that of an explanation but that of a statement of fact."[3] In other words, through connotation the meaning of representation is reduced to seemingly self-evident and uncontested myth, inviting an uncritical reading.

The 1955 *Paris Match* cover used by Barthes immediately comes to mind when looking at two 2003 magazine covers featuring the same picture of Jessica Lynch, the American soldier who was heroically rescued by the American Special Forces after being captured by the Iraqi army. Both *Newsweek* (14 April 2003) and *People* magazine (21 April 2003) use an undated army picture of Lynch in uniform in front of the American flag, an image which has become iconic by now, showing her face in close-up, smiling directly into the camera. There are great similarities between these two covers and the *Paris Match* cover. In both cases, the national flag is present in the left corner. The French flag is implied through the use of its colors, while the American flag is explicitly present. Moreover, the gender of the American soldier works similarly to the racial identity of the French soldier. As the blackness of the French soldier implied wide solidarity for French imperialism, the smiling face of the female soldier suggests broad support for the American war effort.[4] Yet, there are also important differences. The French soldier remained anonymous, while the American soldier has a name: Jessica Lynch, an innocent young woman who ends up being a soldier on duty in Iraq. More than just a name, Jessica Lynch has become an adventurous tale. As the headline of the *People* magazine cover reads: "POW Jessica Lynch – Her Incredible Story: An inside account of the young soldier's midnight rescue, her joyful family reunion, and the long road home." The cover of *Newsweek* uses fewer words to achieve a similar result by presenting the headline "Saving Private Lynch," an obvious reference to the Hollywood blockbuster *Saving Private Ryan* (Steven Spielberg, 1998). Thus, in stark contrast to the anonymous soldier on the 1955 cover of *Paris Match*, the American soldier on the 2003 covers of *Newsweek* and *People* magazine is not only personalized but also transformed into a highly dramatized "true" story, a dramatization which has been taken a step further by the NBC television movie *Saving Jessica Lynch* (Peter Markle, 2003). Through her passive heroism by being both a brave soldier and an innocent victim, Jessica Lynch not only becomes the "face" of the second Gulf War, she also embodies an uncontested positive justification of the American military presence in Iraq.

In his essay "Culture, US Imperialism, and Globalization," John Carlos Rowe compares the "story" of Jessica Lynch – as constructed by the American media, both the factual news and the fictional television film – to the Hollywood film *Wag the Dog* (Barry Levinson, 1997), in which a Hollywood producer helps to cover up a presidential sex scandal by inventing a war with Albania, a fabricated story which includes the saving of an American soldier who is left behind enemy lines. As Rowe argues, *Wag the Dog* "satirizes Americans' chronic ignorance of world events, thanks to news structured around entertainment and commercialism, but it also reinforces the assumption that the US is the center of the world and that even a 'fictional' war can have meaning and value, as long as it is waged by the US."[5] The media coverage of the second Gulf War, and the saving of Private Jessica Lynch in particular, reconfirms the fiction of *Wag the Dog*, especially after the British BBC documentary *War Spin* (originally broadcast on May 18, 2003) revealed that the spectacular rescue of Lynch, which was filmed, appeared to have been scripted by the Pentagon.[6] However, whether or not the saving of Jessica Lynch was "real" is beside the point. When Roland Barthes speaks of myth, he does not imply that myth is by definition untrue or unreal. Myth works because its connotations remain uncontested and uncritically accepted. The smiling face of Jessica Lynch in the media continues to provide an innocent justification of the American invasion of Iraq, in spite of the critical reading that the fictional *Wag the Dog* scenario may invite. As Rowe suggests: "Rather than *Wag the Dog*'s satire overwhelming and thus neutralizing the Jessica Lynch story on the evening news, Jessica Lynch's narrative, now made into a television biopic, has undone the irony of Barry Levinson's film, especially its 'rescued soldier' device."[7] Even if the Jessica Lynch story is recognized as a real-life enactment of the *Wag the Dog* scenario, that does not undermine the effectiveness of the mechanism which the film satirizes.

Neal Gabler also refers to *Wag the Dog* when discussing the way in which the administration of President George H.W. Bush staged the first Gulf War as a "multibillion-dollar movie blockbuster," broadcast by the television networks, featuring heroic soldiers, dark mustachioed villains, and spectacular visual effects of "smart bombing," with a triumphant parade of the homecoming troops in the streets of New York as grand finale.[8] Aptly titled *Life: The Movie*, Gabler's study builds on David Boorstin's *The Image* (1961), in which Boorstin argues that the fantasy of advertising, Hollywood, and television has replaced reality in American culture, becoming more "real" than reality itself. *Life: The Movie* also shares the rather cultural pessimism of Neal Postman's *Amusing Ourselves to Death* (1985), suggesting that, particularly because of commercial television, American culture has been reduced to entertainment. Moreover, *Life: The Movie* can be read as a popular adaptation of Jean Baudrillard's concept of hyperreality, suggesting that reality merely exists as a simulacrum, constructed through its simulation: "The real is hyperrealized. Neither realized, nor idealized: but hyperrealized. The hyperreal is the abolition of the real not by violent destruction, but by its assumption."[9] Baudrillard's hyperreality is not the opposite of reality ("unreal") but a continuous simulation that creates the real

FABRICATING THE ABSOLUTE FAKE

as just another sign in a chain of signs which endlessly refer to each other. If indeed American life *is* a movie rather than being *like* a movie, American life can be perceived as a hyperreality, in which the actual reality of life has become part of the stream of images mediated by Hollywood and television, as Jean Baudrillard convincingly shows in *America*, his fascinating account of his travels through the USA. "In America cinema is true because it is the whole of space, the whole way of life that are cinematic," he writes. "The break between the two … does not exist: life is cinema."[10]

The significance of Baudrillard's *America* lies not so much in the claim that America is the ultimate simulacrum, which can be contested. Concluding whether or not America is in fact a hyperreality is less relevant than trying to understand the way American culture works by perceiving America as a hyperreality. From a Baudrillardian perspective, America is a space where the myth of the American Dream does not come true but is true already through its mythic construction. In a paradoxical way, America is a "utopia achieved," the impossible made possible, because of its fictional character. As Baudrillard explains:

> When I speak of the American "way of life," I do so to emphasize its utopian nature, its *mythic* banality, its dream quality, and its grandeur. That philosophy which is immanent not only … in the reality of everyday life, but in the hyperreality of that life which, as it is, displays all the characteristics of fiction. It is this fictional character which is so exciting. Now, fiction is not imagination. It is what anticipates imagination by giving it the form of reality. … The American way of life is spontaneously fictional, since it is a transcending of the imaginary in reality.[11]

Here Baudrillard's hyperreality and myth overlap, as the fiction that shapes American reality is constituted by myth in the Barthesian sense. In this manner, the American Dream turns out to be an uncontested hyperreality rather than an idealized or imagined desire. American pop culture is instrumental in the shaping of hyperreality through fictionalization, as movie and pop stars are the mythical embodiment of the American Dream, its living examples.

In *The Gulf War Did Not Take Place*, composed of three essays originally published before, during, and immediately after Operation Desert Storm in the British *Guardian* and the French *Libération*, Baudrillard proposes that, similar to his reading of America, the first Gulf War should be perceived as a hyperreality, a simulacrum which transforms the actual war into a virtual one, a spectacle of information. This simulation of the Gulf War, broadcast live on television, is made out of symptoms, images of reality which can no longer be recognized as either true or false, real or fake. "We must learn to read symptoms as symptoms, and television as the hysterical symptom of a war which has nothing to do with its critical mass."[12] Baudrillard's claim that the actual Gulf War had not taken place provoked strong objections, most explicitly by Christopher Norris who accused Baudrillard of being nihilistically uncritical, as by reducing the war to a hyperreal event, Baudrillard escapes the ethical responsibility of speaking out against the physical reality of the Gulf War.[13] However, Baudrillard never suggests that the Gulf War is not real in the sense of denying its materiality of real Iraqi civilians and soldiers being killed by real bombs. Quite the contrary, he strongly criticizes that the "100,000 Iraqi dead" are being misused to recognize the Gulf War as a real war: "What is worse is that these dead still serve as an alibi for those who do not want to have been excited for nothing, nor to have been had for nothing: at least the dead would prove that this war was indeed a war and not a shameful and pointless hoax, a programmed and melodramatic version of what was the drama of war."[14] Rather than being nihilistically uncritical, Jean Baudrillard's *The Gulf War Did Not Take Place* forces us to recognize that the symptomatic images of computerized warfare and smart bombing as broadcast by television are not merely representations that can be judged to be either real or fake, but images that construct the Gulf War as a hyperreality, thereby not denying the physical reality of the Iraqi victims but rendering them invisible.[15]

Although critical of Baudrillard's claim, Ella Shohat and Robert Stam have described the Gulf War as a multigeneric television miniseries, drawing "on the codes of the war film (soldiers silhouetted against the sky, thrilling martial music, *Top Gun* visuals); of the PBS educational show (military pedagogs with pointers, maps, and video blackboards); of sports programming (instant replay, expert-running commentary); and of the western (lines were drawn in the sand, the implacable logic of the showdown)."[16] Not only the images of computer warfare and smart bombing themselves but also the way they were broadcast shape the fictionalization of the Gulf War into hyperreality, based on the conventions of pop culture. As I will show in the remainder of this chapter, the fictionalization was not limited to the news coverage by television news programs, but also occurred through the ritualistic annual performances of the national anthem at the Super Bowl, and in fact still continues today through Hollywood films such as *Three Kings* and *Jarhead*. My analysis of these pop-cultural performances by pop and movie stars will suggest that the Gulf War that did not take place presents and reconfirms America as an uncontested mythical hyperreality.

Whitney Houston was not the first internationally famous pop star to sing "The Star-Spangled Banner" at the Super Bowl. Since the early 1980s, it has become a Super Bowl tradition to invite pop music stars to sing the national anthem, including performances by Diana Ross (1982), Billy Joel (1989 and 2007), Cher (1999), Faith Hill (2000), and *American Idol's* Jordin Sparks (2008). Unlike some of the performances by pop stars at other occasions, none of the Super Bowl performances have been considered controversial. In addition to the earlier-mentioned rendition by Roseanne Barr, controversial performances of "The Star-Spangled Banner" range from José Feliciano's slow and melancholic rendition at the 1968 World Series and Jimi Hendrix's guitar solo at the 1969 Woodstock festival, to the soulful renditions by Aretha Franklin at the 1968 Democratic National Convention and Marvin Gaye at the 1983 National Basketball Association All-Star Game. In 2001, at the start of the Indianapolis 500 racing event, Steven Tyler of the rock band Aerosmith caused controversy by changing the words "the home of the brave" into "the home of the Indianapolis 500." Such controversies have been absent from the annual Super Bowl performance of "The Star-Spangled Banner," which emphasizes its status as *the* performance of the national anthem. Each year the performance is tightly scripted and monitored, the vocals often pre-recorded, to ensure that no unwelcome surprises interfere with its almost ritualistic status, different than can happen during the extravagant halftime performances that are more susceptible to controversy, of which the 2004 performance by Janet Jackson and Justin Timberlake (as discussed later on in this chapter) is the most obvious example.

Several scholars have pointed out the significance of sports events, and the Super Bowl in particular, in the construction of a national identity.[17] Being the "crucible of [the] nation," to quote Toby Miller, sports are often used as a metaphor for the nation.[18] Not only is nationhood essential to international sports events such as the World Cup Soccer and the Olympics, and also American national events such as the Super Bowl and the World Series, the rhetoric of sports and the military are intertwined and often interchangeable. Football coaches use military metaphors to plan the strategies that will lead their uniformed athletes to victory, while army officials, politicians, and journalists talk about military operations – led by generals coaching their uniformed soldiers – by referring to sports. Similar to the way a national identity can be reinforced through the patriotic sentiments of war, sports events can bring national communities together in patriotism and nationalism. Perhaps this "natural" connection between the military and sports explains the relatively easy way, without any resistance or commentary, in which the Super Bowl performances bring together sports and explicit expressions of military power.

Whitney Houston herself recognized the patriotic character of her performance of "The Star-Spangled Banner." In an interview, she recalled:

> If you were there, you could feel the intensity. You know, we were in the Gulf War at the time. It was an intense time for a country. A lot of our daughters and sons were overseas fighting. I could see, in the stadium, I could see the fear, the hope, the intensity, the prayers going up, you know, and I just felt like this is the moment. And it was hope, we needed hope, you know, to bring our babies home and that's what it was about for me, that's what I felt when I sang that song, and the overwhelming love coming out of the stands was incredible.[19]

As the use of the plural personal pronouns "we" and "our" implies, Houston speaks of her performance as a collective experience. Not the American nation-state as an abstract entity but "we" as a "country" are at war. Moreover, she uses the metaphor of the family to express the collective national identity. In spite of the strong presence of the military, Whitney Houston recognizes the expression of explicit patriotism as "overwhelming love," fitting within the perspective of the Barthesian myth, which, in this case, means that the American participation in the first Gulf War remains unquestioned.

Bombastic may be the best word to describe Houston's performance of "The Star-Spangled Banner." Rather than being dressed as the glamorous diva, Whitney Houston wears a white tracksuit, with a red and blue print, an athletic uniform that refers to the national tricolor red, white, and blue. The connection to patriotism and the Gulf War is made explicit by the announcer, as he asks the audience to join in the honoring of "America" and "especially the brave men and women serving our nation in the Persian Gulf and throughout the world." The emphasis on the military is reinforced by the presence of military personnel on the field, while the athletes are notably absent. The military personnel, dressed in various uniforms to signify the solidarity among different army units, display the flags of the different American states, which emphasizes that the USA consists of states all unified in a national war effort. Two male members of the military are singled out through the use of close-ups: an African-American officer and a white officer. The second close-up of the African-American officer uncannily resembles the saluting young black soldier on the cover of the *Paris Match* magazine, as analyzed by Roland Barthes. Similar to his example, the explicit inclusion of African-American military (in addition to Houston's blackness) implies that there is wide support for the war effort among the American population, how ethnically diverse the population may be. This is reinforced by the way in which the close-up of Whitney Houston dissolves into the close-up of the white officer, and back again. For a second, both Houston and the white officer are captured within the same frame (almost like a split screen), a conventional way to emphasize their similarity over their differences. In other words, through the suggestion that Houston and the white officer are one, their shared identity as Americans is brought forward.

The American flag is omnipresent in all shots, either explicitly in the form of an actual American flag, or implicitly through the use of its colors red, white, and blue. In addition to the waving American flags, a group of people at the center of the football field display a gigantic American flag, best visible when shot from a distance. On several occasions, the presence of the flag is emphasized through the use of close-ups in connection to the words Whitney Houston sings. When she sings, "... see, by the dawn's early light," a close-up of an American flag dissolves in and out of the close-up of Houston. Houston does not leave the frame, but for a second, the image of the American flag is transparently placed over her image. At the point when Whitney Houston sings "through the night that our flag was still there," the camera cuts to a close-up of the American flag proudly waving at the top of the stadium – a television convention found in many broadcasts of the Super Bowl national anthem performances.

Perhaps most important is the way in which the audience is presented as a collective of American patriots who wholeheartedly support their nation's war effort. Throughout the performance, there are medium shots and close-ups of the audience waving small American flags. While at international sports events the audience is divided between two or more competing nations, the audience at the Super Bowl supports just one: the American nation. No signs are shown in the support of one of the two teams competing. In fact, any mention of either team is absent (in 1991, the New York Giants beat the Buffalo Bills). Instead, rather than cheering on the individual teams, the red-white-and-blue signs in the audience support the American war effort. "America's Bravest Citizens: Support Our G.I.'s" reads one, followed by two other red-white-blue signs reading "God Bless America" and "Go USA." Particularly the latter sign, "Go USA," emphasizes the intertwinement of sports and the military. The American war effort is supported in the same way as an audience cheers on a sports team. In this way, the Super Bowl becomes a pep rally to cheer on the American military in the Gulf. Moreover, this military connection is made complete with four F-16 fighting jets from the 56th Tactical Training Wing at MacDill Air Force Base flying over as the performance's grand finale.

The intertwinement of sports, patriotism, and pop culture, all supporting the war effort, ties American nationalism to consumerism. Jean Baudrillard has suggested that the USA is "a society that is endlessly concerned to vindicate itself, perpetually seeking to justify its own existence," adding that the "American flag bears witness to this by its omnipresence, ... not as a heroic sign, but as a trademark of a good brand."[20] The American flag is not only a symbol of the American nation-state and its people, but an advertising logo as well, a sign that refers both to the nation-state and to an endless chain of signs of American pop culture. Although already functioning in this manner during the first Gulf War, this has become even clearer after the terrorist attacks of September 11, 2001. As Susan Willis shows, after 9/11 the American flag is omnipresent, displayed at places ranging from Ground Zero to homes, cars, storefronts, and government buildings, and eventually also at Kandahar Airport in Afghanistan. Moreover, the flag functions as a patriotic fashion statement:

> Emblazoned across our chests, the flag becomes one with the rock bands and sports teams that also claim our allegiance and warrant a T-shirt's stamp of approval. ... With flags on our shirts, we express the heartfelt desire to contribute our individual pledge to the collective endeavor, even while we simultaneously recognize that the American endeavor is to consume commodities and ensure their worldwide distribution.[21]

Rather than seeing the flag's double function as a contradiction, Susan Willis suggests that American patriotism and consumerism reinforce each other. In her introduction to *The Selling of 9/11*, Dana Heller makes a similar argument by perceiving the flag as a "national-corporate logo," one which does not invite a questioning of the American nation-state and its international politics, concluding that "the flag erupts upon the national scene like a neurotic symptom, a repetition of our hysterical deafness to any criticism or any idea that might get in the way of our rights to unlimited consumption, and our national duty to employ military measures, if necessary, to protect that right."[22] The performance of "The Star-Spangled Banner" at the Super Bowl functions in the same way, as the American flag and the national anthem have become intertwined as both a conventional reference to the nation-state USA and a free floating sign, an advertising logo of American consumer culture. Performed by Whitney Houston, "The Star-Spangled Banner" is both a national anthem and a pop song, bringing patriotism and consumerism together.

After the Super Bowl performance, Whitney Houston's "The Star-Spangled Banner" was released as a single, reaching number 20 on Billboard's Hot 100. The single was also released in other countries, including the Netherlands, but failed to make the pop charts outside of the USA. Copies of the single (in addition to complementary copies of *Playboy* magazine) were sent to the American troops stationed in Kuwait. Dressed in blue military overalls, Houston gave another performance of "The Star-Spangled Banner" on March 31, 2001, on her *Welcome Home Heroes with Whitney Houston* HBO television special, recorded before an audience of homecoming soldiers and family members. In 2001, one month after 9/11, Houston's record company Arista re-released "The Star-Spangled Banner" as a single, with "America the Beautiful" as an additional song, this time reaching number 6 on Billboard's Hot 100. The cover art of the 2001 single is particularly significant. While the 1991 single features a picture of Houston performing at the Super Bowl, the re-release merely shows a pop art styled picture of the American flag, functioning as a conventional patriotic symbol signifying the nation-state USA, but also as a trademarked brand of pop-cultural America and as an advertising logo to sell Houston's single, perfectly revealing how patriotism, pop culture, and consumerism have become intertwined.

America at the Super Bowl after 9/11

Writing about the 2003 Super Bowl performance of "The Star-Spangled Banner" by the Dixie Chicks, Tobias Peterson has argued that it was a reenactment of the 1991 Super Bowl, as each was "a massive wartime pep rally, cheering not only the players on the field, but the soldiers in the Gulf and elsewhere." He also compares the Dixie Chicks' performance to the 2002 performance by Mariah Carey, claiming that the 2003 one was "far removed from last year's pervading sense of victimization" and that "war and revenge are now more the focus of national discussion than grief and remembrance."[23] Yet, when taking a closer look at all performances, the similarities become striking. Not only the 2003 performance by the Dixie Chicks, but also the 2002 performance by Mariah Carey and the 2004 performance by Beyoncé Knowles prove to be very similar to Whitney Houston's 1991 performance. These four Super Bowl performances can be seen as American national rituals, which, as Rob Kroes suggests, "increasingly blended mass spectator sports with displays of military prowess and martial vigor that paralleled the gestation of the new [neo-conservative] foreign policy views," constituting a "trend [that] may herald a militarization of the American public spirit, propagated through the mass media."[24] Since the pivotal performance by Whitney Houston, most of the Super Bowl performances of "The Star-Spangled Banner" have included an explicit presence of the military.

At a press conference before her 2002 Super Bowl performance, Mariah

Carey explained that she, similar to Whitney Houston, recognized the patriotic symbolism of the ceremony. "Definitely after the events of September 11, I think that people obviously have been much more focused on the patriotic nature of this event and what it's going to mean."[25] Only a couple of months after 9/11, the Super Bowl performance was intended to remember the tragedy and pay respect to the 9/11 victims. However, the performance was also part of a larger spectacle that was more than merely an act of remembrance. As Douglas Kellner has analyzed in his study *Media Spectacle*, the 2002 Super Bowl could be seen as a continuation of the display of military power and patriotism as originally presented at the 1991 Super Bowl:

> Super Bowl 2002 featured Bush I and former US Navy and NFL star Roger Stauback flipping the coin to decide which team would receive the first kickoff. A hi-tech spectacle featured US troops watching live in Kandahar, and military personnel punching in statistical graphics, making the screen appear like a computer in a military system. Stars of each team were periodically shown in front of a waving US flag with a graphic announcing that "they were proud to be a part of SB36, of this great nation, and that they were thankful for the troops' courage in Afghanistan." Broadcast by the ultra-right Fox network, the computer graphics featured red, white, and blue banners and the transition graphics involved the use of an exploding fireworks scene with the triad of patriotic colors blasting across the screen. The Super Bowl logo in the center of the field was in the shape of the United States, and the Fox network used a patriotic logo with the flag's colors and images, imitating NBC, which had transformed its multicolored peacock into the flag's tricolors after the September 11 terrorists attacks.[26]

I quote from Kellner's analysis at length, as it shows how the broadcast of the 2002 Super Bowl, similar to the 1991 Super Bowl, has effectively included the display of military power within a sports event. Rather than merely remembering the 9/11 victims, the 2002 Super Bowl proves to be another example of how the collectivity of the sports event is used to bring together the nation in wartime patriotism and to cheer on the army in its war effort.

Compared to Whitney Houston's performance, the performance by Mariah Carey seems much less bombastic. The stadium is shot in relative darkness, emphasizing a mood of mourning and seriousness. While the audience was clearly visible during the broadcast of Houston's performance, here the audience is visually almost absent. Only in one shot, as the camera is placed among the audience in the stands, is the audience is shown, though

78   FABRICATING THE ABSOLUTE FAKE

individuals are not recognizable. Without medium shots or close-ups of the audience, the audience is reduced to a cheering mass, for the most part hidden in darkness. Similar to Whitney Houston's performance, no athletes are shown and the competing teams (in 2002, the New England Patriots beat the St. Louis Rams) are not mentioned. Instead, the segment starts with a medium pan shot of five uniformed officers of the U.S.S. Cole, the U.S. Marine Corps, the New York New Jersey Port Authority, and the New York City Police and Fire Department. The link to international terrorism is immediately made explicit, as not only the victims of 9/11, but also the military victims of the terrorist attack on the U.S.S. Cole in the Yemen harbor are remembered. This not only shifts the tribute from the national into the international sphere, but also makes an explicit connection between the military and the civilian uniformed personnel. By honoring the victims among uniformed personnel, without explicitly including the civilian victims, the performance reduces 9/11 to a military event of international politics, ignoring its also being a national civilian tragedy. Moreover, it is this shift from the national to the international, from the civilian to the militaristic, that makes the Mariah Carey performance similar to the Whitney Houston performance. Even though the audience in Houston's performance is shown to be more active in the actual support of the war effort (compared to the relatively visual absence of Carey's audience), both performances can be perceived as an explicit support of military action, respectively in the Gulf and Afghanistan.

Similar to most Super Bowl broadcasts of the national anthem, the American flag is omnipresent in the performance by Mariah Carey, again both explicitly through the display of the actual American flag, as well as implicitly through the use of the national tricolor red, white, and blue. For example, in the first close-up of Carey, these three colors are dominant, in the combination of Carey's blue dress, the conductor Keith Lockhart's white shirt, and the red music standard (the only other color is black), which is repeated in the banner containing the Super Bowl logo, the Fox logo, and Carey's name. A group of children dressed in white display a gigantic American flag in the geographical shape of the United States of America. When Carey sings, "... that our flag was still there," the camera zooms into a close-up of the American flag held by one of the five uniformed officers. Perhaps most significant, two American flags are prominently featured in two tableaux vivant: the first being a live enactment of the Iwo Jima monument, with five soldiers in battle fatigues planting the American flag in the soil, and the second being six uniformed officers of the New York Police and Fire Department displaying – in Iwo Jima style – the torn "original" American flag of the World Trade Center. In both shots, the camera zooms into a close-up of the American flag.

The Super Bowl performance is not the first time that the imagery of the Iwo Jima monument, which in its turn is based on the famous 1945 photograph by Joe Rosenthal, has been used in connection with 9/11. Immediately after the attacks on September 11, photographer Thomas Franklin shot an Iwo Jima-style picture of three white firemen raising the American flag on Ground Zero.[27] Franklin's picture instantly became an icon of 9/11, reproduced in many ways, including as official stamp of the U.S. Postal Service and as life-size wax statue at Madame Tussauds in New York City. The picture also inspired the controversial proposal for a bronze statue to be placed at the New York Fire Department, which never materialized because no agreement could be reached on replacing the three white men with a multicultural team – white, African-American, and Hispanic – of firefighters. The attempt to make the proposed statue multicultural follows the logic of Barthesian myth, suggesting broad consensus among the ethnically diverse American population in perceiving the firefighter as a positive embodiment of the nation-state USA. Referring to a model version of the statue, Susan Willis has argued: "In the guise of New York's firefighters the statue embodies the nation and facilitates a shift from the local to the international, from the work of recovery to the work of war. As a sliding signifier, the statue enables the nation's attention to move from Lower Manhattan to the new Iwo Jima in Kabul and Kandahar."[28] The two tableaux vivant at the Super Bowl performance reinforce this shift through the explicit juxtaposition of the live enactment of the "original" Iwo Jima image with the live enactment of the raising of the American flag at Ground Zero. Again, this shift emphasizes the move from the national to the international, from the civilian to the militaristic. In this way, the performance becomes a patriotic support of the American war effort.

One year later, on January 26, 2003, the Dixie Chicks sang "The Star-Spangled Banner" at the Super Bowl, broadcast live by ABC. In retrospect, the patriotic character of their performance may seem atypical, as the Dixie Chicks are now best known for their anti-war announcement made at a concert in London, on March 10, 2003, stating that they were ashamed that President Bush is from Texas, the home state of the Dixie Chicks. As a result, the Dixie Chicks were boycotted by the major country radio channels, heavily criticized by fans, and shunned by fellow country singers, a backlash which has been documented in the film *Shut Up & Sing* (Barbara Kopple and Cecilia Peck, 2006). Yet, before the controversy, the Dixie Chicks were considered to be the most popular female singers of country, a music genre that has a long tradition of explicit pro-military patriotism.[29] At the next Super Bowl, broadcast live by NBC on February 1, 2004, "The Star-Spangled Banner" was performed by Beyoncé Knowles. As a young African-American R&B singer, Beyoncé was

FABRICATING THE ABSOLUTE FAKE

immediately compared to Whitney Houston, including by Beyoncé herself on *The Oprah Winfrey Show* (20 February 2004), telling the audience that singing "The Star-Spangled Banner" became her dream after seeing Houston's performance live on television.

The connection to the military is made explicit immediately at the opening of both ceremonies. The national anthem by the Dixie Chicks starts with a medium shot of the crew of the U.S.S. Preble, a guided missile destroyer of the U.S. Navy, with the announcer stating that the performance is "to honor America and our service men and women around the world." The performance by Beyoncé starts with the announcer introducing the Vice Chairman of the Joint Chiefs of Staff, General Peter Pace, who is shown in close-up, "representing our sailors, soldiers, airmen, marines, and coast guards serving our nation with pride around the world," followed by a word of gratitude: "To our military services we say thank you for your dedication and professionalism in protecting America's freedom." Subsequently, General Pace escorts Beyoncé to the stage, where she, dressed in an elegant white women's suit, sings "The Star-Spangled Banner." When Beyoncé sings "… so proudly we hailed …," a live connection is made to American soldiers stationed at Camp Freedom Rest in Bagdad, Iraq, watching the performance. Similar to Whitney Houston's grand finale in 1991, the explicit connection to the military is repeated at the end of the ceremonies with military aircrafts flying over the stadium. The performance by the Dixie Chicks ends with a fly-over of Super Hornet strike fighters by the VFA-122 Flying Eagles from the Naval Air Station Lemoore, while the Beyoncé performance ends with a fly-over of four Apache attack helicopters by the Texas National Guard.

Different than those of 1991 and 2002, however, the performances by the Dixie Chicks and Beyoncé do include the athletes of the football teams (in 2003, the Tampa Bay Buccaneers beat the Oakland Raiders; in 2004, the New England Patriots beat the Carolina Panthers). In the case of the Dixie Chicks, eleven close-ups of both black and white football players from both teams alternate with shots of military personnel, including a veteran in the audience, emphasizing the connection between the athletes and the military. During the 2004 performance by Beyoncé, the military is not present on the field, with the exception of the uniformed flag bearers. Also here the main focus is on the athletes, with seven close-ups of football players, again both black and white from both teams. In addition, the American flag is less prominently present in the performances of 2003 and 2004 than in those of 1991 and 2002. The Dixie Chicks performance does include two medium shots of a giant American flag on the field and one close-up of the American flag when the Dixie Chicks sing "… of the brave." In the Beyoncé performance, the conventional giant

American flag on the field has been replaced by the giant red-white-and-blue logo of the National Football League, which does include the flag's stars and stripes. Yet, like the Whitney Houston performance, the audience is prominently visible, holding (rather than waving) American flags as banners in their hands, thereby creating a large visual sea of red, white, and blue. On the one hand, the performances by the Dixie Chicks and Beyoncé differ from the performances by Whitney Houston and Mariah Carey, as they emphasize the athletes over explicit signs of military prowess, suggesting that the performances of 1991 and 2002 are stronger expressions of American patriotism, connected to specific moments in history which warrant such support, respectively the Gulf War and 9/11. On the other hand, however, the similarities between all four performances remain striking, showing that American patriotism and the military presence have become generic elements of the annual Super Bowl performance of "The Star-Spangled Banner."

The 2004 Super Bowl performance by Beyoncé was overshadowed by the controversy of the halftime show. When pop star Justin Timberlake tore off a part of singing partner Janet Jackson's costume, thereby exposing her naked right breast, the incident became a hot international news item and a topic of public debate about the lack of decency on American national television. The Federal Communication Commission (FCC) announced that it would investigate the incident. In a hearing before the Senate Commerce Committee, FCC chairman Michael Powell stated that the "now infamous display during the Super Bowl halftime show, which represented a new low in prime-time television, is just the latest example in a growing list of deplorable incidents over the nation's airwaves." Making an explicit reference to the American nation-state, Powell added, "Our nation's children, parents, and citizens deserve better."[30] This incident is significant as it exposes the lack of public discussion about the use of the Super Bowl as a forum for American patriotism and support for the American war effort. While a nude breast at the Super Bowl can lead to heated public debate and senatorial investigation, the overwhelming display of military power at the very same sports event remains uncontested. This suggests that the Barthesian myth is indeed effective, as, through the Super Bowl performances, the positive representation of American military power and American patriotism becomes naturalized and justified, without being contested or countered by oppositional arguments.

Although negotiated and oppositional readings of the four performances of "The Star-Spangled Banner" are possible (not all Americans watching the Super Bowl will recognize themselves in the national identity that is being constructed, and not all non-Americans watching the Super Bowl will accept the presented national identity as representative of "America"), the intertwining

FABRICATING THE ABSOLUTE FAKE

of sports, the military, patriotism, and popular entertainment presents a combination that remains difficult to resist. Bordering on propaganda, these performances of "The Star-Spangled Banner" use the double function of the American flag as national symbol and as advertising logo to represent American patriotism, to paraphrase Roland Barthes, as innocent and natural, not as an explanation, but as a statement of fact. In the end, the performances of the national anthem by Whitney Houston, Mariah Carey, the Dixie Chicks, and Beyoncé do not provide an invitation to question the role of the nation-state USA in international politics, but instead justify its military action of "protecting freedom around the world" by assuring the audience that the American flag is indeed still there.

AMERICA IN THE DESERT OF HOLLYWOOD

In *Imagining America at War*, Cynthia Weber analyzes war films that were shown in the American cinemas immediately after 9/11, ranging from *Pearl Harbor* (Michael Bay, 2001) and *We Were Soldiers* (Randall Wallace, 2002) to *Black Hawk Down* (Ridley Scott, 2001) and *Minority Report* (Steven Spielberg, 2002), suggesting that these films help to understand what it means to be American. As Weber points out, while both World War II and the Vietnam War are prominently present in the American cinematic discourse, the Gulf War remains conspicuously underrepresented.[31] Compared to the amount of Hollywood movies set during War War II and the Vietnam War, including recent ones, the absence of the Gulf War in Hollywood film is indeed significant. Exceptions include the action film *The Finest Hour* (Shimon Dotan, 1991), starring Rob Lowe as an American Navy SEAL who goes to Iraq in search of biomedical weapons, and the courthouse drama *Courage under Fire* (Edward Zwick, 1996), starring Denzel Washington and Meg Ryan. One could also perceive the science fiction of *Starship Troopers* (Paul Verhoeven, 1997) as an allegory of the Gulf War. Yet, the notable exceptions are *Three Kings* (David O. Russell, 1999), which is set in Iraq right after the Gulf War has ended, and *Jarhead* (Sam Mendes, 2005), based on the memoirs by former Gulf War soldier Anthony Swofford. Although the films differ significantly, they do share two important characteristics. First, both *Three Kings* and *Jarhead* present the Gulf War in a surrealist setting, emphasized by the way the films use visual special effects and saturated colors to portray the desert as an alienating space. Second, both films use Hollywood cinema and American pop music as main points of reference, thereby explicitly connecting the international politics of the Gulf War to the globally mediated American pop culture.

Jean Baudrillard's notion that the Gulf War did not take place is present in both films. *Three Kings* starts with the onscreen text "March 1991. The war just ended," followed by the voice of soldier Troy Barlow (Mark Wahlberg), shouting "Are we shooting?" right before he kills his first and only Iraqi soldier. "I didn't think I'd see someone get shot in this war," his fellow soldier Conrad Vig (Spike Jonze) dryly comments, not realizing that the war is in fact over. By setting all the action immediately after the war has ended, *Three Kings* emphasizes that the preceding Gulf War in itself was a non-event. *Jarhead*, in its turn, takes place before, during, and after Operation Desert Storm, but most of the film focuses on the American soldiers waiting in the desert for the war to begin, spending their time alternating between masturbating and cleaning their rifles, a rather obvious but effective analogy which reinforces the connection between masculinity and warfare, foregrounding the frustrating male impotence of not being able to fulfill the act of "real" sex and "real" war. Baudrillard also makes such a connection by discussing the Gulf War as a striptease inviting futile masturbation, "following the calculated escalation of undressing and approaching the incandescent point of explosion (like that of erotic effusion) but at the same time withdrawing from it and maintaining a deceptive suspense (teasing), such that when the naked body finally appears, it is no longer naked, desire no longer exists and the orgasm is cut short."[32] Indeed, once Operation Desert Storm eventually begins, the *Jarhead* soldiers soon realize the war is being fought – literally – over their heads, by the air force's smart bombing. When Anthony "Swoff" Swofford (Jake Gyllenhaal), trained as a Marine Corps Scout Sniper, is finally about to kill his first Iraqi officer, he does not get permission to shoot, as the whole military base will be bombed soon anyway. Thus, after months of anticipation, Swoff does not get to fire his rifle. His orgasmic shot is cut short.

While *Jarhead* uses the non-eventness of the Gulf War as backdrop to the main protagonist's coming-of-age narrative ("every man has his own war" is the film's tagline), *Three Kings* replaces the non-event with an exciting in-search-of-the-hidden-treasure adventure which evolves into a conventional American-as-savior narrative. In their search for the hidden gold, looted from Kuwait by the Iraqi army, Archie Gates (George Clooney), Chief Elgin (Ice Cube), Troy Barlow, and Conrad Vig encounter a group of dissident Iraqis who, with their families, try to flee Iraq. When a dissident Iraqi woman is executed by the Iraqi army, in front of her husband and her children, the American soldiers make a choice. Although initially motivated by their greed for gold, the American soldiers heroically save the refugees by guiding them into freedom, which, rather ironically, is found across the border in Iran. This storyline can be viewed as a criticism of American international policy, as the film suggests that the interests of the USA are based solely on securing the oil supply, in spite of its rhetoric of promoting democracy around the world. Moreover, *Three Kings* explicitly states that the American government has let the Iraqi people down by not following up its promise to protect them. As Archie Gates, played by the film's main movie star George Clooney, tells his soldiers (and, in extension, the audience): "Bush told the [Iraqi] people to rise up against Saddam. They thought they'd have our support. They don't. Now they're getting slaughtered." In other words, the film does not criticize American imperialism in itself, but merely its execution by the Bush administration. The choice made by Archie Gates and his fellow military men conforms to the Hollywood convention of the independent hero who defies the power of the authorities so he can do the right thing. In this way, *Three Kings* ends up reinforcing the image of an ideal America as the protector of freedom and democracy, not questioning if the American presence in Iraq was justified, but why the USA failed to do its job. In his analysis of the film, Jude Davies suggests that such a reading is too limited, as *Three Kings* contains "ideological structures of sameness and difference [which] continue to play along and across the film's narratives to create multiple and sometimes contradictory poles of Americanness."[33] Although at moments the film does satirize its genre, thereby inviting a less hegemonic reading, its overall American-as-savior narrative, which favors an ideal America over the nation-state USA, remains dominant.

Compared to *Three Kings*, *Jarhead* is less explicit about the role the USA plays, focusing more on the senselessness of the war experience in general than on the specific politics of the Gulf War. Perhaps the most critical moment of the film is when Swoff's unit comes across the infamous Highway of Death, the road between Kuwait and Basra that was heavily bombed by the American air force, leaving a long trail of burnt-out vehicles and charred corpses. On the one hand, the scene works as a reminder that smart bombing causes real death, which is emphasized when Swoff is isolated from his unit and joins a circle of "sitting" burned dead bodies. This scene prompted Cynthia Fuchs to comment: "The effect is more harrowing than any battle sequence, underlining *Jarhead*'s anguished point: war is not heroic or rousing. It is only devastating."[34] Yet, on the other hand, such portrayal of devastation and, in particular, Swoff's identification with the dead Iraqi bodies, can also function as, repeating Baudrillard's earlier quoted words, "an alibi for those who do not want to have been excited for nothing," an attempt to prove that "this war was indeed a war and not a shameful and pointless hoax."[35] The scene says more about Swoff's character development (his realization that he is involved in "real" war) than the actual politics of the Gulf War, and, in extension, more about America than Iraq.

Here a connection can be made between Hollywood films depicting the war in Vietnam and the two Gulf War films. In *America*, Jean Baudrillard argues that the Vietnam War was won by both sides: "by the Vietnamese on the ground, [and] by the Americans in the electronic mental space. And if the one side won an ideological and political victory, the other made *Apocalypse Now* and that has gone right around the world."[36] The significant point is that the "real" Vietnam War has been taken over by the Vietnam War as mediated by Hollywood, as the latter has shaped its global perception. In a similar way, the hyperreality of the Gulf War, as broadcast live on television and as fictionalized by Hollywood with *Three Kings* and *Jarhead*, reduces the war's political reality to an American conception of the Gulf War. Moreover, such a perception is framed by the cinematic experience of the Vietnam War. In *Three Kings*, the American soldiers drive their Humvee through the desert, throwing footballs in the air as shooting targets, referring to the scene from *Apocalypse Now* (Francis Ford Coppola, 1979) in which the American soldiers are waterskiing and firing at Vietnam locals while going down the river on an army patrol boat. In *Jarhead*, the soldiers clap and cheer when watching *Apocalypse Now*'s famous scene in which the American military violently attacks a Vietnamese village while Richard Wagner's "Ride of the Valkyries" is blasting out of helicopter loudspeakers as form of psychological warfare. Vietnam films function like pornography for a soldier in training, "getting him ready for his First Fuck," writes Anthony Swofford in his memoirs, and thus "Vietnam films are all pro-war, no matter what the supposed message, what Kubrick or Coppola or Stone intended."[37]

While during the Vietnam War the psychological warfare by the American army included loud broadcasts of Wagner, during the Gulf War they played rock music of the 1960s and 1970s, such as "Beach Boys, AC/DC, and Jimi Hendrix's shrill 'Star-Spangled Banner,' repeated ad nauseam until the enemy submits out of sheer annoyance."[38] When in *Jarhead* "Break on Through" by the Doors is blasting out of a helicopter's speakers, Swoff complains: "That's Vietnam music, man. Can't we get our own fucking music?" In his memoirs, Anthony Swofford expands on why this music does not belong in his Gulf War. "It was fine in the movies, ... but I don't need the Who and the Doors in my war, as I prepare to fight for or lose my life. Teenage wasteland, my ass. This is the other side."[39] In both *Three Kings* and *Jarhead* the Gulf War soldiers eventually do get their "own music," shifting from the cinematic Vietnam War to contemporary American pop culture. Countercultural rock became Vietnam music, African-American rap the sound of the Gulf War. The opening sequence of *Three Kings*, after Troy Barlow has killed the Iraqi soldier, starts with Rare Earth's "I Just Want To Celebrate" from 1971, a song from the Vietnam era, its upbeat rhythm emphasizing the playful images of hunky bare-chested soldiers sunbathing and jumping around, followed by the soldiers singing along to Lee Greenwood's patriotic country hit song "God Bless the USA," originally released in 1984 and revived as a Gulf War anthem. The celebration continues with the soldiers dancing to two contemporary rap and dance songs, Public Enemy's "Can't Do Nuttin' for Ya Man" and Snap!'s "The Power." In *Jarhead*, the end of the war is celebrated in a similar way. When Swoff and fellow soldier Troy (Peter Sarsgaard) return from their special mission, they first wander through the desolate desert, only to stumble upon their unit partying around a large bonfire in the middle of nowhere, dancing to Public Enemy's "Fight the Power," and firing their rifles into the air. The irony is not lost. The soldiers only get to shoot their rifles once the war is over, while they celebrate the American victory by chanting along to a rap song that induces its listeners to "fight the power" of American authority and its white patriotism as embodied by its pop-cultural heroes Elvis Presley and John Wayne.

This diegetic music, both the psychological warfare and the dance songs of the victory parties, enhances the surrealist quality of desert, which, as mentioned before, is expressed in *Three Kings* and *Jarhead* through the use of visual special effects and saturated colors. *Three Kings* even provides a warning that its "visual distortion and unusual colors" are intentional, meant "to enhance the emotional intensity of the storyline." The desert functions as an empty space, in which the combination of surrealist visuals and overwhelming sounds evokes a feeling of alienation. The desert can also be perceived as a Baudrillardian hyperreality, as a space without an origin. Its hyperreality lies not so much in the fact that both films were shot in the deserts of southern California and in Hollywood studios, thus "really" being part of the American rather than the Iraqi landscape. More relevant is the symbolic quality of the desert as the embodiment of an imagined America, like Baudrillard encountered when traveling through the USA. Deserts are so fascinating, writes Baudrillard, "because you are delivered from all depth there – a brilliant, mobile, superficial neutrality, a challenge to meaning and profundity, a challenge to nature and culture, an outer hyperspace, with no origin, no reference-points."[40] Applied to the Gulf War, the Iraqi desert becomes a Hollywood desert, just another image in the endless stream of images that American pop culture mediates globally. In his review of *Three Kings*, *Sight & Sound* film critic Jim Hoberman recognizes such a connection: "Operating at the far frontier of television space, [the] heroes cannot help but find America."[41] This America that Hoberman refers to is not the nation-state USA, but an imagined America consisting of consumer goods and media images. The heroes of *Three Kings* enter bunkers all filled with western consumer goods, looted by the Iraqi army during its invasion of Kuwait. One of the looted televisions shows footage of the Rodney King video, containing images of the African-American taxi driver being beaten by four white Los Angeles police officers. Shot on March 3, 1991, and televised worldwide almost immediately, the video sparked protests against racism and police brutality, eventually leading to the Los Angeles riots of 1992. As several scholars have suggested, the televised violence against Rodney King cannot be disassociated from the mostly non-televised violence by the American army in Iraq.[42] In this way, the Gulf War desert becomes another part of America where the *Three Kings* and *Jarhead* soldiers encounter a seemingly empty space that is not only being penetrated by the American military, but which also has been permeated with American media and pop culture.

The global presence of American pop culture is made even more explicit when, in addition to Rodney King, Michael Jackson pops up in the desert of *Three Kings*. While in 1985 Michael Jackson (when "We Are the World" was recorded, as discussed in chapter one) could be viewed as an embodiment of the American Dream, by 1991 his star image had become tarnished. Michael Jackson came to be known as "Wacko Jacko" based on rumors about him sleeping in a hyperbaric chamber, the alleged whitening of his skin, and the cosmetic alterations to his nose and body. His controversial image intensified later on in the 1990s with his self-proclaimed title of being the "King of Pop," his short marriage to Lisa Marie Presley, daughter of that other American "king," Elvis, and accusations of child molestation. In a 1987 *Village Voice* essay, entitled "I'm White!: What's Wrong with Michael Jackson," Greg Tate perceives Jackson as "a casualty of America's ongoing race war – another Negro gone mad because his mirror reports that his face does not conform to the Nordic ideal."[43] In *Three Kings*, the issue reappears when Mark Wahlberg's character Troy Barlow is captured and tortured by the Iraqi army officer Captain Said, the latter played by the Moroccan-French actor Saïd Taghmaoui. "What is the problem with Michael Jackson?" asks Said, giving the answer himself: "Your country make him chop up his face. Michael Jackson is pop king of sick fucking country. A black man make the skin white and the hair straight, and you know why? Your sick fucking country make the black man hate hisself just like you hate the Arab and the children you bomb over here." Similar to the Rodney King video, the appearance of Michael Jackson ties the American presence in Iraq to practices of racism in the USA, thereby giving Jackson's initial role as an ideological ambassador of the American values propagated by "We Are the World" an ironic twist.[44] Yet, the use of Jackson to suggest that the American military presence in Iraq is rooted in racism also reinforces the global dominance of American pop culture, continuing to render the devastation in Iraq invisible by shaping the Gulf War within an American conception of the world.

"Welcome to the desert of the real," says Orpheus (Laurence Fishburne), when he reveals to Neo (Keanu Reeves) that his idea of the world is actually a computer-generated virtual reality called "the matrix," masking a complex system of artificial intelligence which uses living humans as source of energy. The desert of the real, as shown to Neo, consists of a burnt and desolate landscape, an American city ruined by war. With this pivotal scene, the Hollywood blockbuster *The Matrix* (Andy Wachowski and Larry Wachowski, 1999) makes an explicit reference to Jean Baudrillard's concept of hyperreality, as Morpheus is quoting from his *Simulacra and Simulation*, originally published in French in 1981. The film knowingly cites Baudrillard, as in an earlier scene, Neo is shown owning a copy of the book.[45] "Welcome to the Desert of the Real!" is also the title of an essay by Slavoj Žižek, published right after the terrorist attacks of September 11, 2001, and later expanded to a five-essay book edition. As Žižek suggests, 9/11 could function as a "Welcome to the desert of the real" moment, enabling American citizens to realize that they, like Neo, have been living in some sort of virtual reality, far removed from the reality of global politics:

> Either America will persist in, strengthen even, the attitude, "Why should this happen to us? Things like this don't happen *here!*" ... or America will finally risk stepping through the fantasmatic screen separating it from the Outside World, accepting its arrival into the Real world, making the long-overdue move from "Things like this should hot happen *here!*" to "Things like this should not happen *anywhere!*" America's "holiday from history" was a fake: America's peace was bought by the catastrophes going on elsewhere. Therein resides the true lesson of the bombings.[46]

Just like Truman Burbank (Jim Carrey) in *The Truman Show* (Peter Weir, 1998) realizes that his life so far has been a television reality show, Žižek suggests that America may come to perceive American life as a hyperreality, as a blockbuster movie which has been surpassed by the reality of 9/11.

Jean Baudrillard recognizes a similar function for 9/11 in his essay "L'Esprit du Terrorisme," written only a few days after September 11, by describing the terrorist attacks on the World Trade Center not as a non-event (as he did with the first Gulf War), but as "the absolute event, the 'mother event,' the pure event that concentrates in itself all the events that never took place."[47] This does not mean that 9/11 signifies "a resurgence of the real," but an accelerated state of hyperreality, taken to its fullest extreme.[48] With 9/11, Baudrillard suggests, reality has "absorbed fiction's energy, and has itself become fiction," in the form of an absolute media event existing of the televised image, to which "the real is superadded ... like a bonus of terror, like an additional *frisson*: not only is it terrifying, but, what is more, it is real."[49] Similar to his aforementioned argument that fiction shapes imagination in the form of reality, Jean Baudrillard argues that the "fictional" media event of 9/11, the repeated images of planes flying into the Twin Towers, shot from many different angles, has turned the imagination of the Hollywood disaster movie into images of reality.

In retrospect, however, America seems to have taken Slavoj Žižek's first option, remaining behind its fantasmatic screen of Hollywood and television. By 2006, 9/11 has been fictionalized and dramatized in films like *United 93* (Paul Greengrass, 2006) and *World Trade Center* (Oliver Stone, 2006), which, conform the conventions of Hollywood, emphasize the heroism of individual Americans, such as common plane passengers and New York City firefighters. On television, the controversial two-episode miniseries *The Path to 9/11* (ABC, 10 and 11 September 2006), although more critical of the role of the American government, also focused on the personalized story of the real-life John P. O'Neill, played on the small screen by Harvey Keitel, who had just started his job as head of security at the Twin Towers a couple of days before being killed. Even counter-narratives, such as the documentary *Fahrenheit 9/11* (Michael Moore, 2004), stay behind the fantasmatic screen, using similar strategies of fictionalization and dramatization as Hollywood cinema. In spite of being critical of the politics of the nation-state USA, these counter-narratives reconfirm rather than undermine the idealism of an imagined America.

Although belonging to different genres, the pop-cultural performances that have been analyzed in this chapter all contribute to an American conception of the world, yet in distinctive different ways. The Super Bowl performances of "The Star-Spangled Banner" by Whitney Houston, Mariah Carey, the Dixie Chicks, and Beyoncé turn an American national event into an expression of support of the international politics of the nation-state USA, whereas films like *Three Kings* and *Jarhead* turn the international event of warfare into a personalized American experience. Nevertheless, in all cases, American pop culture, embodied by these pop and movie stars, is used to shape the American conception of international politics, thereby not only reinforcing the myth of the American Dream as an uncontested universal ideal but also rendering other perspectives invisible. In this manner, these pop-cultural artifacts can be perceived as being part of a hyperreal America, as they express the American experience as fiction which shapes, as Baudrillard suggests, imagination into the form of reality. Moreover, this hyperreal America transcends the geographical boundaries of the nation-state USA, as it is being mediated through pop culture around the world.

The global dominance of American pop culture unexpectedly became clear in an incident during the first Gulf War, when the female American soldier Melissa Rathbun-Nealy was captured by the Iraqi army. In stark contrast to the widely publicized story of Jessica Lynch, who became the face of the second Gulf War, little attention has been paid to the Rathbun-Nealy story. Rather than being heroically saved by the American Special Forces, Rathbun-Nealy was released by the Iraqi army after the Gulf War was officially over. Back in the USA, she did not have much to say about her experience, merely stating that the Iraqi officials had treated her well. Moreover, they had complimented her for being as "brave as [Sylvester] Stallone and as beautiful as Brooke Shields."[50] It is this power of American pop culture, irresistible for Americans and non-Americans alike, which will assure that America's holiday from history is far from over.

CHAPTER FOUR

Americans We Never Were:

Dutch Pop Culture as Karaoke Americanism

"Dear wonderful, beautiful Europe. I know we've had our disagreements in the past, but I'm here to tell you, I have never stopped loving you Europe." These words are spoken by President George W. Bush on January 26, 2005, at a special press conference in the Netherlands, broadcast on the television comedy show *Kopspijkers* (VARA, 1995-2005). Then Bush starts to sing: "Maybe I didn't treat you, quite as good as I should have. Maybe I didn't love you, quite as much as I could have. I'm so sorry about Abu Ghraib, and Kyoto I should have signed. But you were always on mind, Europe, you were always on my mind." Obviously, this is not the real President Bush singing, but a parody, performed by the Dutch comedian Thomas van Luyn. Sung in American English with a slight country twinge and subtitled in Dutch for the viewers at home, Bush's rendition of the Elvis Presley classic "Always on My Mind" plays with the stereotype of American ignorance versus European intellectualism. Admitting that he has never cared much for "those little countries you live in, with your museums and those books you read," President Bush delivers a melodramatic plea, with vocal harmonies provided by his bodyguards, asking Europe to "give me one more chance to get you on my side." The parody works not only because American pop culture is used to satirize American international politics, but also because of the (easily overlooked) factor that the Dutch viewers must be familiar with American pop culture. Knowing the original version of "Always on My Mind," or recognizing its genre conventions, is crucial for getting the joke.

"America is the original version of modernity," writes Jean Baudrillard in *America*, adding: "We [in Europe] are the dubbed or subtitled version."[1] His use of dubbing and subtitling as metaphor is striking, as the cultural appropriation of "America" in European pop cultures is most explicitly visible in audiovisual media such as film, television, and internet. In this chapter, I will use Dutch pop culture as a starting point to examine how such appropriation takes place.

"America" is omnipresent in Dutch pop culture, not only through the consumption of products that are actually made in the USA, but also through the production of pop-cultural artifacts such as movies, television programs, and music videos that are made in the Netherlands and seem to imitate American pop culture. Even in times of renewed European anti-Americanism, American pop culture continues to be popular, functioning as the "original" to which the local "national" pop culture is compared. How should we perceive these "American" but "made in Holland" artifacts? Are they merely imitations, the one more successful than the other, or have we instead made the American audiovisual language and genre conventions our own to such an extent that we can take the comparison with the American original for granted? "We are always the last link in these chains of mediation, the final recipients of messages from America," suggests Rob Kroes. "In that position we are never purely and only passive, gradually losing our Dutchness while becoming even more American. We make room for 'America' in a context of meaning and significance that is ours."[2] It is within this context of meaning and significance that I want to explore how "we" redefine "America" through the appropriation of the American original in Dutch pop culture.

To address these questions, I will use the concept of "the American I never was," borrowed from Chris Keulemans, the concept of the absolute fake, as coined by Umberto Eco, and the concept of karaoke Americanism, as coined by Thomas Elsaesser. These concepts can help to discuss Americanized Dutch pop culture as a form of hyper-Americanness without having to fall back upon too essentialist notions of what should be considered American or Dutch, thereby leaving room for more ambivalent and overlapping identities. Subsequently, I will apply these concepts to four different case studies of Dutch celebrities: singer Lee Towers, media personalities Adam Curry and Patricia Paay, actress Katja Schuurman, and Moroccan-Dutch rapper Ali B. Together, these four examples of "Americans they never were" show different ways in which American pop culture has been translated within a Dutch pop-cultural context.

Hyper-Americanness and Karaoke Americanism

Immediately after the terrorist attacks of September 11, 2001, "we were all Americans," as suggested by the famous headline of the French newspaper *Le Monde*.[3] On the political level, this transatlantic solidarity between Europe and the USA proved to be a short-lived sentiment, as soon it was challenged by the unilateral stance of the Bush administration – with its War on Terror and the subsequent war in Iraq – resulting in a revival of European anti-Americanism.

As Rob Kroes has pointed out, such anti-Americanism is not new, but rooted in two long European traditions. On the one hand, there is a European anti-Americanism which despises the alleged shallowness of American pop culture, but admires the "prowess, idealism, and optimism" of American politics, whereas on the other, there is a European anti-Americanism which "rejects an American political creed that, for all its missionary zeal, is perceived as imperialist and oppressive, while it admires American culture, from its highbrow to its pop varieties."[4] Politically, Europeans might no longer be Americans, but culturally "we" remain, to use the concept of Chris Keulemans, "Americans we never were," living within a society that is permeated with American pop culture. As Europeans, we have grown up with Walt Disney, Hollywood, Coca-Cola, and American television programs, and we recognize these pop-cultural artifacts as belonging both to "America" as well as to our own culture in which we have lived all our lives.

The ambivalent position of political anti-Americanism combined with a very personal investment in American pop culture was the focus of the art exhibition *This is America: Visions on the American Dream*, held by the Centraal Museum Utrecht in 2006. The exhibition takes as its starting point that "we all carry the American Dream within us, yet, similar to this dreamed America, we also cannot break loose from the America that we despise."[5] By bringing together artwork by contemporary international artists, ranging from Candice Breitz and Aernout Mik to Tom Sachs and the Guerrilla Girls, with American photorealistic paintings from the 1960s and 1970s, the exhibition emphasizes how images of American consumerist culture have become iconic representations of an imagined America around the world. In addition to these works, the exhibition includes a book with autobiographical perspectives on the American Dream written by Dutch writers, journalists, and scholars. These essays show how, in spite of possible objections to the politics of the nation-state USA, most authors remain personally connected to the pop culture of their imagined America. The essay by Joost Zwagerman, for example, argues that the America of one's youth cannot be disassociated from the contemporary one, as there remains a strong familiarity with America, one which is rooted in American pop culture, and, regardless of the great distance, is not "virtual or imaginary," but "intensely sensual and passionate," inviting us to identify ourselves as being "American."[6]

With his multimedia project *The American I Never Was*, Chris Keulemans shows how American pop culture, and specifically film (*West Side Story*, *Taxi Driver*), pop music (James Brown, Bruce Springsteen, USA for Africa), and pop-cultural icons (Batman and Robin, Muhammad Ali), has shaped his life and colored his memories.[7] Although born in the Netherlands, Keulemans grew up in different international places, including Tunisia, Iraq, and Indonesia, and more importantly, attended international American elementary schools where he was taught to be "a little American patriot, ready for Junior High." However, instead of "returning" to New Jersey, the American state that had become his imagined home (although he never actually had been there), Keulemans returned to the Netherlands, where, eventually, he became more critical of the nation-state USA: "I was raised with the stereotypical, unabashed, happy and heroic image that the USA could export of itself with impunity until 1968. After that I learned, like my whole generation, the darker sides of America: from Irangate to the Gulf War, from the permanent segregation to the omnipresent commercialization. Still, I never completely lost touch with that little boy's paradise."[8] Once, as part of his project, Keulemans finally does visit New Jersey, his imaginary home, it proves to be an ambivalent experience. On the one hand, he recognizes "home" from all the images embedded in his memory, yet, on the other, the confrontation with the "real" New Jersey, especially when he attends a local 9/11 memorial, makes Keulemans realize he is not an American after all.

Even though Chris Keulemans uses "the American I never was" to express his own personal experience, the concept can be applied more generally to look at the way Dutch people have grown up with American pop culture, incorporating "America" within their everyday lives, histories, and memories. Indeed, as Rob Kroes points out: "Generation upon generation of Europeans, growing up after the war, can all tell their own story of a mythical America as they constructed it, drawing on American advertisements, songs, film, and so on."[9] In this sense, we are all Americans we never were, experiencing American pop culture as both foreign and local. The distinction between what is American and what is Dutch has become blurred and seemingly irrelevant.

To grasp this blurred Dutch American pop culture, I need to go beyond the rigid dichotomies that traditionally mark the divide between America and Europe, including – but not limited to – American shallowness versus European depth, American artificiality versus European authenticity, American populism versus European intellectualism, and American lack of history versus European sense of history.[10] In *European Cinema*, Thomas Elsaesser recognizes a similar distinction in the relation between European cinemas and Hollywood. Rightfully arguing that we should move beyond such dichotomies, Elsaesser identifies them to show how the divide between Europe and Hollywood continues to be applied:

> Europe stands for art, and the US for pop; Europe for high culture, America for mass entertainment; Europe for artisanal craft, America for

industrial mass production; Europe for state (subsidy), Hollywood for studio (box office); European cinema for pain and effort, Hollywood for pleasure and thrills; Europe for the auteur, Hollywood for the star; Europe for experiment and discovery, Hollywood for formula and marketing; Europe for film festival circuit, Hollywood for Oscar night; Europe for the festival hit, Hollywood for the blockbuster.[11]

Although seemingly antagonistic, the two poles of this rigid distinction actually complement each other, being two sides of the same coin. As Thomas Elsaesser shows, European national cinemas develop not so much in opposition to, but in relation with Hollywood, "existing in a space set up like a hall of mirrors, in which recognition, imaginary identity and mis-cognition enjoy equal status, creating value out of pure difference."[12] Applied to pop culture in general, the distinction between a highbrow Europe versus a lowbrow America, defined in opposition to each other, sustains the cultural industries on both sides of the Atlantic.

How this divide works is shown by the way both American and Dutch film critics review the Dutch film *Antonia* (Marleen Gorris, 1995), internationally released as *Antonia's Line*, which celebrates female independency with a story of four generations of women living in a small Dutch village. American film critics tend to perceive *Antonia* as a European art film. The *Boston Review*, for example, recognizes *Antonia* as "Mozartian in its beauty – so artfully made that we are carried along by the surprising flow of the narrative without being forced to recognize the intellectual daring and craft of the filmmaker."[13] Dutch film critics, on the contrary, and writing after the film has won the Academy Award in the best foreign language film category, accuse *Antonia*'s director Marleen Gorris of having made a Hollywood movie. In his article "Why Americans love *Antonia*," Hans Kroon suggests that Americans love the escapism which *Antonia* provides, as its simplistic and folkloric portrayal of life in an imaginary countryside enables its spectators to find temporary relief away from their own hectic existence. Tom Ronse sees the American popularity as proof of *Antonia*'s American shallowness, claiming that its one-dimensional character makes the film "ready to eat, easily digestible." According to Ab van Ieperen, *Antonia* is a Dutch feminist version of the American pioneer western, including its convention of letting the plot prevail over character development.[14] Regardless of whether or not these film critics, both the American and the Dutch ones, are correct in their judgments, they all reinforce the traditional distinction between America and Europe. However, they also reveal its limitations, as *Antonia* embodies, on the American side, European depth, and, on the Dutch side, American shallowness.

This traditional Europe versus America divide is further undermined by the "American" pop culture produced in Europe. Throughout the twentieth century, Europeans often have denounced American pop culture as empty and shallow, as superficial and artificial. However, simultaneously, Europeans have denounced European expressions of pop culture – particularly pop music and commercial "feel good" cinema – as weak imitations of the American "real thing." The result is a peculiar reversal. Although American pop culture continues to be perceived as artificial, when discussing European commercial pop culture, the American artificiality suddenly becomes American authenticity. As discussed in chapter one, the perception of American pop culture as being authentic is based on its initial role as a rebellious form of expression for European youth subcultures, which recognized that it was not empty and shallow, but open to new meanings and liberating values.[15] Winfried Fluck suggests that "even the most conventional and maligned symbols of American consumer culture such as Coca-Cola or McDonald's bear a connotation of informality that can still be experienced as liberating by young people in many parts of the world."[16] The attractiveness of American pop culture and the recognition of its authenticity are today no longer limited to youth subcultures (although new forms of American popular culture, like hip-hop, may still function in this way), but tend to be widely accepted among different generations. Especially when compared to Dutch pop-cultural artifacts, American pop culture has become the authentic standard.

To understand how a pop culture that traditionally had been perceived as shallow and artificial can become a sign of authenticity, it is helpful to use the concept of hyperreality. Based on their travels in the USA, Umberto Eco and Jean Baudrillard both have used hyperreality to describe how they have experienced "America." Yet, these two European intellectuals use hyperreality in significantly different ways. Eco, in his *Travels in Hyperreality*, focuses on how American culture consists of perfect copies of original cultural artifacts. Citing Disneyland and Las Vegas as well as the full-scale copy of the Oval Office in the LBJ Library and the copy of the Manhattan Purchase Act (in English rather than in its original Dutch) at the Museum of the City of New York, Eco shows that these artifacts are not merely copies, but are even more perfect than the originals. "To speak of things that one wants to connote as real, these things must seem real. The 'completely real' becomes identified with the 'completely fake.' Absolute unreality is offered as real presence." It is this search for "realness" – or better, as Eco recalls the Coca-Cola slogan, "the real thing" – that makes American popular culture hyperreal. According to Eco, "the American imagination demands the real thing and, to attain it, must fabricate the absolute fake."[17] The absolute fake is not merely an imitation, but a hyperbole of the original, more "real" and "authentic" than the original. Umberto Eco's hyper-reality differs significantly from Baudrillard's, as Eco's still refers to an original, while Baudrillard perceives the hyperreal America as living "in perpetual simulation, in a perpetual present of signs."[18] In Baudrillard's *America*, as discussed in chapter three, the original no longer exists, as it is already a copy of a copy, a simulacrum, just another sign in an endless chain of signs that only refer to each other.

Rob Kroes rightly points out that both Eco's and Baudrillard's notion of American hyperreality remains quintessentially European. Whereas, on the one hand, Europeans tend to perceive American culture as "empty" (thus shallow, superficial, lacking the historical and artistic depth that allegedly constitutes traditional European culture), on the other, the "emptiness" of America enables Europeans to fill up this space with their own images of America, an imagined America, often using the images provided by American pop culture. In this way, America functions as a mirror image of Europe, as an empty screen on which such "liberating" concepts as lack of history and lack of significance can be projected.[19] Yet, the concept of hyperreality proves useful when discussing the Americanization of Dutch pop culture and the appropriation of American pop-cultural signs in Dutch pop-cultural production. Eco's hyperreality may turn out to be the most effective, as it still recognizes the "original" – in this case the American pop-cultural artifacts that, as hyperreality, are perceived by the Dutch public as "the real thing." Dutch pop-cultural artifacts that imitate American pop culture, on the contrary, are easily recognized as "fakes." To paraphrase Eco, "the Dutch imagination demands the real thing and, to attain it, must fabricate the absolute fake" through presenting a hyperreal imitation of American pop culture. I use the term "hyper-Americanness" to describe this Dutch absolute fake, which is, after all, a hyperreal copy of an American original that, in its turn, is also a hyperreal copy. Hyper-Americanness is so "American" that Dutch people may recognize it as "really American," while Americans may not recognize it as "American" at all. Again, an ironic twist of argument is the result, as now Europe signifies artificiality, while America is its authentic original. By naming America the "original version of modernity," even Jean Baudrillard had to admit that in this case an original copy does exist. "We merely imitate them, parody them with a fifty-year time lag, and we are not even successful at that."[20]

Yet, the perception of Dutch pop-cultural artifacts as absolute fakes, rather than mere imitations or parodies, makes room for interpretations that rely less on the question of whether or not the dubbed or subtitled version is a successful copy of the American "original" one. Instead, the focus shifts to how American pop culture – its genre conventions and audiovisual language – can function as an international lingua franca in the shaping of national or other cultural identities. By recognizing the hyper-American character of the absolute fake, its explicit Americanness can be analyzed as part of a larger pop-cultural discourse, without getting trapped in the Europe versus America divide. Moreover, by approaching Dutch pop culture in this way, both sides of the Americanization debate – emphasizing either its being a form of cultural imperialism or instead a form of cultural appropriation – can be acknowledged, as well as the ambiguity between anti-Americanism and a personal investment in American pop culture. A similar approach is suggested by Thomas Elsaesser, who defines what I call hyper-Americanness as a discourse of karaoke Americanism. As Elsaesser explains, "besides the discourse of anti-Americanism and of counter-Americanism, we may have to find the terms of another discourse: let me call it, ... the discourse of karaoke-Americanism – that doubly coded space of identity as overlap and deferral, as compliment and camouflage."[21] The use of the karaoke metaphor – which places much more emphasis on the performative character of Americanization than Baudrillard's metaphor of subtitling or dubbing does – may appear to be rather pejorative, but is actually an effective tool to grasp the ambiguities captured within the absolute fake. As a performance based on clichéd pop-cultural conventions yet inviting creative participation, karaoke signifies both faithful imitation and playful parody, both mimicking and mockery, enabling a cultural appropriation of American pop culture in which "fakeness" is its most defining characteristic.

To explore this notion of hyper-Americanness in Dutch pop culture further, I will apply the concepts of the absolute fake and karaoke Americanism to four specific examples of Dutch stardom. As discussed in chapter one, American stars can be viewed as ideological ambassadors of American pop culture, embodying many different and often contradictory values. Building on Richard Dyer's notion that the star myth is heavily invested in the American Dream, I want to explore how Dutch celebrities fit within such an American-inspired star myth.[22] The focus on stars rather than (only) on specific films, television programs, or music videos has the advantage of recognizing the values of Americanness that the star myth embodies. The four case studies of Dutch stardom – Lee Towers, Adam Curry and Patricia Paay, Katja Schuurman, and Ali B – are all related to American pop culture, albeit each in a different way. By approaching them as "Americans they never were," as examples of hyper-American absolute fakes performing karaoke Americanism, I am able to analyze how these Dutch stars appropriate the signs, genre conventions, and audiovisual language of American pop culture in their performances and in the construction of their star images. Without suggesting that these particular stars present the only way in which American pop culture has been appropriated in the Netherlands, or that they are representative of the whole of Dutch pop culture, these four case studies of Dutch "Americans they never were" do present telling examples of pop-cultural appropriation.

LEE TOWERS: LIVING THE AMERICAN DREAM

The ultimate American he never was in Dutch pop culture is undoubtedly singer Lee Towers, whose stage name in itself is a reference to American pop culture. The Dutch National Pop Institute describes him as "the Dutch cross between Frank Sinatra, Tony Bennett, and Elvis Presley in his Las Vegas years."[23] Always dressed in a black tuxedo and black tie, and holding a golden microphone, Lee Towers has appropriated the American image of the Las Vegas crooner as an easily recognizable trademark. His repertoire consists primarily of cover versions of American show tunes and evergreens, including "You'll Never Walk Alone," "I Can See Clearly Now," and "New York, New York." In the 1980s, Towers became widely credited for being an "un-Dutch" performer with an international style and grandeur, being the first national pop artist to perform in large stadiums like the Rotterdam Ahoy', which previously had hosted only international stars. In 1995, Towers received the Graceland Award from the Estate of Elvis Presley (and the honor to call himself "one of the King's men") for his album *Lee Towers Sings Elvis* (1994). When, in 2002, former President Bill Clinton visited Rotterdam, the hometown of the Holland-America Line, Lee Towers performed especially for him, singing Neil Diamond's "America," a song celebrating America as the "sweet land of liberty" for immigrants coming from all over the world. In spite of not being an American immigrant himself, Lee Towers has made the American rhetoric his own to such an extent that his praise of America as the Beacon of Freedom and Democracy almost naturally befits his star image.

Lee Towers is a significant example of Americanization, not only because his imitation is so explicit that it becomes almost like a parody, a pastiche, but also because his star myth is based on American iconography, and the American Dream in particular. In his biography entitled "Why he believed in his dream," published on his official website, Towers is described as the "Rotterdam realist who fulfilled his American Dream."[24] His American Dream is a rags-to-riches story of "the singing crane operator" Leen Huyzer who becomes the famous star Lee Towers. The website makes an explicit distinction between "the star" and Leen Huyzer, "the man behind Lee Towers … [who] has remained an ordinary human being," reinforcing the notion that his hyper-Americanness is an imitative performance. When, on March 25, 2002, he is the celebrity guest on the Dutch television talk show *Kevin Masters Starring Tom Rhodes* (Yorin, 2001-2003), Lee Towers exclaims that he is living his own American Dream right here in the Netherlands. That Towers makes his exclamation on *Kevin Masters* is fitting, as this talk show can also be perceived as hyper-American. Hosted by the American stand-up comedian Tom Rhodes and his side-kick E-Life, a Dutch black hip-hop artist, *Kevin Masters* can best be described as an – almost literal – imitation of the *Late Show with David Letterman* (CBS, 1993–present). Although both the audience and the celebrity guests are Dutch, the whole show is done in American English, with Dutch subtitles for the viewers at home. The show's premise is based on the interaction between American and Dutch culture, playing with the stereotypes of both. Its imitative character is emphasized by the talk show's title: Kevin Masters is not a real-life person, but a fictional American talk show host being performed by an American comedian. But it is Lee Towers who makes the show's hyper-Americanness most visible, appearing to be more "American" than its host. As Tom Rhodes later recalled: "Lee learned how to speak English from Elvis Presley. This guy is who Elvis should have been. 'I believe in my dreams,' he said that about three times. 'How did this happen for me? I believe in my dreams, Tommy.' I'm like sitting there talking to Elvis, man."[25]

More than merely imitating American pop culture, however, Lee Towers translates his hyper-Americanness into a local and national idiom. His live shows may be "American," Towers remains the "Rotterdam realist" who lives his Dutch American Dream. As his nickname "the singing crane operator" emphasizes, his star image is strongly rooted in Rotterdam working-class culture, exemplified by his identification with the Rotterdam harbor and the local soccer club Feyenoord, for which he recorded the club song "Mijn Feyenoord" (1997). Lee Towers starred in a 1999 television commercial for the local brand of Van Nelle coffee, sipping coffee on a tugboat in the Rotterdam harbor. On his album *My Port of Rotterdam* (2003), he pays tribute to Rotterdam with American classics like Tina Turner's "The Best" and Otis Redding's "(Sittin' on) The Dock of the Bay," as well as with original songs, including the album's title track and "Rotterdam Is the City." In his bombastic Las Vegas style, Towers sings, with a strong American English accent, "I've seen the land of good old Uncle Sam, … but to tell the truth, no matter where I am, wherever I roam, my home sweet home is Rotterdam." In this manner, Lee Towers does not merely imitate but appropriates American pop culture, in a hyper-American form, to express his local identity.

That the hyper-Americanness of Towers is translated not only into a local but a national idiom as well is shown by his performance of "One Moment in Time," originally recorded by African-American pop diva Whitney Houston for the 1988 Olympic games. Lee Towers sang his rendition of the song at his final "Legendary Gala of the Year" in the Rotterdam Ahoy' stadium in October 2000. As the music starts, Towers gives a speech in Dutch: "Not that long ago, we were glued to our television screens during the Olympic games. We watched our heroes win gold medals. We were crying with pride as the Dutch flag was raised. We are such a tiny country. An absolute all-time record for Holland." Lee Towers is referring to the 2000 Olympic games in Sydney, where the Dutch athletes won a relatively large number of medals. He continues to talk about how great "our heroes" are and how long it takes to prepare for such an event. Then Towers shifts into English, stating: "At that moment in time, you got it."[26] During his subsequent bombastic performance of "One Moment in Time," a large screen behind him on stage shows images of the Dutch athletes, alternated with images of the Dutch flag. The combination of American pop music, sports, and patriotism makes this Towers performance very similar to the annual Super Bowl performances of "The Star-Spangled Banner," albeit without the presence of the military. Yet, while the Super Bowl celebrates the "greatest nation in the world," Towers used the genre conventions and audiovisual language of American pop culture to celebrate the extraordinary achievement of "our tiny country," thereby effectively translating the generic American original into a specifically Dutch national context.

Five years later, Lee Towers gives another performance which combines American pop culture with Dutch patriotism, this time connecting the Dutch national soccer team to the Dutch royal family, both of which are symbolized by the national and royal color orange, explaining why Dutch patriotism is often referred to as the "orange sentiment." During the national television broadcast to celebrate the twenty-fifth anniversary of Queen Beatrix as the reigning monarch of the Netherlands (TROS, 30 April 2005), Towers performs "You'll Never Walk Alone," surrounded by a group of young children dressed in the orange uniform of the Dutch national soccer team. The song, which was a hit single for Towers back in 1976, is originally from the American Rodgers & Hammerstein musical *Carousel* (1948), but, as television host Ivo Niehe reminds the viewers, is now best known as, rather paradoxically, "the international soccer national anthem." While Lee Towers is giving his trademark Las Vegas style performance, the camera zooms in on individual audience members, waving their arms to the beat of the music, including Crown Prince Willem Alexander and his wife Princess Máxima. In one sweeping performance, Lee Towers connects the love for the national sports team to an uncontested support of the Dutch monarchy, using American pop culture to join the audience in a collective orange sentiment, an unbridled expression of Dutch patriotism. Thus, Lee Towers can use the same American conventions and rhetoric to praise "America" in front of former President Bill Clinton, to express his local identification with the city of Rotterdam, and to celebrate Dutch patriotism in front of Queen Beatrix, all based on his being an embodiment of the American Dream in the Netherlands.

ADAM CURRY AND PATRICIA PAAY: THE GLAMOUR OF AMERICA

One evening in early 2003, on the Dutch talk show *Barend & Van Dorp* (RTL4, 1990-2005), two wars are being discussed. The main discussion is focused on the pending war in Iraq. Should the Dutch politicians support or oppose the American military intervention? Subsequently, the second topic is introduced as the "War of the Divas." The only female guest, Connie Breukhoven, a former pop singer better known as Vanessa, has been invited to express her heartfelt discontent about the reality television show *Adam's Family* (SBS6, 2003), based on the daily life of former MTV veejay Adam Curry and singer Patricia Paay (who, like Vanessa, is often referred to as a "diva" – hence the topic's title). According to Vanessa, the main problem of *Adam's Family*, in addition to being an absolute bore, is its fakeness. Not only are Paay's hair extensions fake, but also the way Curry and Paay talk, a peculiar mixture of Dutch and American English. The talk show's juxtaposition of these two very different "wars" is striking, revealing how easily television can make a connection between the seriousness of international warfare to something trivial like hair extensions and fake accents. Eventually both discussions focus on American dominance, in international politics as well as in Dutch pop culture. Supporting the war in Iraq means giving into the pressures of the USA, the talk show's hosts suggest, while Adam Curry and Patricia Paay are pretentious fakes because they act American rather than Dutch.

In the pilot episode of *Adam's Family* (SBS6, 28 December 2002), Adam Curry and Patricia Paay are sitting on the couch watching the *Top of the Pop Awards* on television. Seeing the young British pop stars perform makes Paay remark that stardom surely has changed over the years. "There isn't a difference anymore between an ordinary person and a star," she tells Curry in Dutch. "In the old days, you didn't become a star unless you were really special, different than the others." Paay is referring to the 1970s and 1980s, when she herself was a Dutch pop star, with hit singles such as the disco song "Who's that Lady with My Man" (1976), the ballad "Tomorrow" (1982) from the Broadway musical *Annie,* and, with the Star Sisters, "Stars on 45 Proudly Presents" (1983), a medley of songs made famous by the Andrew Sisters. As radio deejay and television host, Adam Curry also has a background in pop stardom, both in the Netherlands, where, in the 1980s, he hosted the pop music television show *Countdown* (Veronica), and, subsequently, in the USA as veejay on MTV. Born in the USA but raised in the Netherlands, Curry quite easily fits in his role of being a "real" American, which was reconfirmed, at least for Dutch viewers, by his cameo appearance in the Madonna documentary *Truth or Dare* (Alek Keshishian, 1991). For Patricia Paay, being the American she never was contributes to the authentication of her star myth, her being a "real" star.

Throughout her singing career, Patricia Paay has made explicit references to American pop culture in her songs and in the way she presented herself as a pop singer. The compact disc *Patricia Paay: Good for Gold* (1996) contains all the hit singles Paay released during the 1970s and 1980s, many being cover versions of American pop songs, ranging from a disco rendition of Walt Disney's "Someday My Prince Will Come" to Neil Sedaka's "Solitaire." However, *Good for Gold* also contains original songs, some co-composed by Paay, which closely follow the American pop conventions. In one of the self-composed songs, called "Take Me Back to Denver," Patricia Paay sings that she wants to go back to Colorado, "the place where I was born." In "The Best Friend I Know," a duet with her sister Yvonne Keeley, Paay recalls how they used to create a "fantasy world" based on Hollywood movies, pretending that her sister was Clark Gable and she was Marilyn Monroe. Patricia Paay reinforces the Monroe connection by releasing the single "A Tribute to Marilyn Monroe" (1984) and by posing nude for the Dutch edition of *Playboy* magazine three times (September 1984, November 1986, and May 1996), including one cover shot reminiscent of the first American *Playboy* featuring Monroe in 1953.[27] Paay's album *Time of My Life* (1995) consists of her renditions of Hollywood movie themes, including the title track, the theme of *Dirty Dancing* (Emile Ardolino, 1987), sung in duet with the American television star David Hasselhoff from *Baywatch* (NBC, 1989-1999). With her pop repertoire, her overall presentation as a sexy starlet, and, arguably, her marriage to MTV veejay Adam Curry, Patricia Paay recreates a fantasy world of American stardom in the Netherlands, tapping into the American star myth.

When, in 1987, Adam Curry and Patricia Paay migrate to the USA, their American Dream materializes. In an interview with the Dutch edition of *Playboy* magazine, Paay explains that living in the USA offers them the opportunity to fulfill their ambitions, while in the Netherlands their potential was curtailed by a prevailing attitude of Dutch parochialism. "I love America and I have always known that I would end up here, one way or another."[28] From the perspective of the Dutch audience, however, Curry and Paay's American life remains a fantasy world, an imagined America of glamour and luxury. The Dutch tabloids report stories about their New York jet-set life and their socializing with

American stars such as Madonna, Cher, and Jon Bon Jovi. Adam Curry's career move from MTV veejay to internet entrepreneur is described by the tabloids as a classic American Dream narrative, the self-made man who became a millionaire. Even the birth of their "love child" Christina in September 1990, featured on the covers of all Dutch tabloids, is presented as a glamorous American experience, as their baby is reported to have been delivered under anesthetic by Caesarean section in an expensive private hospital, with classical music playing in the background. By portraying the couple as examples of how the rich and famous live, the Dutch tabloids made Adam Curry and Patricia Paay into embodiments of American glamour. For example, the Dutch glossy magazine *Avant Garde* (October 1995) devotes its cover story to "Patricia Paay's American Dream: A House Full of Love with Adam and Christina," showing Paay in a seven-page photo spread, shot by Dutch photographer Govert de Roos, posing in and around "her American dream house," located in New Jersey, a half-hour drive away from New York City. One photo shows Patricia Paay next to her kidney-shaped swimming pool, which, as the byline reads, is an exact replica of Elvis Presley's original one at Graceland. Another photo shows Paay leaning against the hood of her luxurious Lincoln limousine (with the license plate reading "CURRY 1") in the streets of Manhattan, while her private chauffeur stands nearby. Whereas Lee Towers translates his American Dream into an identity that encompasses the local and the national, the glamorous fantasy world of Adam Curry and Patricia Paay remains an explicit American experience, reinforced by their living in the USA.

That their American Dream is not confined to the geographical boundaries of the USA, however, becomes clear when, after twelve years, Adam Curry and Patricia Paay return to Europe. Like *Avant Garde*, the Dutch glossy magazine *Beau Monde* (27 July 2001) presents a seven-page photo spread, again shot by Govert de Roos, featuring "glamour queen" Patricia Paay posing in haute couture dresses in and around her luxurious mansion. Although the mansion is located in Belgium rather than the USA, the depicted glamorous lifestyle is identical to the one in *Avant Garde*. As Paay makes clear in the accompanying interview, she intends to bring American glamour to the Netherlands, using the association with her imagined America to promote her La Paay cosmetic line. "Americans are very happy people," Patricia Paay explains. "Always positive, always complimentary. That is no act, that's the way they are. They are less realistic. Dutch people are so down-to-earth. Americans believe in dreams and they love fantasy."[29] Rather than including the American glamour within her definition of being Dutch, Paay uses her position of the American she never was as a quality that makes her stand out and thus exceptional within Dutch pop culture.

Perhaps it is this implicit claim of being exceptional that prompted Vanessa to denounce Curry and Paay's reality television series as a fake. True or not, the same American fantasy world that Adam Curry and Patricia Paay have showcased throughout their careers also forms the basis of *Adams Family*. Although its title refers to the American television series *The Addams Family* (ABC, 1964-1966) and the later film version (Barry Sonnenfeld, 1991), *Adam's Family* is inspired by the American reality television series *The Osbournes* (MTV, 2002-2005), which follows the daily life of hard rock star Ozzy's Osbourne's "dysfunctional family" (Ozzy and his wife Sharon, daughter Kelly, and son Jack) in Los Angeles. Edited according to the conventions of the situation comedy, *The Osbournes* presents "real life" in a fictionalized form, thereby blurring the lines between actual living persons and the fictional characters they portray.[30] Similar to *The Osbournes*, *Adam's Family* provides a behind-the-scenes look at the way celebrities live their everyday lives as members of a family, facing the same problems that ordinary families do. Instead of performing as famous stars, Adam Curry and Patricia Paay play the role of husband and wife, as parents of teenage daughter Christina. In this way, an illusion of reality is created through the suggestion that the viewers get a glimpse of the "real" person behind the façade of the famous star. Such a perspective is supported by Paay, who, in an interview promoting *Adam's Family*, announced that "I believe the time is right for the people in the Netherlands to come to know the real Patricia Paay, as obviously at home I'm not the glamorous diva."[31] However, conform to Richard Dyer's stars theory, the "real" Patricia Paay as shown on television is actually part of her star image, which reconfirms rather than exposes the construction of the star myth.

Whereas other Dutch celebrity reality shows such as *Patty's Posse* (Yorin, 2003-2004) and *De Bauers* (RTL4, 2003, 2007) emphasize the ordinariness of celebrity life, thereby downplaying the importance of glamour, *Adam's Family* showcases the lifestyle of the rich and famous. Living in their luxurious Belgian mansion dubbed Curry's Castle, Adam Curry and Patricia Paay are shown driving their expensive sports cars, preparing lavish dinner parties, flying in their private helicopter, and going on holiday to the Bahamas. As the show's grand finale, also featured on the covers of all Dutch tabloids, Curry and Paay renew their wedding vows with a romantic ceremony set in a small Italian village, which, as one of the tabloids notes, is "such an American thing to do." The show's hyper-American character is enhanced by the use of classic American pop songs as soundtrack, including "Happy Together" by the Turtles as the show's opening tune, Aretha Franklin's "(You Make Me Feel Like) A Natural Woman" when Paay is shown doing her make-up, and the theme of the television series *Dynasty* (ABC, 1981-1989), underscoring the establishing shots of Curry's Castle. By showing the glamorous lifestyle that Dutch viewers will recognize from Hollywood and television series like *Dynasty*, *Adam's Family* reconfirms the American fantasy world that Adam Curry and Patricia Paay have come to personify.

COSTA! AND KATJA: EMBODYING POP CULTURE

The Dutch teenage romantic comedy *Costa!* (Johan Nijenhuis, 2001) takes place in Spain, telling the story of a group of Dutch youth who work at Costa, a trendy discothèque that primarily caters to Dutch teenage tourists. When MTV's annual dance contest comes to town, the youngsters are determined to win, desperate to beat their rivals, the dancers of the discothèque Empire. Although the majority of the film's dialogue is in Dutch, in one scene the Scandinavian discothèque owner Ian, sitting in his wheelchair, gives a motivational speech in English to his young employees, ending with two rhetorical questions: "Do you wanna hold on to the dream? Do you wanna work hard to keep it alive?" At first glance Ian's foreign nationality seems rather arbitrary and unnecessary, as all the other characters are Dutch and speak Dutch. Moreover, the part is played by a Dutch actor (Victor Löwe) who speaks an unidentifiable English with a heavy Dutch accent. The only reason for his foreign nationality seems to be the content of his motivational speech: the discothèque owner is encouraging his young employees to believe in the dream of meritocracy, so they can escape their working-class backgrounds by working hard to make their dreams come true as winners of the MTV dance contest. Obviously, the message of the American Dream is better expressed in English, as a literal Dutch translation loses it connotations, or "just doesn't sound right." To justify his delivering these remarks in English rather than Dutch, Ian has to be a foreigner, enabling him to evoke the rhetoric of the American Dream, even if he speaks English with a heavy, fake accent.

Costa! is only one of many Dutch commercial films that appropriate the genre conventions and audiovisual language of Hollywood. Some of these films are explicitly targeted at an international mainstream audience, such as *Do Not Disturb* (1999) and *Down* aka *The Shaft* (2001), both directed by Dick Maas and starring Hollywood actors like William Hurt and Naomi Watts, and the films by Roel Reiné, *The Delivery* (1999) and *Adrenaline* (2003).[32] As Thomas Elsaesser points out, only a few European films have "the budgets, stars and production values even to try to reach an international mainstream audience," concluding that "often enough these films fail in their aim, not least because they have to disguise themselves to look and sound as if they were American."[33] That the abovementioned films by Dick Maas and Roel Reiné proved to be commercial and critical failures may be explained by the plausible factor that their disguises as "real" American movies are obvious to such an extent that the films become less convincing to audiences and critics alike. The Dutch self-acclaimed "feel good" movies like *Costa!*, on the contrary, are targeted at a national and often younger audience and tend to be commercially successful, including romantic comedies like *Phileine zegt Sorry* (Robert Jan Westdijk, 2003) and *Het Schnitzelparadijs* (Martin Koolhoven, 2005), teenage comedies such as *All Stars* (Jean van de Velde, 1997) and *Shouf Shouf Habibi!* (Albert ter Heerdt, 2004), and action films such as *Lek* (Jean van de Velde, 2000) and *Vet Hard* (Tim Oliehoek, 2005). Even though these films also rely heavily on the often clichéd genre conventions of Hollywood cinema, they do not disguise themselves as American, but instead explicitly emphasize their national or local character, thereby often using actors from national television who are well known by the larger Dutch audience. In this way, these films appropriate Hollywood within their own national context, rather than being mere imitations of the American original.

Although also referring to popular American films like *West Side Story* (Jerome Robbins and Robert Wise, 1961) and *Grease* (Randal Kleiser, 1978), *Costa!* is most of all an updated Dutch version of *Dirty Dancing* (Emile Ardolino, 1987), the latter being the romantic story of a young shy teenage girl, played by Jennifer Grey, who, while on holiday, experiences her sexual awakening and becomes a confident woman after competing in a dance contest with her hunky lower-class dance instructor, played by Patrick Swayze. In *Costa!*, the young shy teenage girl Janet, played by former soap opera actress Georgina Verbaan, is on holiday in Spain, where she meets Rens (Daan Schuurmans), the leader of the Costa dancers. Similar to the plot of *Dirty Dancing*, their romance blossoms when Rens' regular dance partner cannot perform and is replaced by Janet, who transforms into a wonderful dancer. Particularly the scene in which Rens, who, like Patrick Swayze's character, teaches Janet the dance's choreography in the water at a desolated beach is almost identical to the *Dirty Dancing* original. Conform to the genre convention of the happy ending, Rens and Janet win the MTV dance contest. However, *Costa!* does differ from *Dirty Dancing* in one significant aspect. While the role of the former dance partner Penny in *Dirty Dancing* is of minor importance, the role of Frida, the sexy young woman who is replaced by Janet, is played by the film's biggest star, Katja Schuurman. Simply known as Katja, her star appeal is emphasized by her recording of the movie's main love theme, "Lover or Friend," which became a big hit on the Dutch pop charts. One could even argue that it is Katja's star image which connects *Costa!* to the Hollywood star myth, albeit one which is implicitly rather than explicitly American.

Similar to most young stars of the Dutch "feel good" cinema, Katja initially started out as a television actress, being one of the most popular characters on the first Dutch daily soap *Goede Tijden, Slechte Tijden* (*Good Times, Bad Times*, RTL4, 1990–present), in which she played from 1995 to 1999. Her credibility as "serious" actress increased when she appeared in the low-budget film *No Planes, No Trains* (Jos Stelling, 1999). Since the film's director had no clue who she was, he was surprised to see that Katja was treated as a true movie star. Although she only played a minor role, the film's distributor Warner Brothers promoted *No Planes, No Trains* by emphasizing the star image of Katja. Moreover, interviews with Katja were only granted if the magazine would feature the new movie star on its cover, prompting the Dutch film magazine *de Filmkrant* to note that, while beyond the borders of the Dutch small towns no one actually knew her, Warner Brothers was letting Katja "play Hollywood in Holland" anyway.[34] In other words, Katja "plays" the Hollywood starlet she never was, using the star myth traditionally associated with the American Dream. Throughout her acting career in both television and film, Katja has toyed with her sexy starlet image. Like many other Dutch female celebrities, including Patricia Paay, she has posed nude in the Dutch *Playboy* (September 2002). However, rather than posing as her personal self, Katja poses as Thera, the nightclub dancer she portrays in the Dutch film *Oesters van Nam Kee* (Pollo de Pimentel, 2002). In contrast, Katja plays "herself" in the fictional reality television series *BNN Family* (BNN, 2003), a parody of *Adam's Family* and *Patty's Posse*. In this way, the boundaries between the "real" Katja and Katja the Hollywood starlet she never was are continuously crossed.

This blurred distinction between the "real" Katja and her star image as projected in Dutch pop culture is the starting point of the Dutch low-budget film *Interview* (Theo van Gogh, 2003). In *Interview*, Katja plays the soap actress Katja who is being interviewed at home in her Amsterdam apartment by the political correspondent of a Dutch quality newspaper, Pierre Peters, a role played by the renowned stage actor Pierre Bokma. The casting of the most popular starlet in combination with a serious actor is reminiscent of the classic Hollywood film *The Prince and the Showgirl* (Laurence Olivier, 1957), starring Laurence Olivier and Marilyn Monroe, a connection which is emphasized by a large picture of Monroe hanging in Katja's apartment. The suggestion that Katja is playing "herself" is enhanced by the fact that the film has been shot in the apartment of the "real" Katja and by references to her "real" life, including the ring tone of her cell phone which, ringing several times during the film, plays the tune of *Goede Tijden, Slechte Tijden*. At the same time, however, Katja is also presented as a fictional character, made clear by the fictional Katja being blond, conform to the stereotype of the dumb blonde starlet, rather than having the manes of dark curly hair which have become a trademark of the "real" Katja. Moreover, in one scene Katja is watching herself on television, the daily episode of her soap, in which she is crying hysterically. The fictional soap scene is overacted to such an extent that it becomes a parody, not only poking fun at the melodrama of soap, but also emphasizing that Katja is giving a performance. In this way, the film suggests that, similar to the fictional Katja in the fictional soap, the film's fictional Katja is performing the act of being a stereotypical soap actress by portraying Katja as an overindulgent, coke-snorting, man-seducing starlet, thereby mocking the way the Dutch tabloids tend to present the "real" Katja in their gossip stories.

With the contrast between the serious newspaper correspondent and the frivolous soap actress, *Interview* presents a clash between highbrow and lowbrow culture. Pierre embodies highbrow culture, being masculine, mature, arrogant, yet boring, focused on serious issues such as warfare and politics. Katja, on the contrary, embodies lowbrow pop culture, being feminine, young, exciting, yet less naïve than she appears at first sight, focused on frivolous issues such as entertainment and gossip. Perhaps most important, through Katja pop culture is presented as a sex bomb, dangerously seductive and hard to resist. The contrast between highbrow and lowbrow culture echoes the rigid dichotomies which make up the Europe versus America divide, as discussed earlier in this chapter. In this way, Katja could be perceived as signifying American pop culture, whereas, in such a comparison, Pierre would signify European intellectualism. However, in *Interview*, pop culture is never explicitly connected to Americanness, with the exception of the Marilyn Monroe picture in Katja's apartment. As the Hollywood starlet she never was, Katja embodies pop culture, regardless of whether or not her star myth is still associated with the American Dream.

That the star image of Katja (and other Dutch stars) does not travel easily across geographical boundaries becomes apparent with the American remake of *Interview* (Steve Buscemi, 2007). While the role of Pierre is played by the film's American director Steve Buscemi, Katja has been replaced by the Hollywood actress Sienna Miller, who, unlike Katja, does not play "herself" but a character named Katya, thereby losing the play with reality and fiction which is such a significant element of the Dutch version. The "real" Katja does make a cameo appearance in the American film as "the lady in the limo," showing that, outside of the national context, Dutch Hollywood starlets they never were remain anonymous. Five years earlier, Katja made a one-second cameo appearance in the Hollywood film *The Rules of Attraction* (Roger Avary, 2002), based on the novel by Bret Easton Ellis, as "a Dutch television actress" drinking absinthe in an Amsterdam bar with one of the film's characters. In the Dutch comedy *Shouf Shouf Habibi!* (Albert ter Heerdt, 2004), also discussed in chapter five, one of the Moroccan-Dutch characters tells his friends that he wants to marry a virgin who is as beautiful and sexy as Katja. In the film's international edition, the English subtitles translate his comments as "Horny as J-Lo, but a virgin." For the implied international viewers, Katja has been translated as the American star Jennifer Lopez. They both embody the sexy starlet, yet J-Lo's star image travels globally, whereas Katja continues to "play Hollywood in Holland," appropriating the star myth within a limited national context.

ALI B: IN THE DUTCH GHETTO

"President, stupid fucking moron / now listen, a child must go to school / through rebellion I reach my goal / I use a mike, you a gun / boom pow, just shoot me down / in your nightmares you will see me again / I will not leave you alone / … motherfucker."[35] These words, in Dutch, are rapped by the Moroccan-Dutch hip-hop artist Ali B, featured in the music video "Fok de Macht" (2005) by the Dutch rap duo the Opposites. Like the song's title, which translates as "fuck the power," the performance is inspired by classic African-American rap songs like N.W.A.'s "Fuck tha Police" (1988) and Public Enemy's "Fight the Power" (1989). In this way, Ali B appropriates not only the rhetoric and audiovisual language of African-American rap, but also its provocative message of rebelling against the authorities and protesting against racism, police brutality, and poverty in the American urban ghettos. However, Ali B is not rapping about the social-economic conditions in his home country the Netherlands. Featured in the Dutch MTV's *Rap Around the World* documentary series, "Fok de Macht" is a protest against the practice of child labor in Ecuador. In fact, the song is part of a political awareness campaign by the charity foundation Plan Nederland, formerly known as the Dutch chapter of Foster Parents Plan. Thus, quite peculiarly, the Moroccan-Dutch Ali B, as the African-American rapper he never was, uses oppositional African-American pop culture to criticize the politics of a South American country, with a rap song commissioned by a Dutch charity organization.[36]

Ever since his first hit single in 2004, Ali B has become the most popular and commercially successful hip-hop artist of the Netherlands. Not only does he succeed on the pop charts, he is also spokesperson for several charities, appears in television commercials, and is the first Dutch rapper to have his own statue in the Amsterdam Madame Tussauds wax museum. His reputation of representing "the voice of the street" is reconfirmed on October 26, 2006, when he verbally challenges the Dutch Prime Minister Jan Peter Balkenende on the talk show *Pauw & Witteman* (VARA, 2006-present). Yet simultaneously, Ali B is included within the Dutch national discourse, as shown in August 2007 with the announcement by the Amsterdam Rijksmuseum that Ali B will be featured in its exhibition on heroes, commemorating the four-hundredth birthday of the Dutch sea admiral Michiel de Ruyter. Being the first Moroccan-Dutch star in Dutch pop culture, Ali B is often read as a success story of ethnic integration, which can be perceived as a star myth, prompting the question of how American pop culture, and in particular African-American hip-hop, helps to construct Ali B's star image.

Although his full name is Ali Bouali, Ali B uses only the first initial of his last name to mimic, as explained on his website, "the way in which the Dutch media refer to Moroccan criminals."[37] By doing so, Ali B challenges the connotation of the negative media depiction, as "Ali B" now no longer immediately evokes the negative image of Moroccan-Dutch youth as potential criminals (or worse, as potential terrorists), but rather the positive image of a successful rapper. Yet, the connotation of a life of crime remains, and thus "Ali B" also implies authenticity and street credibility, which is part of the image that he presents with his *Ali B vertelt het leven van de straat* album and theater show (2004), an assumingly autobiographical account of Moroccan-Dutch youth street life. Heavily inspired by the imagery of African-American "gangsta" rap, Ali B takes on the persona of the tough and streetwise rapper, or "thugmarokkaan" ("thug Moroccan"), as he identifies himself. This street image is enhanced by the pictures on his first album cover and its promotional material. Ali B is pictured in a gloomy urban landscape, which seems closer to the American urban ghetto as featured in African-American 'hood films and hip-hop music videos than Ali B's relatively mundane Dutch hometown Almere. However, in addition to boasting about his being an authentic gangsta, Ali B raps about being refused entrance to a local disco because he is Moroccan, a common practice of discrimination that has become a recurring theme in Dutch pop culture. Moreover, Ali B addresses his newfound popularity as Moroccan-Dutch hip-hop star, receiving the attention of white Dutch women who previously avoided him because they assumed he was a criminal. By doing so, Ali B translates the image of the African-American hip-hop gangsta into a specific local context, using its rebellious rhetoric to express his anger about occurrences of structural racism in Dutch society.

That Ali B can be perceived as the African-American rapper he never was becomes clear with the song "Ghetto" which he and his cousin Yes-R recorded with the African-American rapper Akon. Peculiarly subtitled "the international mix" (the song was only released in the Netherlands), this version consists of Akon's original American one with overdubs by Ali B and Yes-R in Dutch. In the original version, Akon raps about the hard life in American ghettos. Akon's original music video makes a connection between ghetto life in a black inner city in New Jersey, a white trash trailer park in New Mexico, and the Native American Navajo Nation reservation in Arizona, thereby explicitly suggesting that the hardship of ghetto life is not an African-American experience, but rather a social-economic condition shared by a diverse group of underprivileged Americans. The Dutch version of the music video adds images of ghetto life in Amsterdam Zuidoost (South-East), also known as the Bijlmer. Recognizing that such a comparison may seem a bit farfetched, Ali B raps: "Look, I don't want to say that the Bijlmer is like New York / but a lot of people treat it as if it were a village / where nothing ever happens while the apartment buildings are occupied by junks on crack / you are fooling yourself."[38] By translating Akon's ghetto to the Dutch situation, Ali B suggests that there is an international similarity and potential solidarity not only among the underprivileged in the USA and the Netherlands, but also among the different ethnic groups living in the ghetto of the Amsterdam Bijlmer. Tellingly, it is the image of ghetto life as represented by American pop culture, in African-American 'hood films and hip-hop music videos, through which such solidarity is expressed; this is thus rooted in an imagined America, rather than the USA.

In interviews, Ali B stresses his social and economic success, being a role model for other Moroccan-Dutch teenagers, while simultaneously maintaining his "ghetto" background: "I've always kept to the straight and narrow and never was a hanger-on. I'm really proud of that. The boys in the neighborhood accepted me for who I was. A lot of my friends weren't so lucky. One is doing time for murder, another for burglary, and some are still hanging around on the streets and delivering pizzas."[39] Again, the image of the American urban ghetto is evoked, although in a local version, with the stereotypical image of the Moroccan-Dutch teenage boy on a moped delivering pizzas replacing the stereotypical image of the African-American drug dealer. Moreover, in some interviews, Ali B's success story is told using the rhetoric of the American Dream, yet without making its Americanness explicit. For example, in the special "Dutch Dream" issue of *LINDA*. (February 2005), a glossy magazine based on the media personality of Linda de Mol, Ali B is featured as one of the "ethnic" Dutch celebrities who are being showcased as examples of successful integration. As will be discussed in chapter five, *LINDA*. appropriates the connotations of the American Dream to present these success stories of non-white stars, suggesting that Dutch multiculturalism has not failed. Conform to the American rhetoric of self-reliance and meritocracy, Ali B is portrayed by *LINDA*. magazine as a proud, hardworking, and determined individual, who hopes that his peers will follow his example.

His increasing mainstream popularity, however, has challenged the street credibility of Ali B's image as a thug Moroccan rapper. Especially his 2005 duet with the popular white Dutch singer Marco Borsato "Wat Zou Je Doen" ("What Would You Do"), recorded for the charity organization War Child and, in that same year, his widely publicized encounter with Queen Beatrix, with whom he did the hip-hop handshake before hugging her, have made Ali B susceptible to criticism of tokenism, suggesting that Al B has become the "pet Moroccan" of the white Dutch establishment.[40] In the popular media, such criticism of tokenism tends to be explained as a conflict between being an "authentic" rapper or a "sellout," suggesting that commercial success endangers hip-hop authenticity. In her essay on Dutch hip-hop, Mir Wermuth confirms that in the Dutch hip-hop subculture, "there is a tendency to stick to the dichotomy of commercial versus anticommercial."[41] However, another explanation might be the incompatibility of the image of the thug Moroccan rapper with the image of being a commercially successful rapper, revealing a significant difference between the star myths of African-American rappers and those of their Dutch counterparts. The African-American role models of Ali B, such as rapper 50 Cent, can sustain their image as ghetto gangsta while simultaneously embodying the rags-to-riches star myth of the American Dream, as is exemplified by 50 Cent's film *Get Rich or Die Tryin'* (Jim Sheridan, 2005), loosely based on his "real" life, in which he plays a drug dealer in the ghetto who succeeds in becoming a major hip-hop star. In stark contrast, to become accepted as a rapper who enjoys mainstream success, Ali B has to distance himself from his reputation as thug Moroccan rapper, an image that remains connected to the negative media representation of Moroccan-Dutch youth as potential criminals. Decriminalizing his image by emphasizing a "softer" image of the huggable pop star enables Ali B to be embraced by the white Dutch establishment, ranging from Queen Beatrix to Linda de Mol, as an embodiment of the Dutch Dream success story.

Conclusion: The Real Thing

"This is really cool, the Universal logo. … When I saw that I thought 'wow, a real movie.' … It's the best part of the film." These are comments, originally in Dutch, made by the actors of the Dutch hit comedy *Het Schnitzelparadijs* (2005), who, together with its director Martin Koolhoven, give frame-by-frame commentary on the DVD edition of the film. Before the movie actually starts, the screen shows the revolving globe of the Universal film studio, which stops at the moment the American continent is on front, with "Universal" stamped in big letters on the screen. Although undoubtedly meant to be funny, the comments bring to the foreground two important elements of Dutch pop culture which is based on the American example of Hollywood. First, American pop culture is often perceived as being "universal," an audiovisual language that can be globally interpreted and appropriated. Second, American pop culture can function as a sign which can provide authentication. *Het Schnitzelparadijs* may not have been shot in the "real" Hollywood, yet the Universal trademark provides the association with Hollywood and thereby makes the hit comedy a "real" movie.

Similar to the way the Universal trademark provides *Het Schnitzelparadijs* with a suggestion of authenticity, the hyper-Americanness of the four examples of Americans they never were – Lee Towers, Adam Curry and Patricia Paay, Katja Schuurman, and Ali B – makes them just like "the real thing." Each of them appropriates similar elements of American pop culture, but with different aims and different results. With his bombastic performances, Lee Towers as the Las Vegas crooner he never was uses the rhetoric of the American Dream to express both his local identity, rooted in the working-class culture of Rotterdam, and his national identity, based on a rather patriotic and traditional interpretation of Dutchness. Adam Curry and Patricia Paay, on the contrary, appropriate American pop culture not to express a local or national identity, but instead to present themselves as living examples of a fantasy world of the rich and famous, in which hyper-Americanness signifies the glamour traditionally associated with Hollywood. Being the Hollywood starlet she never was, Katja Schuurman embodies pop culture, translating the American star myth within a specific national context by "playing Hollywood in Holland." Yet, in contrast to Lee Towers, Adam Curry, and Patricia Paay, the star myth of Katja is no longer explicitly American. Finally, the Moroccan-Dutch rapper Ali B uses the genre conventions and audiovisual language of African-American hip-hop and gangsta rap to comment not only on Dutch multiculturalism, but also on international politics, suggesting that African-American hip-hop can result in international solidarity among different ethnic groups which find themselves in similar social-economic conditions. However, Ali B is trapped between the image of being a thug Moroccan and the image of being a commercially successful star accepted by mainstream white society. In spite of their differences, these four case studies share the appropriation of American pop culture to express their specific local and national identity by performing karaoke Americanism as Americans they never were.

By perceiving them as absolute fakes, I am not suggesting that Lee Towers, Adam Curry and Patricia Paay, Katja Schuurman, and Ali B are fake Americans. It is neither my intention to judge whether or not they succeed in presenting a convincing imitation of American pop culture, nor to claim that Dutch pop culture has been taken over by American pop culture or that we are all becoming global Americans. On the contrary, subtitled or dubbed, karaoke Americanism enables Dutch artists in pop music, film, and television to form and express their cultural identity by appropriating American pop culture within a local and national context. Moreover, I am interested instead in those moments in Dutch pop culture when its Americanness is taken for granted, when it no longer seems obvious to question why American pop culture is being imitated. The metaphor of karaoke Americanism enables a perception that goes beyond imitation, as karaoke implies an active performance of mimicking and mockery, based on the clichéd conventions of pop culture, yet also paying tribute to the original in a specific local or national manner. In this way, American pop culture proves to be a source of signs that provides us with a lingua franca to create our own "America," which is not an identical copy, but an appropriation, often expressed with a heavy, "fake" accent. However, it is the space where the imitation is slightly off, where the copy becomes a hyperbole of the original, an example of hyper-Americanness, which enables the creation of new meanings. As a form of active cultural appropriation, American pop culture is neither merely a form of American cultural imperialism, nor merely a liberating source of agency. Instead, the signs provided by American pop culture are part of our own pop culture as we live it day by day, and while we still may recognize them as "American," or ascribe more meaning to them because we view them as being "American," they remain "Dutch" at the same time.

Chapter Five

The Dutch Dream:

Americanization, Pop Culture, and National Identity

On July 27, 2005, the day after Mohammed B., the convicted murderer of the controversial Dutch filmmaker and columnist Theo van Gogh, was sentenced to life imprisonment, the Boomerang company released a free postcard featuring graffiti by Van Gogh's teenage son.[1] Inspired by urban American hip-hop culture (often defined as African-American), the graffiti uses American iconography – the text "Theo Forever" in English, Donald Duck, and the prominently pictured American flag with the name Theo spelled out in little stars – to provide a very personal expression of both remembrance and protest. On the one hand, the graffiti can be interpreted within a post-9/11 political discourse, in which Samuel Huntington's polarizing thesis of the "Clash of Civilizations" has been accepted by many as self-evident. By connecting him explicitly to American symbolism, Theo van Gogh is placed on the side of the USA in its War on Terror, against the Muslim extremists who took his life. On the other hand, the graffiti can also be perceived as an example of American iconography as an international lingua franca, which is no longer connected to a specific American context but free to be appropriated and interpreted on local levels.[2] In that case, the American flag does not function as a symbol of the nation-state USA, but instead has become a sign of "America," connoting, in this example, the freedom of expression.

The two interpretations of the Van Gogh graffiti do not contradict each other, but they do show how a distinction can be made between the nation-state USA and an imagined America. The first interpretation fits the unilateral stance of the nation-state USA, best exemplified by the now-famous words of President George W. Bush, spoken in a televised address to the American Congress nine days after 9/11: "Either you are with us, or you are with the terrorists."[3] The second interpretation fits the notion of an imagined America as a symbol of the freedom of expression, thereby suggesting that the American conception of such a value has come to be accepted as universal. In this chapter, I will discuss specific Dutch pop-cultural artifacts which appropriate elements of American pop culture – images, genre conventions, and audiovisual language – to comment on the Dutch political reality since 9/11, and, in particular, the assassinations of the controversial Dutch politician Pim Fortuyn on May 6, 2002, and of Theo van Gogh on November 2, 2004. As has been suggested in the Dutch media, the horrifying murders of Fortuyn and Van Gogh can be perceived as "our 9/11," a connection which was immediately recognized by conspiracy theorists who pointed out that Van Gogh was murdered exactly 911 days after Fortuyn. More important, just as 9/11 prompted debates in the USA about redefining what it means to be American, the murders of Fortuyn and Van Gogh have been interpreted as marking a drastic change in the Dutch political climate, shifting from the celebrated principle of multicultural tolerance towards a renewed patriotism and a more restrictive view on Dutch national identity.[4] Similar to the post-9/11 debates in the USA, there is a strong call for a return to the history of the nation-state as the foundation of a collective national identity, often envisioned, evoking Benedict Anderson's concept, as a Dutch imagined community.

To explore how an Americanized Dutch pop culture adds to the post-9/11 political discourse about national identity in the Netherlands, I will present five case studies: an episode of the television talent show *Idols* presenting national identity as a theme in pop culture, the pop tributes to Pim Fortuyn remembering him as the Dutch Kennedy, hip-hop songs by Moroccan-Dutch and white Dutch rappers commenting on Dutch society, the special "Dutch Dream" issue of the glossy magazine *LINDA.* featuring successful "ethnic" celebrities, and the movies *Shouf Shouf Habibi!* (2004) and *Kicks* (2007), both directed by Albert ter Heerdt, which use Hollywood conventions to address Dutch multiculturalism. By analyzing these specific pop-cultural artifacts, I suggest that "America" can function as a shared point of reference, connecting different positions within the political debate through the common language of American pop culture, rather than falling back upon an imagined community based on Dutch national history.

Pop Culture and National Identity

Similar to its counterparts in other countries, the Dutch version of the television talent show *Idols* (RTL4, 2003-present) consists of contestants performing cover versions of classic, most often American, pop songs, which can be seen as a literal form of karaoke Americanism. Each broadcast is centered around

FABRICATING THE ABSOLUTE FAKE

one particular theme, ranging from "The 1980s" and "Motown" to "Disco" and "Top 40 Hits." Although themes may vary during each season, the "Dutch Hits" theme always returns, as one broadcast is dedicated to the contestants singing original Dutch pop songs, either in Dutch or English. In this manner, Dutchness is just another theme among others, which is reconfirmed by the way *Idols* presents the theme in its opening segment. During the second season, for example, the "Disco" episode (27 March 2004) shows the contestants dressed in platform-soled shoes, bellbottom pants, and big Afro wigs. In the "Dutch Hits" episode (3 April 2004), they are wearing traditional Dutch costumes. At first sight, the black Columbian-born contestant JK wearing a folkloristic Dutch costume looks particularly out of place, giving the impression of a drag performance, as his blackness contradicts the traditional whiteness of Dutch folklore. However, JK's hypervisibility actually reveals that the same could be said of the white Dutch contestants, showing that they too are in "drag" by donning traditional Dutch dress. In the global pop television format of *Idols*, there is no real difference between disco revivalism and Dutch national folklore, as both offer just another occasion to dress up in fancy costumes.

The "Dutch Hits" episode of *Idols* is significant because it shows how through pop culture the presentation of national identity can be reduced to the clichéd and stereotypical images of global tourism. As host Reinout Oerlemans tells the audience, to "get into the right mood," the contestants are placed in a "typically Dutch setting" as they are being tested on their knowledge of Dutch national heritage. In addition to the contestants wearing traditional Dutch costumes, this "typically Dutch setting" is created through the use of the color orange in combination with the red-white-and-blue of the national flag and images of Dutch tourism: tulips, windmills, wooden shoes, and cheese. The conventional orange sentiment is evoked with footage of the national soccer team and the Dutch royal family. That such a stereotypical expression of national identity should not be taken too seriously becomes clear when the contestants are quizzed about Dutch national history. None of them recognize the name of national hero Michiel de Ruyter, the famous Dutch sea admiral of the seventeenth century, jokingly suggesting instead that he must be a fishmonger or a bicycle repairman. Since the general frame of reference of both *Idols* and its contestants, in all the episodes, is pop culture – and American pop culture in particular – it is not surprising that the depiction of Dutch national identity conforms with the clichéd images that pop culture provides. Moreover, the performance of Dutchness fits within the overall karaoke Americanism of *Idols*, in which Dutchness is treated as just another theme, in spite of being performed by Dutch contestants on a Dutch television show.

By perceiving this particular performance of Dutchness on *Idols* as a form of karaoke Americanism, I am not suggesting that any stereotypical expression of pop culture is by definition American or should be considered as such. Also the question of whether or not *Idols* (based on an originally British format) is American is beside the point. The significance of this particular example is found in the notion that the Dutch edition of *Idols* uses its international format to present a national identity which is based on clichéd images of Dutchness taken from a global, yet American-dominated, pop culture. In this way, *Idols* does not present Dutchness as an explicit local or national form of self-depiction but rather as a pastiche based on how Dutchness is believed to be globally perceived. The Dutchness as presented on *Idols* may be an extreme example of how pop culture reduces a national identity to such a clichéd image. Nevertheless, it is telling that in a time when the redefinition of national identity has become a topic of political urgency, the depiction of Dutch nationality on *Idols* is taken for granted.

Since 9/11 and the assassinations of Fortuyn and Van Gogh, the political debate on Dutch national identity is predominantly focused on the danger of Muslim extremism and the issue of ethnic integration. The fear that the national identity could be undermined by the cultural imperialism of Americanization has conspicuously disappeared from the political agenda. Quite the contrary, now the USA is often mentioned as a successful multicultural society to be emulated.[5] As Peter van der Veer has argued, the political debate says more about a changing Dutch culture than about Islam, even if most discussions are limited to the issue of Muslim fundamentalism. Particularly the assassinations challenged preexisting notions of Dutchness, as these "events did not fit the Netherlands's global image and tourist brand as a wealthy, tolerant, and perhaps excessively liberal society."[6] A catchphrase in the debate is "the multicultural drama," based on an influential essay of the same name, published on January 29, 2000 (thus before 9/11) by left-wing intellectual Paul Scheffer.[7] In the essay, Scheffer argues that the seriousness of the situation has been underestimated. The Dutch policy of multiculturalism has resulted in ethnic segregation and the exclusion of ethnic minorities from a collective Dutch history and identity, comparable to Anderson's notion of imagined community. The celebrated Dutch principle of tolerance through respecting ethnic, cultural, and religious diversity often turned out to be an indifference toward the immigrant population instead. As a result, first-generation immigrants have recreated their homeland cultures separately from mainstream Dutch society, leaving second-generation immigrants torn between the traditional culture of their parents and an indifferent Dutch mainstream culture. Although Paul Scheffer wrote the essay before 9/11, he believes that the multicultural drama has been reconfirmed by 9/11 and the assassinations of Fortuyn and Van Gogh. "Once

　　　　　　　　　　　　FABRICATING THE ABSOLUTE FAKE

you accept that multicultural argument against teaching them *our* history, you are excluding them from collective memory, from an enormous chance for renewal," as Scheffer explained the Dutch multicultural drama to a reporter of *The New Yorker* in 2006, adding that "September 11th gave many of them their narrative."[8]

While "The Multicultural Drama" can be credited for exposing some of the actual problems facing Dutch multiculturalism, including the possibility of ethnic segregation and the social exclusion of ethnic groups from mainstream society, the essay does imply a rigid distinction between "our" and "their" culture, and thereby limits "our" culture to an identity which is predominantly formed by a collective national history. Even though national history is important, such a perspective, including the added comments after 9/11, is problematic for two reasons. First, the multicultural drama perspective presents the collective national identity as an uncontested given, suggesting that both "our" and "their" culture are fixed entities. Second, such a perspective tends to ignore that 9/11 and the assassinations of Fortuyn and Van Gogh not only gave "many of them their narrative" but also "us" a range of narratives, including ones that polarize the debate, as well as others that instead challenge the rigid "us" versus "them" divide. This wide range of narratives can be found in the political and public debates, but also in literature, the arts, academic discussions, and in pop culture. I focus specifically on pop culture, as within this realm, the notion of national identity (including the question of who belongs to "us" and who belongs to "them") is often expressed through the appropriation of American genre conventions and audiovisual language. Inspired by popular African-American hip-hop, national identity has been addressed in Dutch hip-hop songs by both "white" and "ethnic" rappers, including Ali B, Brainpower, Lange Frans & Baas B, Raymzter, and Postman.[9] On television, drama series such as *Najib en Julia* (AVRO, 2002), directed by Theo van Gogh, and *Dunya & Desie* (NPS, 2002-2004) deal with romance and friendship between white Dutch and Moroccan-Dutch teenagers, whereas sitcoms like *Bradaz* (NPS, 2001-2002) and *Shouf Shouf* (VARA, 2006-2007) take the multicultural society as the setting for amusing cultural misunderstandings among characters of different ethnic backgrounds, only to return to a state of ethnic and national harmony. Popular Dutch movies like *Shouf Shouf Habibi!* (Albert ter Heerdt, 2004), *Het Schnitzelparadijs* (2005), and *'n Beetje Verliefd* (2006), the last two directed by Martin Koolhoven, use the genre conventions of the Hollywood comedy to present the "funny" side of Dutch multiculturalism, showing that it is not always a multicultural drama, but often a multicultural comedy as well.

As Thomas Elsaesser has suggested, Theo van Gogh – and, to a lesser extent, Pim Fortuyn – also operated within the realm of pop culture, as he used television, film, the internet, and the popular press as "fields of symbolic action, deploying a language of signs, clichés and stereotypes as the common code of a culture that lives its differences in the realm of discourse, rather than by force."[10] Although the assassinations of Fortuyn and Van Gogh may suggest that these fields of symbolic action no longer provide space for a pop-cultural discourse, having been replaced by the political "reality" of Muslim extremism, both 9/11 and the assassinations also operate within these fields of symbolic action. The murder of Pim Fortuyn, for example, inspired Van Gogh to make the political thriller *06/05*, released posthumously in 2005, in which actual news footage of Fortuyn's political rise, his assassination, and its aftermath are combined with a fictional conspiracy narrative. Dutch film reviewers immediately made the rather obvious comparison between Van Gogh and the American filmmaker Oliver Stone by perceiving *06/05* as a Dutch version of *JFK* (1991), the Hollywood film about the conspiracy behind the assassination of President John F. Kennedy. Moreover, the assassination of Theo van Gogh too can be interpreted within the fields of symbolic action as, suggested by Elsaesser, "the murder itself, with its ritualistic overtones and easily decodable symbolism, had the performative dimension of other acts of barbarity deliberately staged to produce shocking media images and atrocity events."[11] Without denying the political reality of these events, one can also perceive the assassinations of Fortuyn and Van Gogh as part of a pop-cultural discourse on Dutch national identity, functioning as symbolic references in films, television programs, websites, and pop songs.

Like the depiction of Dutchness on *Idols*, the pop-cultural artifacts that I will discuss below can be analyzed as performances of karaoke Americanism, in which American pop culture is being appropriated to provide commentary on Dutch national identity since 9/11. Starting with the appraisal of Pim Fortuyn as the Dutch Kennedy, I will analyze how the genre conventions and audiovisual language of American pop culture are applied to discuss notions of belonging in Dutch society, questioning the explicit or implicit "us" versus "them" divide which all these artifacts address. Operating within fields of symbolic action that are heavily inspired by the American original, these pop-cultural objects tend to refer to an imagined America, rather than the nation-state USA or a Dutch imagined community, thereby possibly opening up space for a shared sense of belonging across different cultural and ethnic identities.

THE POP SENTIMENTALITY OF THE DUTCH KENNEDY

In the television program *De Waarheid* (SBS6, 2002-2003), the Dutch pop singer Gerard Joling visits national celebrities to check whether or not the stories in that week's tabloids are telling the truth. In the episode broadcast on May 4, 2002, Joling interviews politician Pim Fortuyn, the controversial independent candidate whose sudden popularity is dominating the national elections campaign at that moment. Running on a populist anti-immigration and anti-Islam platform, Fortuyn seems to attract the votes of a "silent majority" fed up with traditional politics. Yet, Joling and Fortuyn are not talking about politics. Both men are openly and quite flamboyantly gay, and they frankly discuss the lack of romance in their lives, concluding that, if neither of them finds Mister Right, they might have to grow old together. Two days later, Pim Fortuyn is assassinated at the Hilversum Media Park, the center of Dutch media, shot to death by a white Dutch animal rights activist. "Everyone is sad, the message was so bad, democracy has died, and everybody cried," sings Gerard Joling in English on his single "At Your Service," paying tribute to the slain politician he had interviewed so recently. "At 6.09, the sixth of May, became an awful day."

That Pim Fortuyn was shot at the center of Dutch media emphasizes the notion that Fortuyn was a media phenomenon. As Ian Buruma suggests, Fortuyn not only used "showbiz as a political tool" (in the tradition of politicians such as Silvio Berlusconi, Arnold Schwarzenegger, and Ronald Reagan), he also used "his instinct for pop sentimentality."[12] Peter van der Veer compares Fortuyn to Dutch "campy, extroverted gay entertainers," suggesting that his gayness enabled him to "say things in a strident manner and [to combine] a feminine vulnerability with a sharp and entertaining irony."[13] Unlike most other Dutch politicians, Pim Fortuyn fitted easily within the realm of pop-cultural stardom, using not only the serious press but also the tabloids (including a photo session of Fortuyn relaxing in his luxurious bathroom at home) to present himself to the larger public. His death led to a massive collective mourning, reminiscent of the death of Princess Diana and befitting his charismatic star image. In both the serious and popular press, Fortuyn's death was also immediately compared to the assassination of John F. Kennedy. Although Kennedy had been shot four decades earlier (and several European political leaders had been assassinated in the intervening years), the Kennedy assassination has become part of the global audiovisual collective memory, through the Zapruder film and Hollywood movies like Oliver Stone's *JFK* (1991). Moreover, Fortuyn also has been compared to Kennedy as the symbol of a political promise that could not be fulfilled. Dutch television repeatedly showed a fragment of an interview with Fortuyn in which he pointed at a portrait, hanging in his own living room, of John F. Kennedy, saying that he took the American president as one of his role models. The Dutch tabloids quickly picked up this connection by remembering Pim Fortuyn's attempt to confront conventional politics as "the guts of the Dutch Kennedy."[14]

The day after Fortuyn's assassination, the Dutch commercial radio channel Yorin FM broadcast an adapted version of Tom Clay's "What the World Needs Now Is Love." The original version, released by Motown in 1971, is an audio collage of live radio coverage of the assassinations of John F. Kennedy, Martin Luther King, Jr., and Robert Kennedy played over the music of Burt Bacharach's "What the World Needs Now Is Love" and Dion's "Abraham, Martin, and John." By adding Fortuyn's voice and audio fragments of the live news coverage of his death to this melodramatic plea for peace and racial harmony, Yorin FM places Pim Fortuyn alongside these American political martyrs. However, this connection is not based on the political beliefs of those who were assassinated, but on the similarities in the way they were assassinated, in the way the media portrayed their assassinations, and what they have come to mean in cultural history. Just like Robert Kennedy, Pim Fortuyn was shot during an election campaign, and just like the assassination of John F. Kennedy, the death of Pim Fortuyn tends to be perceived as the end of innocence. In this way, Fortuyn's death is framed within a specific American pop-cultural context, yet one which is used to articulate an equally specific Dutch collective experience. The comparison of Pim Fortuyn to President Kennedy is reinforced by the aforementioned film *06/05*, the Dutch *JFK* directed by Theo van Gogh, suggesting that the conspiracy behind the death of Fortuyn reveals the corrupted nature of politics.

A similar sentiment is expressed by Gerard Joling on his tribute single, as he sings: "Our future went so wrong, our innocence was gone." The song's title refers to the English slogan "At Your Service" which Fortuyn used to express that he represents the voice of "the common people." Singer Connie Breukhoven, better known as Vanessa, also released a tribute single. Instead of singing an original composition, Vanessa reworked "When You Say Nothing At All," an American country song originally recorded by Keith Whitley, which had become a global hit song in the versions by the American country singer Alison Krauss and by the Irish, former Boyzone singer Ronan Keating. In Vanessa's version, "You say it best when you say nothing at all" is changed into "You *said* it best, *but now* you say nothing at all." One may wonder why Dutch singers decide to pay tribute to a slain Dutch politician by singing in English. When these songs were released, however, this question never arose. A possible explanation may be that the Dutch audience expects and thus accepts such songs to be sung in English, as both songs build upon the themes, rhetoric, and melodrama expressed in songs like USA for Africa's "We Are the World" and Elton John's "Candle in the Wind" (both his original tribute to film star Marilyn Monroe and the adapted version in honor of Princess Diana). With these songs as original examples, singing in English may sound more convincing, sincere, and authentic. Moreover, echoing the rhetoric of these originals, Joling and Vanessa take freedom of speech and racial harmony as starting points. "They can never explain what we hear when you just say your thing" sings Vanessa, a reworking of the original line "They can never define what's been said between your heart and mine." Similar to "We Are the World," Gerard Joling calls upon "the people in the street, black or white" to fight together to create a peaceful and respectful society. "As one country we'll go on, together, together, we are strong."

As performances of karaoke Americanism, both tribute singles imitate the American original to such an extent that, if we did not know better, one might think that they are parodies rather than genuinely meant tributes (which could explain why both singles were commercial failures). Nevertheless, they do reinforce the pop sentimentality which has come to define the Fortuyn phenomenon, fitting the depiction of Fortuyn as the Dutch Kennedy, a martyr who not only embodies the good of society, but most of all its unfulfilled promise. In this way, Fortuyn's political agenda of anti-immigration and anti-Islam is pushed to the background, being replaced by the allegedly universal values of an imagined America such as freedom of expression, individual liberty, and racial harmony, all expressed in the hollow rhetoric of the pop-cultural cliché.

The Land of... F___ing Moroccans??!

"It may sound simple what I say, but they look at me as if I flew into the Twin Towers," raps the Moroccan-Dutch hip-hopper Raymzter in Dutch.[15] Released in October 2002, his hit single "Kutmarokkanen??!," translated by *Time* magazine as "F___ing Moroccans," addresses the negative way in which Moroccan-Dutch youth are represented in the Dutch media, particularly since the terrorist attacks of 9/11.[16] The song takes its title from the infamous slip of the tongue by the white left-wing Amsterdam alderman Rob Oudkerk. When he whispered to the mayor of Amsterdam to complain about those "kutmarokkanen," he did not realize that his words were being recorded by television. Although never intended to be broadcast, Oudkerk's use of such a pejorative term shows that, in the then-current political climate, the overt stigmatization of Moroccan-Dutch youth was not limited to the rhetoric of right-wing politicians like Pim Fortuyn. By appropriating the pejorative term, Raymzter effectively counters this negative representation, as the term no longer merely refers to Moroccan-Dutch youth as potential criminals or terrorists, but also to a popular hit single by a rising Moroccan-Dutch hip-hop star.

Similar to other Moroccan-Dutch hip-hop, "Kutmarokkanen??!" – both the song and the accompanying music video – combines the sounds and imagery of African-American hip-hop with local Dutch youth street culture and Arabic pop music. While the Dutch lyrics emphasize how the negative media representation has led to the stigmatization of Moroccan-Dutch youth, the music video presents an alternative scenario by showing white Dutch girls being barred from entering the disco, whereas Moroccan-Dutch girls are allowed to enter and join Raymzter in his performance of the song. The single's cover art presents an even more explicit criticism of the negative media representation. Mocking the front page of the Dutch daily newspaper *De Telegraaf,* known for its alleged sensationalist and populist coverage of ethnic minorities, the cover presents the front page of *De Raymzter,* with a tough-looking Raymzter pictured in close-up under the headline "Kutmarokkanen??!" with the blurb "Moroccans are now also terrorizing the pop charts."[17] The fictional article reports that more and more Moroccan youth are making pop music, much to the dismay of the established radio channels, which, as the quote by an anonymous deejay reveals, may appreciate that Moroccans are making western music, but also claim that there is no room for them on the play lists. The radio channels clearly represent mainstream Dutch culture at large, which tends to tell Moroccan-Dutch youth to actively participate in society, while simultaneously excluding them from the job market. Eventually, "Kutmarokkanen??!" broke through the barrier that it criticizes, at least in the music industry, as the song was included on the play lists of the radio and music television channels, becoming the first Moroccan-Dutch hit single and setting an example for future Moroccan-Dutch pop stars to follow.

That a Dutch rap song about exclusion succeeds in being included within mainstream pop culture befits its hip-hop genre. "Kutmarokkanen??!" can be perceived as a cultural appropriation of African-American hip-hop, a music genre and initial subculture which finds itself in a paradoxical position. On the one hand, hip-hop can be seen as the rebellious voice of a marginalized group within American society, whereas, on the other, hip-hop has become one of the most dominant and profitable genres in American commercial pop culture.[18] As such, hip-hop can be simultaneously rebellious and mainstream, representing positions of both exclusion and inclusion, eventually becoming part of the culture that it criticizes. On the global scale, hip-hop is a very powerful form of Americanization, providing the language and imagery for youth subcultures to shape their rebellion against authority, quite similar to the way rock 'n' roll functioned five decades earlier.[19] Yet, simultaneously, hip-hop is a profitable commodity, selling American pop culture around the world.

Whereas Raymzter appropriates the rebellious rhetoric of African-American hip-hop to protest against structural discrimination in Dutch society, the white Dutch hip-hop duo Lange Frans & Baas B use rap to protest against so-called "senseless violence" in general. Released in October 2004, their number-one hit single "Zinloos" ("Senseless") pays tribute to four different victims who all were killed for no apparent reason and as such became symbols of senseless violence. Immediately after the assassination of Theo van Gogh, with "Zinloos" still on the pop charts, Lange Frans & Baas B added a verse about Van Gogh, wishing that their "homie" Theo may rest in peace. One year later, they released another number-one hit single, "Het Land Van…" ("The Land of…"), an am-biguous ode to their homeland. Presenting the Netherlands as the land of Pim Fortuyn and Volkert van de G. (the convicted assassin of Fortuyn) and of Theo van Gogh and Mohammed B., Lange Frans & Baas B depict a nation of uncer-tainty: "[We] come from the land with the most cultures per square meter / yet where people are afraid to have dinner with their neighbors / and integration is a wonderful word / but shit is fucking bitter when nobody listens."[20] Even though they recognize the country's confused state after the assassinations and its uncritical support of "Uncle Bush" in his War on Terror, Lange Frans and Baas B. also depict the Netherlands as a country which cherishes freedom and where everyone is included within the patriotic orange sentiment when the national soccer team plays.

Through their use of hip-hop to comment on Dutch society, Lange Frans & Baas B are comparable to Raymzter, appropriating African-American hip-hop within a local context. However, by explicitly defining identity on the basis of nationality, the Netherlands as "the land of Lange Frans & Baas B" invites ambiguous interpretations. On the one hand, the nation is presented as a mul-ticultural society, providing a home to people from different ethnic and cultur-al backgrounds. Yet, on the other hand, the song also can be interpreted as im-plying that Lange Frans & Baas B still perceive the Netherlands as their home, in spite of its multicultural character. Here ethnicity proves to be significant. Since Lange Frans & Baas B are white, their Dutchness is uncontested, mak-ing their expression of a confused yet hopeful Dutch national identity seem-ingly representative of the collective Dutch state of mind. Such a perspective is reconfirmed by the music video, which shows Lange Frans & Baas B, dressed in designer suits rather than typical hip-hop attire, performing "Het Land Van…" live at the Amsterdam Uitmarkt in front of a large outdoor audience. Shots of their performance alternate with shots of the audience, showing close-ups of individual audience members listening tentatively, only to erupt in approving cheers at the song's finale. With a few exceptions, like the close-up of a young black woman, the shown audience members are white, emphasizing the white-ness of the traditional Dutch national identity. Moreover, different than "ethnic" rappers, Lange Frans & Baas B do not need to account for their ethnicity, as their Dutchness is taken for granted. One can only wonder, had "Het Land Van…" been performed by a Moroccan-Dutch rapper, whether or not such an explicit expression of a collective Dutchness would have received the same approving response, including the number-one spot on the pop charts.

"Het Land Van…" gets a provocative response with another song entitled "Het Land Van…," rapped in Dutch by the Moroccan-Dutch hip-hop artist Salah Edin, released in 2007. The song can be seen as a counter-narrative, presenting a far more negative perspective on Dutch society. In the song, Edin denounces the Netherlands as a capitalist and materialistic country in which covert racism prevails: "The land where I was born … / the land which calls me the fucking Moroccan."[21] Moreover, the song samples audio fragments of, among others, Pim Fortuyn and Theo van Gogh defending freedom of expression, suggesting, placed within the song's context, that freedom of expression has resulted in hatred against Dutch Muslims. The song's music video shows a conventional white Dutch family whose cozy home is being infiltrated by the media images of Muslim terrorism. Simultaneously, Salah Edin is shown slowly transforming from a mainstream young man into a Muslim extremist, eventually dressed in orange overalls as worn by the prisoners of Guantánamo Bay. The orange overalls signify both the global and the local, as the image of the Muslim terrorist is explicitly connected to the politics of the nation-state USA, whereas the color of the overalls connotes the Dutch orange sentiment.

Although explicitly commenting on Dutch society, both the song as well as the album it's from, *Nederlands grootste nachtmerrie* ("Holland's Worst Nightmare"), can be seen as appropriations of African-American pop culture. The album's promotional material emphasizes the role of its American producer Focus, who is a protégé of the famous African-American gangsta rap producer Dr. Dre. In this way, Salah Edin obtains authenticity as being a real gangsta rapper. However, instead of the stereotypical image of the tough gangsta rapper, Edin adopts the image of the stereotypical Muslim terrorist. His picture on the album cover mimics the widely publicized mug shot of Mohammed B., the convicted assassin of Theo van Gogh. Edin has denied that the cover art is intended as a provocation, saying that instead the imitation of the mug shot is meant to emphasize the tendency in the media to portray all Moroccan-Dutch young men as potential terrorists: "This is the way the average white Dutch citizen sees me, as a young Moroccan Muslim radical. That's why I chose to do this picture and use it for the front cover of my album. It is in no way supporting the deeds of Mohammed B."[22] Yet, as a hip-hop persona, Edin's impersonation of Mohammed B. functions quite similarly to the gangsta image of African-American rappers like 50 Cent, both as a commercial sign of street credibility and hip-hop authenticity as well as a provocative political statement.

Taken together, the rap songs by Raymzter, Lange Frans & Baas B, and Salah Edin show how the genre conventions and audiovisual language of African-American hip-hop have been translated and appropriated into a specific Dutch context, providing perspectives not only on Dutch national identity but also on the experience of structural racism and the negative depiction of Moroccan-Dutch youth in the Dutch media. However, the songs differ greatly in the messages that they convey. The two versions of "Het Land Van…" can be perceived as the two oppositional poles of the "us" versus "them" divide, in which the Dutch "us" perspective is represented by Lange Frans & Baas B and the Moroccan "them" perspective by Salah Edin. Perhaps tellingly, the first became a number-one hit single on the pop charts, whereas the second was banned from the Dutch music television channels MTV and TMF. Moreover, the divide is reinforced by Lange Frans & Baas B explicitly identifying themselves with their "homie" Theo van Gogh, and Salah Edin with Mohammed B. With his single "Kutmarokkanen??!," on the contrary, Raymzter challenges the rigid "us" versus "them" divide, as he counters racism by not only protesting but also crossing the media's ethnic boundaries that have kept Moroccan-Dutch rappers from commercial success. Nevertheless, although coming from different perspectives along the lines of the "us" versus "them" divide, the three songs are significantly similar in the way they appropriate the genre conventions of African-American hip-hop. They may have different stories to tell, yet Raymzter, Lange Frans & Baas B, and Salah Edin have the language of American pop culture in common.

LINDA'S DUTCH DREAM

In February 2005, the monthly *LINDA.* magazine published a special issue on the success of ethnic integration in the Netherlands, using the English title "Dutch Dream" as its main theme. Introduced a year earlier, *LINDA.* is a lifestyle glossy magazine based on the star persona of Linda de Mol, one of the most popular television hosts of the Netherlands. Known as just Linda, she is also an actress, starring in the television drama series *Gooische Vrouwen* (Talpa/RTL4, 2005-present), often described as a Dutch "remake" of the American television series *Desperate Housewives* (ABC, 2004-present). Her initial image of being Holland's favorite daughter-in-law evolved into the far more glamorous image of a "real" star, a transformation which runs parallel to the role she plays in the Dutch film comedy *Ellis in Glamourland* (Pieter Kramer, 2004). By starring alongside Joan Collins, most famous for her glamorous role as Alexis in *Dynasty* (ABC, 1981-1989), Linda, like her character in the film, has become part of the glamour that defines movie stardom, appropriating the star myth of Hollywood. It is Linda's star persona that forms the basis of *LINDA.* magazine, which is clearly modeled after the American glossy *O* magazine, based on the star persona of the African-American talk show host Oprah Winfrey. Like Oprah, Linda is featured on the cover of each issue, and, also like Oprah, she always emphasizes her personal experience and interest in specific topics – ranging from cosmetic surgery, fashion, and dieting, to love, religion and multiculturalism – to help her predominantly female readership relate to these themes.

As Linda explains in her editorial, the idea for a special "Dutch Dream" issue came up in May 2004, as a response to the negative media representation of ethnic minorities in the Netherlands. Although she mentions neither 9/11 nor the popularity and subsequent assassination of Pim Fortuyn, she clearly suggests that these events helped to shape the popular assumption that ethnic integration has failed. To counter such a negative perception, *LINDA.* would focus on the success stories of ethnic minorities and on ethnic products, such as food and fashion, that have enriched Dutch culture. But then, writes Linda, "all went wrong." Theo van Gogh was murdered and everything changed. "I discovered that I had thoughts I'd never had before, and of which I am definitely not proud. Suddenly it was *my* Netherlands and they better not think *they* can tell us to shut up or tell us how to live."[23] By recognizing and expressing her blunt first reaction, Linda opens up to her readers, enabling them to have their own possible feelings of intolerance acknowledged, a typical Oprah Winfrey strategy.[24] Then, countering her own initial reaction, Linda returns to the need for a more positive perspective on ethnic integration, focusing both on the "facts" (in the form of an article based on a report by the Dutch government's Social and Cultural Planning Office) and on the "fun" side: "the success stories, the influence on fashion, culture, and eating habits."

By using the title "Dutch Dream" to highlight the positive side of ethnic integration, *LINDA.* evokes the symbolic rhetoric of the American Dream, including its focus on the economic and social-cultural success of individuals, which is embodied by the featured "ethnic" Dutch celebrities. The magazine's cover shows a festive dinner table, with Linda as the white media queen sitting in the middle, flanked by, on one side, the Moroccan-Dutch rapper Ali B and the Surinamese-Dutch stand-up comedian Jörgen Raymann, and on the other, the Surinamese-Dutch sports anchorman Humberto Tan and the Surinamese-Dutch television host Sylvana Simons. When unfolding the foldout cover (similar to the cover of *Vanity Fair*), the dinner table is extended to in-

FABRICATING THE ABSOLUTE FAKE

clude eight more "ethnic role models," symbolizing that ethnic integration in Dutch society can be successful: the Algerian-Dutch actor Hakim Traïdia, famous for his role on the Dutch *Sesame Street*, the Moroccan-Dutch singer and former *Idols* contestant Hind, the Surinamese-Dutch musical star Stanley Burleson, the Surinamese-Dutch member of Dutch parliament Laetitia Griffith, the Argentinean jewelry maker Rodrigo Otazu, the Surinamese-Dutch singer Ruth Jacott, the Moroccan-Dutch actor Mimoun Oaïssa of *Shouf Shouf Habibi!* fame, and the Moroccan-Dutch soccer player Mohammad Allach. With the exception of Ali B, who wears "his own clothes," all are dressed in designer outfits, befitting the magazine's celebratory focus on social-economic success. Although several white Dutch men are featured inside the magazine, they are conspicuously absent from its cover, or at least visually – they are present in three of the four blurbs printed on *LINDA.*'s cover. Moreover, most of the featured ethnic celebrities are either Moroccan-Dutch or Surinamese-Dutch, while the Antillean-Dutch, the Turkish-Dutch, and the Chinese-Dutch, among others, are not represented.

Inside the magazine, all featured celebrities are interviewed about their individual success. Staying within the rhetoric of the American Dream, most of them stress the importance of hard work and believing in one's destiny. For example, Sylvana Simons argues that there is no relation between one's ethnic background and what one can achieve in life: "You can become successful by working hard, by clearly setting your dreams and goals." Humberto Tan suggests that young "ethnic" men can avoid a life of crime by climbing the social ladder, which requires discipline, stamina, self-criticism, and a support network of family and friends. According to Hakim Traïdia, everyone has the same opportunities to become successful, at least in acting: "Whether you are Dutch or ethnic, your success is determined by the audience." Only the Moroccan-Macedonian-Dutch actress Touriya Haoud (not featured on the magazine's cover) mentions that she has been treated differently because of her ethnic background, as in Dutch films she tends to be typecast as "the headscarf-wearing Moroccan girl." She explicitly states that in that respect the Netherlands is totally different from the USA as, claims Haoud, there is far less typecasting in American films, enabling non-white actors to play a wide range of roles. In none of the interviews are the aftermath of 9/11 or the assassinations of Fortuyn and Van Gogh mentioned. With the exception of the comment about typecasting in Dutch film, the individual success stories do not refer to broader social-political issues like discrimination. Instead, echoing the American rhetoric of meritocracy, the successful "Dutch Dream" as embodied by these Dutch celebrities is presented as a personal achievement which is solely based on individual talent and effort. The use of the English term "Dutch Dream" rather than a literal translation into Dutch ("de Nederlandse droom") is significant, as it not only makes an explicit connection to the American Dream and its connotations, but also shows that the social-economic success story ("making your dreams come true") is based on an American conception of achievement. Similar to Oprah Winfrey, as discussed in chapter two, Linda de Mol functions as an embodiment of the star myth, her Dutch appropriation of the American Dream. As such, Linda includes the ethnic Dutch celebrities within her "glamour land" – her own imagined America – by letting them join her at the festive dinner table on the cover and by interviewing them inside her magazine, and so celebrating Dutch multiculturalism.

However, that the inclusive range of such an imagined America proves to be limited is shown by the other articles in *LINDA.* magazine. While the ethnic celebrities are included within Linda's success story, thereby crossing the "us" versus "them" divide of the Dutch political discourse, the other articles reinforce the rigid distinction instead. The opposition between two cultural identities is present in almost all articles: a fashion photo spread entitled "Morocco meets Holland," six photo portraits of gay Muslim men who "love Allah and men," and an interview with the Surinamese-Dutch female politician Laetitia Griffith by the white Dutch male journalist Jort Kelder, whose impertinent question "Are you a Bounty?" (referring to a candy bar that is chocolate brown on the outside and white on the inside) is used as the interview's title. In the interview, Kelder tells Griffith that she is not as sensual as he expected a Surinamese woman to be, before asking her whether or not it is true that black men are more sexually promiscuous than white men. The feature on "full color" make-up for women with darker skin is not addressed to potential non-white readers, but rather informs white female readers about the difficulties non-white women face in their search for the right make-up. In the explicit *Sex and the City*-style column "Angelique," the columnist claims she cannot be xenophobic, as otherwise she never would have "enjoyed" Baba, a twenty-five-year-old Nigerian black man with a penis of twenty-five centimeters. In this way, although seemingly ethnic boundaries are being crossed, they are reinforced instead, as non-white cultures are reduced to a "colorful," "sensual," or "exotic" quality that enriches white Dutch culture. Moreover, in contrast to the inclusion of the ethnic celebrities, *LINDA.* excludes non-white readers by continuously addressing an implied (and sometimes explicit) white Dutch audience.

THE MULTICULTURAL COMEDY

In *Shouf Shouf Habibi!* (Albert ter Heerdt, 2004), a comedy about a group of young Moroccan-Dutch friends which became the box office hit of the year, there is one reference to 9/11. Main character Abdullah (Mimoun Oaïssa), called "Ap" by his friends, is shooting pool at his local Amsterdam bar, together with his best buddies: the Moroccan-Dutch Mustafa or "Mussi" (Mohammed Chaara), the Moroccan-Dutch Rachid (Mimoun Ouled Radi), and the white Dutch Robbie (Leo Alkemade). Suddenly Ap tells Mussi, "You look like Atta," and then repeats to the others, "Mussi looks like Atta."[25] That Ap refers to the face of Mohammed Atta, the terrorist who piloted the first plane into the Twin Towers, is not coincidental. With the obvious exception of Osama bin Laden, Mohammed Atta has been the most extensively discussed 9/11 terrorist in the media, and specifically the oft-published picture of Atta's face has become an emblem of 9/11.[26] However, the importance of 9/11 is downplayed immediately by a comic exchange between Ap and Rachid. "Atta?" Rachid asks; "The hijacker of September 11," Ap says; "September 11?" Rachid asks; "Those towers, man," Ap says, to which Rachid responds, "Oh, those towers!" By observing that Mussi looks like Atta, Ap mirrors the practice of the white Dutch population of looking at Moroccan-Dutch youth, paraphrasing Raymzter, "as if they flew into the Twin Towers," yet without resulting in the racial profiling and objectification that stigmatizes them as potential terrorists.

This comic reference to 9/11 and the objectification of Moroccan-Dutch youth is intensified by Ap's suggestion that looking like Atta provides a great career opportunity. There are hardly any Arab actors in Hollywood, which means that once the events of 9/11 are turned into blockbuster action movies, Ap and his friends will be in great demand to star as the terrorists. Envisioning a glamorous Hollywood life with beautiful women, private swimming pools, big convertibles, and millions of dollars in his pocket, Ap tells his friends: "Not one! Not a single Arab actor left in America. It might take them a little while but once they start: one war movie after another. *Action in Afghanistan I, Action in Afghanistan II, Action in Afghanistan III*. Who will play them? Who will play Atta? I'll tell you, those towers will go down at least thirty more times." Another comic exchange between Ap and Rachid follows. "Saving Private Saddam," Rachid jokes, pointing at Mussi, to which Ap responds, "They can use a crazy ape like you too. They're not all handsome," suggesting that Rachid, unlike Mussi and Ap himself, does not have the conventional good looks of a Hollywood leading man. Rachid shoots back, "If you say so, Brad Pitt." The joke works, because Rachid's comment exposes the flaw in Ap's dream scenario. Even if they would be able to become actors in Hollywood 9/11 blockbusters, portraying the terrorists thanks to racial profiling, they could never become the leading men, let alone Hollywood stars like Brad Pitt – a joke that, as Thomas Elsaesser rightly observes, "would fall flat indeed were it not contradicted by the film itself, which briefly did make Mimoun Oaïssa into a star."[27] Although the film takes the objectification of Dutch-Moroccan youth after 9/11 out of its local Dutch context into an imaginary Hollywood setting, eventually, as the scene suggests, there is little difference between being looked at as if you are a potential terrorist or being a potential Hollywood actor cast as a terrorist because you look like one.

The 9/11 scene is typical for the film in its entirety, as *Shouf Shouf Habibi!* literally can be considered as a form of comic relief in the debate about national identity and multiculturalism. The movie pokes fun at common stereotypes of both Moroccan immigrant culture and white Dutch mainstream society, although no explicit jokes are made about religion, neither about Islam nor about Christianity.[28] In its opening sequence, *Shouf Shouf Habibi!* presents a parody of the "Clash of Civilizations" on the local level. Traditional Moroccan culture is presented as naïve and backward. Ap and his brothers are shown on holiday in an isolated Moroccan country village, where their father was born. The village is presented as a romantic pre-modern cultural space, where the single television does not work properly and the villagers cannot believe that people have been on the moon. In stark contrast, the Netherlands is shown as an impersonal modern space, where it is always grey and raining. Consumerism and seductive sexuality are omnipresent, as signified by the scarcely clad female models pictured on the H&M fashion billboards which are dominating the cityscape. Ap's voiceover reveals his love-hate relationship with both cultures, as he complains about both Moroccan traditionalism and Dutch superficiality. Yet, rather than presenting a conventional second generation's caught-in-between-two-cultures dilemma, Ap seizes its opportunities. If he ever strikes it rich in the Netherlands, he will move to Morocco where the sun always shines.

Marketed as an "oer-Hollandse" ("typically Dutch") comedy, *Shouf Shouf Habibi!* appears to be the opposite, suggesting that this self-acclaimed label should be taken ironically. The movie closely follows the genre conventions of the Hollywood comedy to comment on multiculturalism in Dutch society. Shot in both Dutch and Arabic, *Shouf Shouf Habibi!* is one of the first Dutch mainstream films which prominently features ethnic minorities as its main characters. Being an American-style multicultural comedy, the movie seems atypical rather than typical of Dutch mainstream cinema. The "oer-Hollands" label, however, can also be read as a statement, suggesting that the multicultural society which the film depicts is "typically Dutch," challenging pre-existing notions of national identity by using the Hollywood genre to present a Dutch identity in which the inclusion of Moroccan-Dutch youth culture is uncontested. By the exaggerated portrayal of both the traditional Moroccan immi-

FABRICATING THE ABSOLUTE FAKE

grant culture of Ap's parents and mainstream white Dutch society consisting of responsible adults, a multicultural space is created for Ap and his friends for whom pop culture constitutes their main frame of reference. In stark contrast to Ap's older brother, a respectful police officer embodying the conventional image of successful integration, Ap and his friends are a group of opportunistic losers who continuously fail to achieve their goal of getting rich without too much effort. Yet, instead of repeating the dominant media image of Moroccan-Dutch youth as being potential criminals, *Shouf Shouf Habibi!* depicts them as just "regular" young men rebelling against the normative responsibility of mainstream society. In this manner, the film challenges the "us" versus "them" divide, as the alliance created among Ap and his friends is formed along the lines of generation rather than nationality or ethnicity, with Hollywood as their shared point of reference.

At a conference discussing the necessity of self-censorship among Dutch filmmakers, held two weeks after the murder of Theo van Gogh, *Shouf Shouf Habibi!*'s director Albert ter Heerdt announced that the filming of its sequel *Shouf Shouf Barakka!* would be postponed, because, as he explained, "at this moment, I can't make a comedy about these issues." In the tense political climate that pervaded Dutch society immediately after Van Gogh's murder, a comedy about Dutch-Moroccan ethnic relations could be misinterpreted. Moreover, the director revealed, "I don't want a knife in my chest."[29] The production company of *Shouf Shouf Habibi!* confirmed the postponement of the sequel, adding that Ter Heerdt and co-writer Mimoun Oaïssa, before returning to comedy, wanted to address the issues faced by Dutch multicultural society in the form of a realistic drama. As Ter Heerdt told *The New York Times*: "Before I can go on in a funny way, I first have to do another film dealing with the serious side of the problem – this time with many more [white] Dutch characters in it."[30] Two years later, the team of *Shouf Shouf Habibi!* produced *Kicks* (Albert ter Heerdt, 2007), a realistic drama starring Mimoun Oaïssa as the Moroccan-Dutch kick boxer Saïd whose younger brother is shot to death by a white Dutch policeman, leading to social tensions between the different ethnic groups of the population. The film's plot develops along various storylines in which the both white Dutch and Moroccan-Dutch main characters are connected through chance encounters, prompting many Dutch film reviewers to perceive *Kicks* as a Dutch version of *Crash* (Paul Haggis, 2005), the Hollywood movie which uses a similar network-based narrative to address social problems related to race relations in Los Angeles. *Kicks* focuses on the social tensions between the white Dutch and Moroccan-Dutch population in the aftermath of the fatal shooting, yet also emphasizes the coming together of both sides through personal interaction, suggesting that ethnic harmony is eventually possible. Although based on different Hollywood genres, *Shouf Shouf Habibi!* and *Kicks* are similar in the way they appropriate the genre conventions of Hollywood to present an optimistic picture of multiculturalism in which the Moroccan-Dutch presence is an uncontested element of Dutch national identity.

The decision by the makers of *Shouf Shouf Habibi!* and *Kicks* to turn to realistic drama rather than staying with comedy reinforces the assumption that lightweight pop culture, such as "feel good" cinema, cannot deal sufficiently with the "serious" side of the debate on national identity but merely, as comic relief, provides a welcome distraction. As these two films show, however, the "fun" and "serious" character of the debate compliment each other. Moreover, in spite of the postponement of its official sequel, the commercial success and popularity of *Shouf Shouf Habibi!* resulted in other multicultural comedies focused on white-Dutch and Moroccan-Dutch cultural interaction, including the popular spin-off television situation comedy *Shouf Shouf* (VARA, 2006-2007) starring most of the film's original actors. The romantic comedy *Het Schnitzelparadijs* (Martin Koolhoven, 2005) is set in the typical Dutch countryside and tells the story of the Moroccan-Dutch teenager Nordip Doenia (Mounir Valentyn) who works at a cheap roadside restaurant and falls in love with Agnes (Bracha van Doesburgh), the pretty white Dutch niece of his boss. As an updated version of the Romeo and Juliet love story, yet with the happy ending conform to the genre conventions of the Hollywood romantic comedy, *Het Schnitzelparadijs* suggests that true love and friendship have no ethnic boundaries. This message of ethnic harmony is repeated in *'n Beetje Verliefd* (Martin Koolhoven, 2006), which focuses on the Moroccan-Dutch teenager Omar, played by the popular rapper Yes-R, who arranges a blind date for his white Dutch grandfather, whereas he himself falls in love with a Turkish-Dutch girl. Staying closer to the American original, the television sitcom *Shouf Shouf* and the two films by Martin Koolhoven turn out to be even more generic and predictable than *Shouf Shouf Habibi!*. Nevertheless, together they show how the multicultural comedy has become a popular Dutch subgenre, thereby continuing to provide a counterweight to the multicultural drama perspective.

Conclusion: The Promise of Pop Culture

Although a strict distinction is often made between the entertainment of pop culture on the one hand and the seriousness of political discourse on the other, both American as well as Dutch pop culture show that in specific cases the two realms can become intertwined. In this chapter, I aimed to explore how Dutch pop culture appropriates elements of its American example to comment

FABRICATING THE ABSOLUTE FAKE

on a political reality. The focus on national identity is then the most obvious choice as, particularly after 9/11 and the assassinations of Pim Fortuyn and Theo van Gogh, the discussion about national identity – specifically in relation to the issues of Islam and multiculturalism – has come to dominate Dutch political discourse. Specifically the idea that a common sense of belonging is to be found in a collective national history, forming an imagined community that provides a clear expression of Dutchness, appears to be widely accepted. Moreover, a traditional fear of Americanization as a form of cultural imperialism which could threaten national culture and identity seemingly has disappeared, partially replaced by a fear for the growing influence of Islam, which may imply that the omnipresence of American pop culture is now perceived as a buffer rather than a threat.

Yet, as my discussion of the Dutch pop-cultural artifacts suggests, other senses of belonging can be found in the shared experience of American pop culture. All the examples – the *Idols* "Dutch Hits" episode, the Pim Fortuyn tribute singles by Gerard Joling and Vanessa, the hip-hop songs by Raymzter, Lange Frans & Baas B, and Salah Edin, the special "Dutch Dream" issue of *LINDA.* magazine, and the films *Shouf Shouf Habibi!* and *Kicks* – translate an American original into a specific local and national context. Although American pop culture is viewed as a model to emulate, none of these Dutch pop-cultural artifacts makes connections to the nation-state USA or to a historical Dutch imagined community, but instead should be perceived as part of an imagined America which transcends geographical boundaries. In other words, here American pop culture provides a common language to discuss political issues as national identity, ethnic integration, and multiculturalism, with the potential of creating alliances among different cultural identities within the Netherlands.

As performances of karaoke Americanism, each of these case studies shows that Dutch pop culture is not merely an imitation of American pop culture, but instead is made up of active cultural appropriations in which mimicking and mocking often go together, presenting different perspectives on the notion of national identity in the Netherlands. The depiction of Dutchness on the "Dutch Hits" episode of *Idols*, based on the worn-out clichés of global tourism, does not only express national identity, but also undermines its authenticity, because it is such a cliché that one cannot take it too seriously. The tributes to Pim Fortuyn use American pop culture to glorify the assassinated politician as the Dutch Kennedy, thereby mystifying his political agenda and implying that collective mourning equals national unity. The Moroccan-Dutch rappers Raymzter and Salah Edin successfully make the stereotypical image of the African-American gangsta rapper their own, using the rebelliousness of hip-hop to critically assess Dutch society. Lange Frans & Baas B, in their turn, use the same language of hip-hop to present an ambiguous yet affirmative ode to the Dutch nation. *LINDA.* magazine borrows the rhetoric of the American Dream to present "ethnic" success stories as examples of the Dutch Dream, intending to prove that ethnic integration can be successful. In this way, the American conception of achievement is introduced to celebrate Dutch multiculturalism. Finally, *Shouf Shouf Habibi!* and its successors apply the genre conventions of Hollywood to present a promising and inclusive perspective on national identity. Yet, although American pop culture functions as a common language, its connotations differ from one pop-cultural artifact to another, thereby questioning its alleged universalism.

As the case studies show, the potential to create alliances among different cultural identities is not always fulfilled. The intention to challenge the "us" versus "them" divide by appropriating the rhetoric of the American Dream and so celebrating Dutch ethnic success stories, as done by *LINDA.* magazine, is undermined by the magazine's continuously reinforcement of the otherness of "their" ethnic culture in opposition to "our" white Dutch culture. Also the two different versions of "Het Land Van…" by Lange Frans & Baas B and Salah Edin suggest that the distinction between white Dutch and Moroccan-Dutch cultural identity is reinforced rather than challenged. Gerard Joling's call for "the people in the street, black or white" to come together is a generic cliché, reducing the message of racial harmony to hollow rhetoric. In the end, the ethnically mixed group of young losers in *Shouf Shouf Habibi!* seems to be the most promising in creating an alliance among "our" and "their" culture. Exposing the ambivalence of the American Dream – and, by extension, the Dutch Dream – by being anti-heroes who, within the film's fictional setting, fail to succeed, they simultaneously have become success stories in their own right by being actors in a commercially successful and critically acclaimed movie.

Sometimes, the promise of multicultural alliance can be found where one expects it the least. In the final scene of *06/05*, Theo van Gogh's political thriller about the conspiracy behind Pim Fortuyn's assassination, the white Dutch main character Jim de Booy (Thijs Römer) is playing soccer on the beach with his teenage daughter and her Moroccan-Dutch boyfriend, who she endearingly describes as "my very own *kutmarokkaan.*" With the bittersweet pop song "Broad Day Light" as soundtrack, the camera presents a pan shot of the beach, moving from the soccer-playing trio to the broad horizon, a typical Hollywood convention that symbolizes an uncertain yet optimistic future. In *06/05*, a multiethnic Dutch national identity is presented as an uncontested given, embodied by two young teenagers in love playing soccer together.

Conclusion:

Let's Make Things Better

"Let's Make Things Better" (best pronounced with a heavy Dutch accent) is the former advertising slogan of the Dutch-based multinational company Royal Philips Electronics, used in its global advertising campaign. Allegedly, the Dutch Philips executive Cor Boonstra himself invented the slogan to inspire his employees on the work floor. Like its successor "Sense and Simplicity," "Let's Make Things Better" is hyper-American, not so much because it is coined in English, but because it refers to the American promise of a better, improved world, that American rhetoric of perpetual progress and positive change which works so well in advertising.[1] At the same time, I cannot help but read the Philips slogan as an attempt to sound American, as an imitation of American rhetoric that just misses a beat. American slogans tend to emphasize that they are already better than the real thing; Philips is merely trying to get better. This – admittedly very subjective – reading seems to be confirmed by the American company American Satellite, owned by RCA, which on its website gives an American "translation" of the slogan: "Let's make things better is the Philips slogan and they've done it with this DIRECTV System."[2] Now Philips is no longer just trying; they have proven that they are better. By focusing on the Philip's slogan missing a beat, I am not suggesting that Philips "got it wrong" or failed to be "authentically American." Rather, Americanization consists of imitation and appropriation, and it is precisely at the point where the slogan is slightly off that its hyper-Americanness becomes most visible.

At a session of the 2002 Salzburg Seminar "The Politics of American Popular Culture: Here, There, and Everywhere," attended by participants from all over the world, we were asked to give an ultimate example of Americanization. When a participant from China named the Philips slogan "Let's Make Things Better," my first reaction was to protest. Like many people in the Netherlands, I grew up with the notion that Philips is part of our national heritage, as are other "Royal Dutch" multinationals such as Heineken, KLM, and Shell. As such, we were told, their global visibility exemplifies "our" presence in the world. Luckily I did not protest out loud, as I realized in time that my first reaction repeated a false sense of patriotism, based on an installed pride in Dutch entrepreneurship which is still strongly present in the Dutch national discourse. On second thought, the example given by my Chinese colleague made sense. Instead of exemplifying a Dutch presence in the world, the advertisement campaign by Philips shows that the language of American advertising transcends the geographical borders of the nation-state USA into the realm of global pop culture. As Rob Kroes points out: "America has replicated itself into icons, clichés of itself that leave their imprint everywhere, on T-shirts, in commercial images, and in our heads. They have lost their lifelines to America and circulate as a free-floating visual lingua franca."[3] The Philips slogan belongs to such a global language, based on an American original, yet open to different interpretations. Moreover, whereas I may read "Let's Make Things Better" as an imitation that's slightly "off," my Chinese colleague clearly perceived the slogan as authentically American, revealing the inherent subjectivity of interpreting "American" pop culture.

That any interpretation of such a free-floating pop culture is by definition subjective, however, should not keep one from trying to grasp its possible meanings. Although definite conclusions about what "America" represents or how it functions within a global pop culture cannot be made, close readings of actual pop-cultural artifacts do provide an opening for analysis, enabling the making of concrete observations about how pop culture could work. Yet too often in the analysis of pop culture, the object is taken for granted, as broad claims are made without including the object itself. If indeed pop culture is a bombardment of signs, as Jean Baudrillard has suggested, a good way to make sense of it is by starting with a specific object, even though the choice of what one analyzes will always be arbitrary and open to discussion. For example, *America First*, a fascinating essay collection that examines how American national identity has been depicted in Hollywood cinema, takes the use of "American" in the film's title as a selection criterion, yet still leaves out obvious choices like *American Beauty* (Sam Mendes, 1999) and *American Psycho* (Mary Harron, 2000).[4] Because pop culture is omnipresent and intertextual, and continuously refers to other artifacts that one may recognize or not, any selection is problematic. The most effective alternative may be to pick an object at random and start analyzing.

The two points of entrance of *Fabricating the Absolute Fake* – a picture by the Dutch photographer Erwin Olaf and USA for Africa's "We Are the World," a pop song and music video made to raise awareness of famine in Africa – are

FABRICATING THE ABSOLUTE FAKE

two distinctively different objects, yet they both refer to an imagined America, an imagined community that goes beyond the geographical boundaries of the nation-state USA. The picture by Olaf enabled me to recognize an America that is made up of images presented by the media. Like myself, Erwin Olaf is an "American he never was," who grew up outside of the USA yet within a culture which is permeated with American pop culture through Hollywood, American television, pop music, and advertisements. His photograph, a telling example of how such images can be appropriated, depicts a pre-9/11 America based on its mediated representations, which Olaf uses to make a statement about the importance of the freedom of expression. A close reading of USA for Africa's "We Are the World" enabled me to question the dominant presence of America in global pop culture, thereby revealing the explicitness of its ideological content which promotes an American conception of the world based on allegedly universal values such as individual liberty and freedom of choice within a free market economy, an overt message which we easily take for granted because "We Are the World" is just another cheery pop song.

An important thread that runs throughout *Fabricating the Absolute Fake* is the distinction between the nation-state USA and an imagined America. Although both Americans and non-Americans may oppose the actual politics of the nation-state USA, that does not necessarily lead to a questioning of the idealism embodied by an imagined America. Particularly after the terrorist attacks of September 11, 2001, this distinction became explicitly visible. In spite of the controversial policies of the Bush administration (the Patriot Act, the War on Terror, Guantánamo Bay), "America" still remains to many the Beacon of Freedom and Democracy, which, as Bono told Oprah, is "an ideal that's supposed to be contagious." Specifically the American Dream – the belief that with talent and hard work all individuals can achieve their goals – is overtly present in American pop culture, forming the basis of the star myth personified by celebrities. The American Dream can be considered as a myth in the Barthesian sense: not necessarily true or false, but often uncritically accepted as self-evident. The suggestion by Jean Baudrillard that America is an utopia achieved is based on the same myth. By perceiving America (rather than the USA) as a hyperreality, Baudrillard does not claim that America is not "real" but argues instead that its fictional character, such as the American Dream as well as Hollywood, makes the American way of life real, as "it is a transcending of the imaginary in reality."[5]

Recognizing the distinction between the nation-state USA and an imagined America is also significant when discussing Americanization, as the pop-cultural appropriation of "America" is predominantly based on the latter. To analyze such an appropriation, I have applied Umberto Eco's concept of the absolute fake. Like Baudrillard, although using a different definition of hyperreality, Eco emphasizes the fictional character of American pop culture, which, as he suggests, consists of absolute fakes that succeed as "the real thing" by being improved copies of the "real" originals. As stated before, fakeness in this sense is not a value judgment, questioning the quality or authenticity of a specific object. Instead, the concept of the absolute fake makes it possible to specify pop-cultural appropriation by perceiving the object as a copy of an original. Even though Eco only recognizes absolute fakes in American culture, I have shown that Dutch pop culture – or, more specifically, those pop-cultural artifacts which are based on an American original – can be analyzed using Eco's concept. However, to avoid the unproductive question of whether or not an object is a successful imitation, I have added Thomas Elsaesser's concept of karaoke Americanism, which is an effective tool for grasping the slippery distinction between sheer imitation and active appropriation. As performances of karaoke Americanism, the wide variety of analyzed Dutch pop-cultural artifacts show that, when translated into specific local or national contexts, "America" can be appropriated in many different ways, ranging from explicit hyper-American-ness to implicit mimicking of an American original in which the association with "America" is almost lost.

Fabricating the Absolute Fake foregrounds the intertwinement of pop culture and politics, arguing that, despite pop culture being "only entertain-ment," it cannot be separated from politics. All pop-cultural artifacts analyzed either explicitly or implicitly refer to a political reality, centered around 9/11 and its aftermath. Recognizing the distinction between the nation-state USA and an imagined America does not imply that the two exclude each other. As the American case studies show, the idealism of an imagined America can be used to justify or even mystify the political actions of the nation-state. Yet, pop culture also can translate the political into a popular and personal experience of the political, bringing the political into people's everyday lives, thereby cre-ating possible room for dissenting voices or oppositional readings. Pop culture can be both manipulative and empowering.

The intertwinement of pop culture and politics is also significant in the debates on Americanization. Whereas the first half of the book deals with the way American pop culture relates to the political reality of 9/11 and its after-math, the second half deals with the way "American" pop culture made in the Netherlands relates to post-9/11 Dutch politics, and in particular the assas-sinations of Pim Fortuyn and Theo van Gogh. 9/11 has prompted discussions around national identity both in the USA and the Netherlands. Just as in the USA, in the Netherlands pop culture can translate the political into a popular and personal experience of the political. Moreover, as a form of Americanization, the Dutch appropriation shows that American pop culture can function as a shared language, with the potential of connecting different cultural identities within the Netherlands and so enabling alliances that are based on other senses of belonging besides solely national identity. This does not mean that one should be uncritical of the dominant American presence in global pop culture, but that one can recognize the potential of "America" as an international lingua franca. Admittedly, that may be a far too optimistic assessment of how pop culture could work, but after all, I too am an American I never was, trying to make things better.

Notes

Introduction

1 Ken Johnson, "Art in Review: Erwin Olaf," *The New York Times* (27 January 2006).
2 Annalisa Cho, "Erwin Olaf: Rain & Hope," *Spread: Art Culture* (1 May 2006); Jhim Lamoreet, "Erwin Olaf: 'Ik trek eruit wat er in zit'," *Het Parool* (12 May 2007): PS16; "Erwin Olaf: Tijd voor bezinning," *Babel* 16:1 (September 2007): 12-13.
3 Francis A. Frascina, "Advertisements for Itself: *The New York Times*, Norman Rockwell, and the New Patriotism," in Dana Heller (editor), *The Selling of 9/11: How a National Tragedy Became a Commodity*, New York: Palgrave Macmillan, 2005, 75-96, quotation on p. 78. See also, Richard Halpern, *Norman Rockwell: The Underside of Innocence*, Chicago and London: University of Chicago Press, 2006.
4 For a comprehensive discussion on pastiche, see: Richard Dyer, *Pastiche*, London and New York: Routledge, 2007. Erwin Olaf's picture explicitly refers to two famous paintings by Norman Rockwell: "He's Going to Be Taller Than Dad" (1939), originally an advertisement featuring a young boy and his dog, and "The Runaway" (1958), originally a cover of *The Saturday Evening Post* featuring a young boy and a police officer sitting at the counter of a diner.
5 Richard Pells, *Not Like Us: How Europeans Have Loved, Hated, and Transformed American Culture Since World War II*, New York: Basic Books, 1997; Sabrina P. Ramet and Gordana P. Crnković (editors), *KAZAAAM! SPLAT! PLOOF! The American Impact on European Popular Culture since 1945*, Lanham and New York: Rowman & Littlefield, 2003.
6 Umberto Eco, *Travels in Hyperreality: Essays*, translated by William Weaver, San Diego, New York, and London: Harcourt, Brace & Company, 1986, 7-8.
7 Neil Campbell, Jude Davies, and George McKay, "Introduction," in Campbell, Davies, and McKay (editors), *Issues in Americanisation and Culture*, Edinburgh: Edinburgh University Press, 2004, 1-38, quotations on p. 2.
8 John Hartley, "Introduction: 'Cultural Exceptionalism,' Freedom, Imperialism, Power, America," in John Hartley and Roberta E. Pearson (editors), *American Cultural Studies: A Reader*, Oxford: Oxford University Press, 2000, 1-13; Rob Kroes, *If You've Seen One, You've Seen the Mall: Europeans and American Mass Culture*, Urbana and Chicago: University of Illinois Press, 1996; Pells, *Not Like Us*.
9 Kroes, *If You've Seen One, You've Seen the Mall*, 36-37.
10 Richard Dyer, *Only Entertainment*, second edition, New York and London: Routledge, 2002, 2.
11 George Ritzer and Michael Ryan, "Americanisation, McDonaldisation and Globalisation," in Neil Campbell, Jude Davies, and George McKay (editors), *Issues in Americanisation and Culture*, Edinburgh: Edinburgh University Press, 2004, 41-60, the two concepts are discussed on pp. 44-45.

12 Stuart Hall, "The Local and the Global: Globalization and Ethnicity" (1989) in Anthony D. King, *Culture, Globalization and the World-System: Contemporary Conditions for the Representation of Identity*, Minneapolis: University of Minnesota Press, 1997, 19-39, quotation on p. 28.

13 Andrew Higson, "The Limiting Imagination of National Cinema," in Mette Hjort and Scott MacKenzie (editors), *Cinema and Nation*, London and New York: Routledge, 2000, 63-74, quotation on p. 69.

14 Kroes, *If You've Seen One, You've Seen The Mall*, 177-178.

15 Rob Kroes, "Advertising: the commodification of American icons," in Annemoon van Hemel, Hans Mommaas, and Cas Smithuijsen (editors), *Trading Culture: GATT, European cultural policies and the transatlantic market*, Amsterdam: Boekman Foundation, 1996, 137-147, 140.

16 George Ritzer, *The McDonaldization of Society: Revised New Century Edition*, Thousand Oaks, London, and New Delhi: Pine Forge Press, 2004.

17 Alan Bryman, "The Disneyization of Society," *The Sociological Review* 47:1 (February 1999): 25-47, quotation on p. 26, emphasis in original.

18 *The American I Never Was* is a multi-media project by Chris Keulemans consisting of a website, a novel, a DVD, and a radio documentary. Website: http://www.deamerikaan.nl (Dutch) or http://www.theamericanineverwas.net (English). Novel: Chris Keulemans, *De Amerikaan die ik nooit geweest ben*, Amsterdam: Augustus, 2004.

19 Thomas Elsaesser, *European Cinema: Face to Face with Hollywood*, Amsterdam: Amsterdam University Press, 2005, 317.

20 Jean Baudrillard, *In the Shadows of the Silent Majorities, or The End of the Social and Other Essays*, translated by Paul Foss, Paul Batton, and John Johnson, New York: Semiotext(e), 1983, 125.

21 Mieke Bal, *Travelling Concepts in the Humanities*, Toronto, Buffalo, and London: University of Toronto Press, 2002, 45.

22 Dyer, *Only Entertainment*, 1-3.

23 Eco, *Travels in Hyperreality*, 3-58; Jean Baudrillard, *America*, translated by Chris Turner, London and New York: Verso, 1988.

24 G. Christopher Williams, "The Death of Jean Baudrillard Did Not Take Place," Popmatters.com, 30 March 2007): http://www.popmatters.com/pm/features/article/32197/the-death-of-jean-baudrillard-did-not-take-place.

25 Kroes, *If You've Seen One, You've Seen the Mall*, quotation on p. 177; Pells, *Not Like Us*.

26 Elsaesser, *European Cinema*, 59-60.

27 Eco, *Travels in Hyperreality*, 7.

28 Jaap Kooijman, "Bombs Bursting in Air: The Gulf War, 9/11, and the Super Bowl Performances of 'The Star-Spangled Banner' by Whitney Houston and Mariah Carey," in Ruud Janssens and Rob Kroes (editors), *Post-Cold War Europe, Post-Cold War America*, Amsterdam: VU University Press, 2004: 178-193. Parts of the essay reappear in revised form in chapter three.

29 Bernard Mergen, untitled book review, *American Studies International* 42:2/3 (June and October 2004): 291-294, quotation on p. 293.

30 Jaap Kooijman, "Karaoke-amerikanisme," *De Groene Amsterdammer* 131:12 (23 March 2007): 25-28; Paul Arnoldussen, "Karaoke-Amerikanen," *Het Parool* (22 March 2007): PS 17.

Chapter 1

1   Thomas Elsaesser, *European Cinema: Face to Face with Hollywood*, Amsterdam: Amsterdam University Press, 2005, 59-60.
2   As quoted in Simon Frith, "The Feast and the Famine," *Sunday Herald*, online edition (7 November 2004): http://www.sundayherald.com/45822.
3   Elsaesser, *European Cinema*, 28.
4   Simon Frith, "The Feast and the Famine," *Sunday Herald*, online edition (7 November 2004): http://www.sundayherald.com/45822.
5   The case of Band Aid and USA for Africa brings to the foreground an important point of discussion in the Americanization debate, namely the role of British pop culture (and particularly pop music). This issue can be avoided, though not solved, by talking about Anglo-Americanization instead of Americanization. Without denying its importance, I will not discuss the British-American distinction in this book, as too often such a discussion leads to unproductive essentialism. Moreover, at least in the case of the Netherlands, consumers do not always recognize or even care whether a pop-cultural product geographically originates in the USA or the UK. Just to give one telling example, Elton John may be British, but his Disney recordings "Can You Feel the Love Tonight" and "Circle of Life" are easily perceived as being "American."
6   Andrew Goodwin, *Dancing in the Distraction Factory: Music Television and Popular Culture*, London: Routledge, 1993, 133; Roy Shuker, *Understanding Popular Music*, second edition, London and New York: Routledge, 2001, 119.
7   Jaap Kooijman, "Michael Jackson: *Motown 25*, Pasadena Civic Auditorium, March 25, 1983," in Ian Inglis (editor), *Performance and Popular Music: History, Place and Time*, Aldershot: Ashgate, 2006, 119-127.
8   There are quite a few academic studies that extensively discuss the connection between Bruce Springsteen's star image and white American working-class masculinity, including: Fred Pfeil, *White Guys: Studies in Postmodern Domination and Difference*, New York: Verso, 1995, 71-104; Gareth Palmer, "Bruce Springsteen and Masculinity," in Sheila Whitely (editor), *Sexing the Groove: Popular Music and Gender*, London and New York: Routledge, 1997, 100-117; Bryan K. Garman, *Race of Singers: Whitman's Working Class Hero from Guthrie to Springsteen*, Chapel Hill: University of North Carolina Press, 2000; Kate McCarthy, "Deliver Me from Nowhere: Bruce Springsteen and the Myth of the American Promised Land," in Eric Michael Mazur and Kate McCarthy (editors), *God in the Details: American Religion in Popular Culture*, New York and London: Routledge, 2001, 23-45; Jefferson Cowie and Lauren Boehm, "Dead Man's Town: 'Born in the U.S.A.,' Social History, and Working-Class Identity," *American Quarterly* 58:2 (June 2006): 353-378.
9   Richard Dyer, *Stars*, London: British Film Institute, 1979; Richard Dyer, *Heavenly Bodies: Films Stars and Society*, second edition, London and New York: Routledge, 2002; Christine Gledhill (editor), *Stardom: Industry of Desire*, London and New York: Routledge, 1991; Paul McDonald, *The Star System: Hollywood and the Production of Popular Identities*, London: Wallflower Press, 2000.
10 Dyer, *Stars*, 42.

11 As quoted in J. Randy Taraborrelli, *Michael Jackson: The Magic and the Madness*, New York: Birch Lane Press, 1991, 412.

12 Hosted by film star Jane Fonda, the thirty-minute *We Are the World: The Video Event* was broadcast on the American cable network HBO in 1985 and commercially released on video that same year. In 2005, an extended edition was released on DVD, entitled *We Are the World: The Story Behind the Song*, to commemorate the twentieth anniversary of USA for Africa.

13 Boze Hadleigh, *The Vinyl Closet: Gays in the Music World*, San Diego: Los Hombres Press, 1991, 59-63.

14 Jaap Kooijman, "From Elegance to Extravaganza: The Supremes on *The Ed Sullivan Show* as a Presentation of Beauty," *The Velvet Light Trap* 49 (Spring 2002): 4-17; Jaap Kooijman, "'Ain't No Mountain High Enough': Diana Ross as American Pop-Cultural Icon of the 1960s," in Avital Bloch and Lauri Umansky (editors), *Impossible to Hold: Women and Culture in the 1960s*, New York: New York University Press, 2005: 152-173.

15 Philip Brian Harper, *Are We Not Men? Masculine Anxiety and the Problem of African-American Identity*, New York: Oxford University Press, 1996, 88-89; Greg Tate, "I'm White!: What's Wrong with Michael Jackson," *Village Voice* (22 September 1987), reprinted in Greg Tate, *Flyboy in the Buttermilk: Essays on Contemporary America*, New York: Simon & Schuster, 1992, 95-99.

16 Charles L. Sanders, "Diana and Michael: They are the undisputed king and queen of entertainment," *Ebony* (November 1983): 29-36.

17 David Breskin, "There Comes a Time When We Heed a Certain Call," *Life* (April 1985), reprinted in the liner notes of the *We Are the World: The Story Behind the Song* DVD.

18 Michael Eric Dyson, *Reflecting Black: African-American Cultural Criticism*, Minneapolis: University of Minnesota Press, 1993, 35-63; Cynthia Fuchs, "Michael Jackson's Penis," in Sue-Ellen Case, Philip Brett, and Susan Leigh Foster (editors), *Cruising the Performative: Interventions into the Representation of Ethnicity, Nationality, and Sexuality*, Bloomington and Indianapolis: Indiana University Press, 1995, 13-33; Harper, *Are We Not Men?*, 88-96; Michelle Wallace, *Invisibility Blues: From Pop to Theory*, London and New York: Verso, 1990, 77-90.

19 Kobena Mercer, "Monster Metaphors: Notes on Michael Jackson's *Thriller*," in *Welcome to the Jungle: New Positions in Black Cultural Studies*, New York and London: Routledge, 1994, 33-51, quotation on p. 35.

20 Garman, *Race of Singers*, 225.

21 Palmer, "Bruce Springsteen and Masculinity," 116.

22 During the presidential elections of 2004, the Democratic candidate John Kerry was pictured playing guitar in front of a huge American flag, obviously mimicking the by-then classic Bruce Springsteen pose.

23 Cowie and Boehm, "Dead Man's Town," 359.

24 Bruce Springsteen initially recorded a slower version of "Born in the USA," intended to be included on his album *Nebraska* (1982). In recent years, Springsteen performs an acoustic guitar version of the song during his live concerts. Both these alternate versions of "Born in the USA" are less ambiguous than the one that was released in 1984.

25 Ronald Reagan, "Remarks at a White House Ceremony Marking Progress Made in the Campaign Against Drunk Driving, May 14, 1984," *The Public Papers of President Ron-*

ald W. Reagan. Ronald Reagan Presidential Library: http://www.reagan.utexas.edu/archives/speeches/1984/51484a.htm.

26 Ronald Reagan, "Remarks at a Reagan-Bush Rally in Hammonton, New Jersey, September 19, 1984," *The Public Papers of President Ronald W. Reagan*. Ronald Reagan Presidential Library: http://www.reagan.utexas.edu/archives/speeches/1984/91984c.htm.

27 Austin Scaggs, "[Interview with] Billy Joel," *Rolling Stone*, online edition (5 December 2005): http://www.rollingstone.com/news/story/8878182/billy_joel.

28 Greil Marcus, "Number One with a Bullet," in *In The Fascist Bathroom*, New York: Harvard University Press, 1993: 280-284, quotation on pp. 283-284.

29 As quoted in Breskin, "There Comes a Time When We Heed a Certain Call," emphasis in original.

30 An essay on the history of the "Hilltop" Coca-Cola commercial can be found on the website of the US Library of Congress, which has an entire section devoted to "Fifty Years of Coca-Cola Television Advertisements" – a remarkable fact in itself: http://memory.loc.gov/ammem/ccmphtml/index.html. "I'd Like to Teach the World to Sing" was also released as single, in two versions, one by The Hillside Singers and another by The New Seekers, although without the explicit reference to Coca-Cola. Both versions became international hits.

31 As quoted in Monica Langley, "Philanthropy: How Turner Decided to Give Away $1 Billion," *The Wall Street Journal* (22 September 1997): B1.

32 Paul Duncum, "Theoretical Foundations for an Art Education of Global Culture and Principles for Classroom Practice," *International Journal of Education & the Arts*, online edition 2:3 (10 June 2001): http://ijea.asu.edu/v2n3.

33 Geoffrey Norman, "We Are the World: Or so we tell ourselves, over synchronized swimming," *National Review*, online edition (16 August 2004): http://www.nationalreview.com/norman/norman200408161148.asp.

34 Sally Price, *Primitive Art in Civilized Places*, second edition, Chicago and London: University of Chicago Press, 2001, 24.

35 Rob Kroes, "Advertising: the commodification of American icons," in Annemoon van Hemel, Hans Mommaas, and Cas Smithuijsen (editors), *Trading Culture: GATT, European cultural policies and the transatlantic market*, Amsterdam: Boekman Foundation, 1996, 137-147, 137. The exact origin of the term Coca-Colonization remains unclear, although it is most often connected to French anti-Americanism of the 1950s and Latin American anti-Americanism of the 1970s. A popular definition available on the internet reads "the spread of western, specifically U.S., popular culture and commercialism to indigenous societies throughout the world, creating a bland uniformity," which leaves out the significant reference to colonialism: http://encarta.msn.com/dictionary_701705147/Cocacolonization.html. The term became highly visible in the European Americanization debate with the publication of Reinhold Wagnleitner, *Coca-Colonization and the Cold War: The Cultural Mission of the United States in Austria after the Second World War*, translated by Diana M. Wolf, Chapel Hill: University of North Carolina Press, 1994. Wagnleitner, however, does not provide a definition of Coca-Colonization, but rather uses the term as a synonym to Americanization.

36 Price, *Primitive Art in Civilized Places*, 25.

37 Mark Pendergrast, *For God, Country, and Coca-Cola: The Definitive History of the Great*

American Soft Drink and the Company That Makes It, second edition, New York: Basic Books, 2000, 240-241; John Tomlinson, Globalization and Culture, Chicago: University of Chicago Press, 1999, 84.

38 Richard Pells, Not Like Us: How Europeans Have Loved, Hated, and Transformed American Culture Since World War II, New York: Basic Books, 1997, 199-201. Pells also discusses the position of Pepsi in the former Soviet bloc countries. While Coca-Cola could not be sold in eastern Europe, Pepsi was widely available, based on an agreement between Pepsi and the Soviet Union: "Because Pepsi had to rely on state-run bottling companies, as the agreement stipulated, it experienced continual problems with deliveries and quality control. Consequently [after the fall of communism], Pepsi could never disentangle its image from the backwardness and inefficiency of the Eastern European and Soviet system as a whole."

39 Ruth Oldenziel, "America made in Europe: De triomf van het Amerikaanse consumentisme," in Meta Knol and Pauline Terreehorst (editors), This is America: Visies op de Amerikaanse droom, Amsterdam: Meulenhoff, 2006, 107-115, 115.

40 Launched in 2002 by the French entrepreneur Taufik Mathlouthi, the Mecca-Cola World Company is now based in Saudi Arabia. Profits of its sales go to provide aid to people in the Palestinian territories. See www.mecca-cola.com.

41 Pells, Not Like Us, 200.

42 Ronald Reagan, "Remarks at a Ceremony Honoring Peace Corps Volunteers for Africa," April 23, 1985, The Public Papers of President Ronald W. Reagan. Ronald Reagan Presidential Library: http://www.reagan.utexas.edu/archives/speeches/1985/42385b.htm.

43 See also, Reebee Garofalo, "Who Is the World?: Reflections on Music and Politics Twenty Years after Live Aid," Journal of Popular Music Studies 17:3 (December 2005), 324-344.

44 The prominent presence of African-American artists was not lost on the African-American magazine Ebony, which headlined Clinton's inauguration as "Black America's biggest inaugural bash" (March 1993). The Lincoln Memorial is not only the place where Martin Luther King exclaimed the legendary words "I Have a Dream" (28 August 1963), but also where African-American singer Marian Anderson performed "Let Freedom Ring" on April 9, 1939, after the Daughters of the American Revolution barred her from performing at the Constitution Hall.

45 Stuart Hall, "The Local and the Global: Globalization and Ethnicity" (1989) in Anthony D. King, Culture, Globalization and the World-System: Contemporary Conditions for the Representation of Identity, Minneapolis: University of Minnesota Press, 1997, 19-39, quotation on p. 28.

46 Elsaesser, European Cinema, 59-60.

Chapter 2

1 Lynn Spigel, "Entertainment Wars: Television Culture after 9/11," American Quarterly 56:2 (June 2004): 235-270, quotation on p. 239; reprinted in Dana Heller (editor), The Selling of 9/11: How a National Tragedy Became a Commodity, New York: Palgrave Macmillan, 2005, 119-154.

2 Eva Illouz, *Oprah Winfrey and the Glamour of Misery: An Essay on Popular Culture*, New York: Columbia University Press, 2003, 2-3.

3 In the Netherlands, *The Oprah Winfrey Show* is broadcast daily by the commercial television channel RTL4, which has also broadcast *The West Wing*. *Ally McBeal* has been broadcast by the commercial television channel Net5.

4 Benedict Anderson, *Imagined Communities: Reflections on the Origin and Spread of Nationalism*, revised edition, London and New York: Verso, 1991, 6.

5 Anderson, *Imagined Communities*, 7, emphasis in original.

6 Thomas Elsaesser, *European Cinema: Face to Face with Hollywood*, Amsterdam: Amsterdam University Press, 2005, 65-67.

7 Elsaesser, *European Cinema*, 60.

8 As quoted in Rob Kroes, "European Anti-Americanism: What's New?," *The Journal of American History* 93:2 (September 2006): 417-431, quotation on p. 417.

9 Dana Heller, "Introduction: Consuming 9/11," in Heller (editor), *The Selling of 9/11*, 1-26, quotation on p. 3.

10 See, for example, Francis A. Frascina, "Advertisements for Itself: *The New York Times*, Norman Rockwell, and the New Patriotism," in Heller (editor), *The Selling of 9/11*, 75-96.

11 White House Press Release, "President Urges Readiness and Patience: Remarks by the President, Secretary of State Colin Powell and Attorney General John Ashcroft, Camp David, Thurmont, Maryland," 15 September 2001: http://www.whitehouse.gov/news/releases/2001/09/20010915-4.html.

12 William Hart, "The Country Connection: Country Music, 9/11, and the War on Terrorism," in Heller (editor), *The Selling of 9/11*, 155-173, quotation on p. 160.

13 Jasbir K. Puar and Amit S. Rai, "Monster, Terrorist, Fag: The War on Terrorism and the Production of Docile Patriots," *Social Text* 72, 20:3 (Fall 2002): 117-148, quotation on p. 126.

14 White House Press Release, "Address to a Joint Session of Congress and the American People," 20 September 2001: http://www.whitehouse.gov/news/releases/2001/09/20010920-8.html.

15 Both quotations in Spigel, "Entertainment Wars," 252-253. For an excellent analysis of the famous televised "coming out" of Ellen Degeneres, see Anna McCarthy, "Ellen: Making Queer Television History," *GLQ: A Journal of Lesbian and Gay Studies* 7:4 (2001): 593-620.

16 White House Press Release, "Statement by the President in His Address to the Nation," 11 September 2001: http://www.whitehouse.gov/news/releases/2001/09/20010911-16.html.

17 Spigel, "Entertainment Wars," 247, emphasis in original. Although Spigel does not name a specific episode of *The Oprah Winfrey Show*, she is most likely referring to "Dr. Phil Helps Grieving Wives" (2 October 2001).

18 Jane M. Shattuc, "The Oprahfication of America: Talk Shows and the Public Sphere," in Mary Beth Haralovich and Lauren Rabinovitz (editors), *Television, History, and American Culture: Feminist Critical Essays*, Durham/London: Duke University Press, 1999: 168-180, quotation on p. 177.

19 On how the talk show genre has enabled the inclusion of alternative voices within the

public debate, see also Joshua Gamson, *Freaks Talk Back: Tabloid Talk Shows and Sexual Nonconformity*, Chicago: University of Chicago Press, 1998.

20 Ien Ang, *Desperately Seeking the Audience*, London and New York: Routledge, 1991, 24-32; Graham Murdock, "Talk Shows: Democratic Debates and Tabloid Tales," in Jan Wieten, Graham Murdock, and Peter Dahlgren (editors), *Television across Europe: A Comparative Introduction*, London: Sage, 2000: 198-220; Laurie Ouellette and Justin Lewis, "Moving Beyond the 'Vast Wasteland': Cultural Policy and Television in the United States," in Robert C. Allen and Annette Hill (editors), *The Television Studies Reader*, London and New York: Routledge, 2004, 52-65.

21 Cecilia Konchar Farr, *Reading Oprah: How Oprah's Book Club Changed the Way America Reads*, Albany: State University of New York Press, 2004.

22 Illouz, *Oprah Winfrey and the Glamour of Misery*, 37-43. See also: Sherryl Wilson, *Oprah, Celebrity and Formations of Self*, New York: Palgrave McMillan, 2003.

23 For example, actress Brooke Shields talked openly on *The Oprah Winfrey Show* about her suffering from postpartum depression after the birth of her daughter, using the opportunity to promote her recent book on the same topic, *Down Came the Rain* (4 May 2005). Two weeks later, actress Kristie Alley discussed her continuous battle with being overweight, while also promoting her book *How to Lose Your Ass and Regain Your Life* and her fictionalized reality television show *Fat Actress*, starring herself (16 May 2005).

24 Eva Illouz, "From the Lisbon Disaster to Oprah Winfrey: Suffering as Identity in the Era of Globalization," in Ulrich Beck, Natan Sznaider, and Rainer Winter (editors), *Global America? The Cultural Consequences of Globalization*, Liverpool: Liverpool University Press, 2003, 189-205, quotations on p. 196.

25 Melissa Crawley, *Mr. Sorkin Goes to Washington: Shaping the President on Television's the West Wing*, Jefferson, North Carolina: McFarland & Company, 2006; Trevor Parry-Giles and Shawn J. Parry-Giles, *The Prime-Time Presidency: The West Wing and U.S. Nationalism*, Urbana and Chicago: University of Illinois Press, 2006; Peter C. Rollins and John E. O'Connor (editors), *The West Wing: The American Presidency as Television Drama*, Syracuse: Syracuse University Press, 2003.

26 See: http://www.nbc.com/The_West_Wing. Jeff Zucker as quoted in Gail Shister, "*West Wing* will address tragedy in a special episode," *Philadelphia Inquirer* (25 September, 2001): C05.

27 The original text reads: "When you think Taliban, think Nazis. When you think Bin Laden, think Hitler. And when you think 'the people of Afghanistan' think 'the Jews in the concentration camps.'" Tamim Ansary, "An Afghan-American Speaks," (14 September 2001): http://archive.salon.com/news/feature/2001/09/14/afghanistan.

28 Spigel, "Entertainment Wars," 244, emphasis in original.

29 As quoted in Myron A. Levine, "*The West Wing* (NBC) and the West Wing (D.C.): Myth and Reality in Television's Portrayal of the White House," in Rollins and O'Connor, *The West Wing*, 42-62, quotation on p. 50.

30 Puar and Rai, "Monster, Terrorist, Fag," 134.

31 Spigel, "Entertainment Wars," 245.

32 Amanda D. Lotz, *Redesigning Women: Television after the Network Era*, Chicago: University of Illinois Press, 2006, 88-117; Joke Hermes, *Re-Reading Popular Culture*, London: Blackwell, 2005, 96-114; Tracey Owens Patton, "Ally McBeal and Her Homies: The

Reification of White Stereotypes of the Other" *Journal of Black Studies* 32:2 (November 2001): 229-260.

33   Two days after the broadcast on *Ally McBeal*, Josh Groban performed his single "To Where You Are" on CNN's *Larry King Live* (12 December 2002). Pictures of 9/11 victims were shown during the performance.

34   Ben Shapiro, "The Oprah schnook club," *Townhall.com* (19 March 2003): http://www. townhall.com/columnists/BenShapiro/2003/03/19/the_oprah_schnook_club;   Fedwa Wazwaz, "Oprah Winfrey: Warmonger?," *CounterPunch* (5 November 2002): http:// www.counterpunch.org/wazwaz1105.html.

35   Wim Wenders, *Emotion Pictures*, London: Faber and Faber, 1986, 142.

36   Lotz, *Redesigning Women*, 178.

37   Spigel, "Entertainment Wars," 260.

38   White House Press Release, "President Holds Prime Time News Conference," The East Room, 11 October 2001: http://www.whitehouse.gov/news/releases/2001/10/20011011-7.html.

Chapter 3

1   George Bush, "Remarks to United States Army Troops Near Dhahran, Saudi Arabia," 22 November 1990, *Public Papers of the Presidency*, George Bush Presidential Library: http://bushlibrary.tamu.edu/papers/1990/90112201.html.

2   George Bush, "Exchange With Reporters aboard Air Force One," 27 July 1990, *Public Papers of the Presidency*, George Bush Presidential Library: http://bushlibrary.tamu.edu/papers/1990/90072701.html.

3   Roland Barthes, *Mythologies*, translated by Annette Lavers, New York: The Noonday Press, 1972, 143.

4   For a discussion of the role of gender in the Jessica Lynch case, see Sara Buttsworth, "Who's Afraid of Jessica Lynch? Or, One Girl in all the World? Gendered Heroism and the Iraq War," *Australasian Journal of American Studies* 24:2 (December 2005): 42-62.

5   John Carlos Rowe, "Culture, US Imperialism, and Globalization," *American Literary History* 16:4 (Winter 2004): 575-595; quotation on p. 586.

6   Deepa Kumar, "War Propaganda and the (Ab)uses of Women: Media Constructions of the Jessica Lynch Story," *Feminist Media Studies* 4:3 (November, 2004): 297-313.

7   Rowe, "Culture, US Imperialism, and Globalization," 586.

8   Neal Gabler, *Life: The Movie: How Entertainment Conquered Reality*, New York: Vintage Books, 1998, 113.

9   Jean Baudrillard, *In the Shadows of the Silent Majorities, or The End of the Social and Other Essays*, translated by Paul Foss, Paul Batton and John Johnson, New York: Semiotext(e), 1983, 84.

10   Jean Baudrillard, *America*, translated by Chris Turner, London and New York: Verso, 1988, 101.

11   Baudrillard, *America*, 95, emphasis in original.

12   Jean Baudrillard, *The Gulf War Did Not Take Place*, translated by Paul Patton, Bloomington: Indiana University Press, 1995, 41.

13 Christopher Norris, *Uncritical Theory: Postmodernism, Intellectuals, and the Gulf War*, Amherst: University of Massachusetts Press, 1992.

14 Baudrillard, *The Gulf War Did Not Take Place*, 72.

15 As William Merrin has pointed out, most critics overlooked the title's reference to the French play *The Trojan War Will Not Take Place*, written in 1935 by Jean Giraudoux, suggesting that "we can read Baudrillard's essays warning of a past war that did not happen but that we know did." William Merrin, *Baudrillard and the Media: A Critical Introduction*, Cambridge: Polity Press, 2005, 87.

16 Ella Shohat and Robert Stam, *Unthinking Eurocentrism: Multiculturalism and the Media*, London and New York, Routledge, 1994, 125. See also Robert Stam, "Mobilizing Fictions: The Gulf War, the Media, and the Recruitment of the Spectator," *Public Culture* 4:2 (Spring 1992): 101-126.

17 Nobuo Kamioka, "Support Our Troops: The U.S. Media and the Narrative of the Persian Gulf War," *The Japanese Journal of American Studies* 12 (2001): 65-81; Lauren Rabinovitz, "Soap Opera Woes: Genre, Gender, and the Persian Gulf War," in Susan Jeffords and Lauren Rabinovitz (editors), *Seeing Through the Media: The Persian Gulf War*, New Brunswick, New Jersey: Rutgers University Press, 1994, 190-201; Lawrence Wenner, "The Super Bowl Pregame Show: Cultural Fantasies and Political Subtext," in Lawrence Wenner (editor), *Media, Sports, and Society*, Newbury Park: Sage, 1989, 157-179.

18 Toby Miller, *Sportsex*, Philadelphia: Temple University Press, 2001, 29-35. As Miller convincingly shows, the connection between the military and sports is strongly intertwined with issues of masculinity.

19 "Interview with Whitney Houston," on DVD *Whitney: The Greatest Hits* (Arista, 2000). The DVD also includes Houston's Super Bowl performance of "The Star-Spangled Banner."

20 Baudrillard, *America*, 86.

21 Susan Willis, "Old Glory," in Stanley Hauerwas and Frank Lentricchia (editors), *Dissent From the Homeland: Essays after September 11*, Durham and London: Duke University Press, 2003, 121-130, quotation on p. 129.

22 Dana Heller, "Introduction: Consuming 9/11," in Dana Heller (editor), *The Selling of 9/11: How a National Tragedy Became a Commodity*, New York: Palgrave Macmillan, 2005, 1-26, quotation on p. 18.

23 Tobias Peterson, "Bulls on Parade," Popmatters.com, 4 February 2003: http://www.popmatters.com/tv/features/030204-superbowl.shtml.

24 Rob Kroes, "European Anti-Americanism: What's New?," *The Journal of American History* 93:2 (September 2006): 417-431, quotation on p. 418.

25 "Super Bowl Press Conference," 1 February 2002, www.mariahcarey.com: http://www.monarc.com/mariahcarey/news/index.las?month=2&year=2002.

26 Douglas Kellner, *Media Spectacle*, London and New York: Routledge, 2003, 23. Kellner's book features a long shot picture of the 2002 Super Bowl "The Star-Spangled Banner" performance on its cover.

27 The picture's copyright is owned by the New Jersey newspaper *The Record*, which also named the picture "Ground Zero Spirit." See the picture's official website: www.groundzerospirit.org.

28 Willis, "Old Glory," 121-122.

29 William Hart, "The Country Connection: Country Music, 9/11, and the War on Terrorism," in Heller (editor), *The Selling of 9/11*, 155-173.
30 Jeremy Pelofsky, "U.S. Watchdog Probes Janet Jackson Bare Breast," 2 February 2004; Jeremy Pelofsky, "FCC on Jackson Stunt: 'Classless, Crass, Deplorable'," 3 February 2004, Reuters News online: www.reuters.com (no longer available).
31 Cynthia Weber, *Imagining America at War: Morality, Politics, and Film*, London and New York: Routledge, 2006, 7.
32 Baudrillard, *The Gulf War Did Not Take Place*, 77.
33 Jude Davies, "'Diversity. America. Leadership. Good over evil.' Hollywood Multiculturalism and American Imperialism in *Independence Day* and *Three Kings*," *Patterns of Prejudice* 39:4 (2005): 397-415, quotation on p. 412.
34 Cynthia Fuchs, "No Glory," PopMatters.com, 4 November 2005: http://www.popmatters.com/film/reviews/j/jarhead-2005.shtml.
35 Baudrillard, *The Gulf War Did Not Take Place*, 72.
36 Baudrillard, *America*, 49. See also: Michael Anderegg (editor), *Inventing Vietnam: The War in Film and Television*, Philadelphia: Temple University Press, 1991; Linda Dittmar and Gene Michaud (editors), *From Hanoi to Hollywood: The Vietnam War in American Film*, New Brunswick: Rutgers University Press, 1990.
37 Anthony Swofford, *Jarhead: A Soldier's Story of Modern War*, London: Scribner, 2003, 6-7.
38 Ian Urbina, "Forked-Tongue Warriors: In the Battle for Hearts and Minds, Watch Out for the Psy-Ops," *Village Voice* (9 October 2002): http://www.villagevoice.com/news/0241,urbina,39047,1.html.
39 Swofford, *Jarhead*, 213.
40 Baudrillard, *America*, 124.
41 J. Hoberman, "Burn, Blast, Bomb, Cut," *Sight & Sound* (February 2000): http://www.bfi.org.uk/sightandsound/feature/12/.
42 Allen Feldman, "On Cultural Anesthesia: From Desert Storm to Rodney King," *American Ethnologist* 21:2 (May 1994): 404-418; George Mariscal, "In the Wake of the Gulf War: Untying the Yellow Ribbon," *Cultural Critique* 19 (Fall 1991): 97-117.
43 Greg Tate, "I'm White!: What's Wrong with Michael Jackson," originally published in *Village Voice* (22 September 1987), reprinted in Greg Tate, *Flyboy in the Buttermilk: Essays on Contemporary America*, New York: Simon & Schuster, 95-99, quotation on p. 95.
44 Fittingly, in his review of *Three Kings*, Jim Hoberman credits director David O. Russell for "rethinking the combat-movie genre in the weird we-are-the-world terms that Desert Storm established."
45 The appropriation of Baudrillard by *The Matrix* and Baudrillard's own views on the film are discussed in Merrin, *Baudrillard and the Media*, 115-132.
46 Slavoj Žižek, "Welcome to the Desert of the Real!," in Hauerwas and Lentricchia, *Dissent from the Homeland*, 131-135, quotation on p. 135, emphasis in original. Several versions of the essay have been published, including an extended edition: Slavoj Žižek, *Welcome to the Desert of the Real!: Five Essays on September 11 and Related Dates*, London and New York: Verso, 2002.
47 Jean Baudrillard, "L'Esprit du Terrorisme," translated by Michel Valentin, in Hauerwas

and Lentricchia, *Dissent from the Homeland*, 149-161, quotation on p. 149. Several versions of the essay have been published, including an extended edition: Jean Baudrillard, *The Spirit of Terrorism*, new edition, translated by Chris Turner, London and New York: Verso, 2003.

48 For an extensive discussion of Baudrillard's essay and its critical reception, see: Merrin, *Baudrillard and the Media*, 98-114.
49 Baudrillard, *The Spirit of Terrorism*, 28-29.
50 Cynthia Nantais and Martha F. Lee, "Women in the United States Military: Protectors or Protected? The Case of Prisoner of War Melissa Rathbun-Nealy," *Journal of Gender Studies* 8:2 (1999): 181-191, quotation on p. 186.

Chapter 4

1 Jean Baudrillard, *America*, translated by Chris Turner, London and New York: Verso, 1988, 76.
2 Rob Kroes, *If You've Seen One, You've Seen the Mall: Europeans and American Mass Culture*, Urbana and Chicago: University of Illinois Press, 1996, 176.
3 As quoted in Rob Kroes, "European Anti-Americanism: What's New?," *The Journal of American History* 93:2 (September 2006): 417-431, quotation on p. 417.
4 Kroes, "European Anti-Americanism: What's New?," 426-427.
5 Text printed on the back of the exhibition catalog, Meta Knol and Pauline Terreehorst (editors), *This is America: Visies op de Amerikaanse droom*, Amsterdam: Meulenhoff, 2006, translation mine.
6 Joost Zwagerman, "Met de vrije slag: Van 'This is not America' tot 'I'm an American'," in Knol and Terreehorst (editors), *This is America*, 2006, 83-90, quotation on p. 90, translation mine.
7 *The American I Never Was* is a multi-media project by Chris Keulemans consisting of a website, a novel, a DVD, and a radio documentary. Website: http://www.deamerikaan.nl (Dutch) or http://www.theamericanineverwas.net (English). Novel: Chris Keulemans, *De Amerikaan die ik nooit geweest ben*, Amsterdam: Augustus, 2004.
8 Quotations on http://www.deamerikaan.nl/amerikaan/html/chris.jsp.
9 Rob Kroes, "Advertising: the commodification of American icons," in Annemoon van Hemel, Hans Mommaas, and Cas Smithuijsen (editors), *Trading Culture: GATT, European cultural policies and the transatlantic market*, Amsterdam: Boekman Foundation, 1996, 137-147, quotation on p. 141.
10 The concept of American exceptionalism, in particular, has been based on these rigid dichotomies, which are often persuasive because they are so recognizable. See for example, Seymour Martin Lipset, *American Exceptionalism: A Double-Edged Sword*, New York: W.W. Norton & Company, 1996.
11 Thomas Elsaesser, *European Cinema: Face to Face with Hollywood*, Amsterdam: Amsterdam University Press, 2005, 300.
12 Elsaesser, *European Cinema*, 47.
13 Alan A. Stone, "A Second Nature: *Antonia's Line* re-imagines life, after patriarchy," *Boston Review* (Summer 1996): http://bostonreview.mit.edu/BR21.3/Stone.html.

14 Hans Kroon, "Waarom Amerikanen van *Antonia* houden," *Trouw* (28 March 1996); Tom Ronse, "*Antonia* in Oscarland," *De Groene Amsterdammer* (3 April 1996); Ab van Ieperen, "*Antonia*: een echte Amerikaanse pionierswestern," *Vrij Nederland* (30 March 1996): 17.

15 Kroes, *If You've Seen One, You've Seen the Mall*, 36-37.

16 Winfried Fluck, "California Blue: Americanization as Self-Americanization," in Alexander Stephan (editor), *Americanization and Anti-Americanism: The German Encounter with American Culture after 1945*, New York and Oxford: Berghahn Books, 221-237, quotation on p. 227.

17 Umberto Eco, *Travels in Hyperreality: Essays*, translated by William Weaver, San Diego, New York, and London: Harcourt, Brace & Company, 1986, 7-8.

18 Baudrillard, *America*, 76.

19 Kroes, *If You've Seen One, You've Seen the Mall*, 39-40.

20 Baudrillard, *America*, 78.

21 Elsaesser, *European Cinema*, 317.

22 Richard Dyer, *Stars*, London: British Film Institute, 1979, 42.

23 See the biography of Lee Towers on the website of the Dutch National Pop Institute: http://www.popinstituut.nl/biografie/lee_towers.1398.html.

24 See the official website of Lee Towers: http.//www.leetowers.nl. The website is in both Dutch and English.

25 Todd Savage, "The Funny American: Interview with Tom Rhodes," *Expatica*: http://www.expatica.com/xpat/xpatsite/index.asp? pad=10,48,&item_id=25670.

26 The performance is included on the DVD: *Lee Towers, Legendary Gala of the Year: Ahoy' Document, Part 2* (2001). The English translation is taken from the DVD's subtitles.

27 For a discussion of how *Playboy* magazine came to be an embodiment of American post-war consumer culture, see: Bill Osgerby, *Playboys in Paradise: Masculinity, Youth, and Leisure-style in Modern America*, New York: Berg Publishers, 2001.

28 Mick Boscamp, "*Playboy* interview: Patricia Paay," *Playboy*, Dutch edition (May 1988): 33-44, quotation on p. 44.

29 Nicolette Wolters, "Patricia Paay: Glamourqueen in haute couture," *Beau Monde* (27 July 2001): 13-19, quotation on p. 17, translation mine.

30 Jennifer Gillan, "From Ozzie Nelson to Ozzy Osbourne: The Genesis and Development of the Reality (Star) Sitcom," in Su Holmes and Deborah Jermyn (editors), *Understanding Reality Television*, London and New York: Routledge, 2004, 54-70; Derek Kompare, "Extraordinarily Ordinary: *The Osbournes* as 'An American Family'," in Susan Murray and Laurie Ouellette (editors), *Reality TV: Remaking Television Culture*, New York and London: New York University Press, 2004, 97-116.

31 Mieke van Wijk, "Heel persoonlijk: Patricia Paay," *TROS Kompas* 52 (28 December 2002): 10-13, quotation on p. 13, translation mine.

32 See for my discussion of *The Delivery* as an absolute fake: Jaap Kooijman, "Let's Make Things Better: Hyper-Americanness in Dutch Pop Culture," in Kate Delaney and Ruud Janssens, *Over (T)here: Transatlantic Essays in Honor of Rob Kroes*, Amsterdam: VU University Press, 2005, 82-95.

33 Elsaesser, *European Cinema*, 76.

34 Dana Linssen, "Jos Stelling: Film is de kunst van het adoreren," *de Filmkrant* 199 (April 1999): http://www.filmkrant.nl/av/org/filmkran/archief/fk199/stelling.html.

35 My translation of: "President domme kutmongool / luister goed een kind moet naar school / door een opstand bereik ik mijn goal / ik met een mike jij met een pistool / poem pauw schiet me maar neer / in je nachtmerries zie je me weer / ik laat je niet met rust / … motherfucker."

36 See also the book, Ali B, *Rap Around the World*, Amsterdam: Rothschild & Bach, 2005, which includes a DVD with the entire MTV documentary series.

37 As stated on Ali B's official website www.alib.nl, translation mine.

38 My translation of: "Kijk, ik wil niet zeggen dat de Bijlmer als New York is / maar heel veel van die mensen die doen net of het een dorp is / waar nooit wat gebeurt terwijl de flats zijn bezet door de junks aan de crack / je houdt jezelf voor de gek."

39 As quoted in Martin Kuiper, "Rapping with a Moroccan accent: Rising Amsterdam rap star Ali B loves the mike, but he's not a mouthpiece," *Amsterdam Weekly* (19 May 2004): http://www.xs4all.nl/~kuiper/news/310504alib.htm.

40 Robert van de Griend and Thijs Niemantsverdriet, "Ali B, fatsoensrapper: De juiste Marokkaan op het juiste moment op de juiste plaats," *Vrij Nederland* (5 February 2005): http://www.vrijnederland.nl/vn/show/id=47084.

41 Mir Wermuth, "Rap in the Low Countries: Global Dichotomies on a National Scale," in Toni Mitchell (editor), *Global Noise: Rap and Hip-Hop Outside the USA*, Middletown: Wesleyan University Press, 2002, 149-170, quotation on p. 157.

Chapter 5

1 Postcard entitled "Boomerang supports Lieuwe," released both digitally and in print on July 27, 2005, featuring graffiti by Lieuwe van Gogh, Ruben Pauw, and Tyron Ballantine, "Theo Forever," 3 November 2004. Lieuwe van Gogh and his friends painted the graffiti on the wall of his bedroom.

2 Rob Kroes, "Advertising: the commodification of American icons," in Annemoon van Hemel, Hans Mommaas, and Cas Smithuijsen (editors), *Trading Culture: GATT, European cultural policies and the transatlantic market*, Amsterdam: Boekman Foundation, 1996, 137-147, 140.

3 George W. Bush, "Address to a Joint Session of Congress and the American People," 20 September 2001: http://www.whitehouse.gov/news/releases/2001/09/20010920-8.html.

4 Political scientist Maarten Vink convincingly shows that the change ascribed to 9/11 and the murders of Fortuyn and Van Gogh is instead the result of a longer historical process. See: Maarten P. Vink, "Dutch 'Multiculturalism' Beyond the Pillarisation Myth," *Political Studies Review* 5 (September 2007): 337-350.

5 See for example: Frans Verhagen, *The American Way: Wat wij kunnen leren van het meest succesvolle immigratieland*, Amsterdam: Nieuw Amsterdam, 2006; Paul Scheffer, *Het land van aankomst*, Amsterdam: De Bezige Bij, 2007, 291-339.

6 Peter van der Veer, "Pim Fortuyn, Theo van Gogh, and the Politics of Tolerance in the Netherlands," *Public Culture* 18:1 (Winter 2006): 111-124, quotation on p. 112.

7 Paul Scheffer, "Het multiculturele drama," *NRC Handelsblad* (29 January 2000): http://www.nrc.nl/W2/Lab/Multicultureel/scheffer.html. Seven years later, Scheffer published *Het land van aankomst* in which he elaborates on his essay.

8   As quoted in Jane Kramer, "The Dutch Model: Multiculturalism and Muslim Immigrants," *The New Yorker* (3 April 2006): 60-67, quotation on p. 64, emphasis in original.

9   I realize that "white" and "ethnic" are problematic categories. In the Netherlands, a distinction is made between "*autochtoon*" (native) and "*allochtoon*" (immigrant), although in practice it is often used to make a distinction between "white" and "non-white." With "white" I mean the *autochtoon* population which is generally not considered to be belonging to an ethnic minority. See also Richard Dyer, *White: Essays on Race and Culture*, London and New York: Routledge, 1997.

10 Thomas Elsaesser, *European Cinema: Face to Face with Hollywood*, Amsterdam: Amsterdam University Press, 2005, 112.

11 Elsaesser, *European Cinema*, 113.

12 Ian Buruma, *Murder in Amsterdam: The Death of Theo van Gogh and the Limits of Tolerance*, London: Atlantic Books, 2006, 65.

13 Van der Veer, "Pim Fortuyn, Theo van Gogh, and the Politics of Tolerance in the Netherlands," 114.

14 Evert Santegoeds, *Professor Pim: Het lef van de Hollandse Kennedy*, Amsterdam: VIPZ Media, 2002. See also: Arendo Joustra (editor), *Het fenomeen Fortuyn*, Amsterdam: de Volkskrant/Meulenhoff, 2002; Dick Pels, *De geest van Pim: Het gedachtegoed van een politieke dandy*, Amsterdam: Anthos, 2003.

15 My translation of: "Wat ik zeg klinkt misschien eenvoudig, maar ze kijken me aan alsof ik vloog in de Twin Towers."

16 Abi Daruvalla, "Rapping from the Heart: Raymzter's Dutch-Moroccan rap is challenging racial stereotypes — and the music is pretty good, too," *Time*, online European edition (3 February 2003): http://www.time.com/time/europe/magazine/article/0,13005,901030203-411386,00.html.

17 My translation of: "Marokkaanse jongeren maken nu ook de hitlijsten onveilig."

18 Tricia Rose, *Black Noise: Rap Music and Black Culture in Contemporary America*, Middletown: Wesleyan University Press, 1994; Greg Tate (editor), *Everything But the Burden: What White People Are Taking from Black Culture*, New York: Harlem Moon, 2003.

19 Rob Kroes, *If You've Seen One, You've Seen the Mall: Europeans and American Mass Culture*, Urbana and Chicago: University of Illinois Press, 1996, 36-37.

20 My translation of: "Kom uit het land met de meeste culturen per vierkante meter / maar men is bang om bij de buren te gaan eten / en integratie is een schitterend woord / maar shit is fucking bitter wanneer niemand het hoort."

21 My translation of: "Het land waar ik geboren ben ... / het land dat mij bestempeld als de kutmarokkaan."

22 As quoted on the website of Salah Edin's international distributor Ringz & Partners Entertainment Group: http://rpeg-ltd.com/news/id/23.

23 Linda de Mol, untitled editorial, *LINDA.* (February 2005): 7, translation mine, emphasis in original.

24 Eva Ellouz, *Oprah Winfrey and the Glamour of Misery: An Essay on Popular Culture*, New York: Columbia University Press, 2003, 62-63.

25 All quotes taken from the film are my translation of the Dutch dialogue.

26 See for example, Andrew Holleran, "The Face of Atta," *The Gay & Lesbian Review Worldwide* 8:6 (1 January 2002): 8-10. According to Holleran, Atta has the face of a bitter drag queen.

27 Elsaesser, *European Cinema*, 113.

28 After the murder of Theo van Gogh, director Albert ter Heerdt revealed that he deliberately refrained from making jokes about Islam, following the advice of the film's initiator and main actor Mimoun Oaïssa. See: "Debat zelfcensuur in Ketelhuis," *de Filmkrant* 261 (December 2004): http://www.filmkrant.nl/av/org/filmkran/archief/fk261/debat-nl.html.

29 The conference, held on November 17, 2004, was organized by *de Filmkrant* magazine and film house Het Ketelhuis (see footnote 26). Van der Heerdt's comments were cited in the national and international media. See for example, "Dutch director 'may postpone film' after murder," *Guardian Unlimited* (November 19, 2004): http://film.guardian.co.uk/news/story/0,12589,1355109,00.html.

30 Alan Riding, "On Screen, Tackling Europe's New Reality," *The New York Times* (18 January 2005): E1.

Conclusion

1 Umberto Eco, *Travels in Hyperreality: Essays*, translated by William Weaver, San Diego, New York, and London: Harcourt, Brace & Company, 1986, 7; Rob Kroes, "Advertising: the commodification of American icons," in Annemoon van Hemel, Hans Mommaas, and Cas Smithuijsen (editors), *Trading Culture: GATT, European cultural policies and the transatlantic market*, Amsterdam: Boekman Foundation, 1996, 137-147.

2 Originally on http://rca.americansatellite.com. Since the introduction of the new Philip's slogan "Sense and Simplicity," the slogan is no longer there. The new slogan cannot be found on the website.

3 Rob Kroes, *If You've Seen One, You've Seen the Mall: Europeans and American Mass Culture*, Urbana and Chicago: University of Illinois Press, 1996, 175.

4 Mandy Merck (editor), *America First: Naming the Nation in US Film*, London and New York: Routledge, 2007.

5 Jean Baudrillard, *America*, translated by Chris Turner, London and New York: Verso, 1988, 95.

Bibliography

Anderegg, Michael (editor), *Inventing Vietnam: The War in Film and Television*, Philadelphia: Temple University Press, 1991.

Anderson, Benedict, *Imagined Communities: Reflections on the Origin and Spread of Nationalism*, revised edition, London and New York: Verso, 1991.

Ang, Ien, *Desperately Seeking the Audience*, London and New York: Routledge, 1991.

Bal, Mieke, *Travelling Concepts in the Humanities*, Toronto, Buffalo, and London: University of Toronto Press, 2002.

Barthes, Roland, *Mythologies*, translated by Annette Lavers, New York: The Noonday Press, 1972.

Baudrillard, Jean, *In the Shadows of the Silent Majorities, or The End of the Social and Other Essays*, translated by Paul Foss, Paul Batton, and John Johnson, New York: Semiotext(e), 1983.

Baudrillard, Jean, *America*, translated by Chris Turner, London and New York: Verso, 1988.

Baudrillard, Jean, *The Gulf War Did Not Take Place*, translated by Paul Patton, Bloomington: Indiana University Press, 1995.

Baudrillard, Jean, "L'Esprit du Terrorisme," translated by Michel Valentin, in Stanley Hauerwas and Frank Lentricchia (editors), *Dissent From the Homeland: Essays after September 11*, Durham and London: Duke University Press, 2003, 149-161.

Baudrillard, Jean, *The Spirit of Terrorism*, new edition, translated by Chris Turner, London and New York: Verso, 2003.

Bryman, Alan, "The Disneyization of Society," *The Sociological Review* 47:1 (February 1999): 25-47.

Buruma, Ian, *Murder in Amsterdam: The Death of Theo van Gogh and the Limits of Tolerance*, London: Atlantic Books, 2006.

Buttsworth, Sara, "Who's Afraid of Jessica Lynch? Or, One Girl in all the World? Gendered Heroism and the Iraq War," *Australasian Journal of American Studies* 24:2 (December 2005): 42-62.

Campbell, Neil, Jude Davies, and George McKay (editors), *Issues in Americanisation and Culture*, Edinburgh: Edinburgh University Press, 2004.

Cowie, Jefferson, and Lauren Boehm, "Dead Man's Town: 'Born in the U.S.A.,' Social History, and Working-Class Identity," *American Quarterly* 58:2 (June 2006): 353-378.

Crawley, Melissa, *Mr. Sorkin Goes to Washington: Shaping the President on Television's the West Wing*, Jefferson, North Carolina: McFarland & Company, 2006.

Davies, Jude, "'Diversity. America. Leadership. Good over Evil.' Hollywood Multiculturalism and American Imperialism in *Independence Day* and *Three Kings*," *Patterns of Prejudice* 39:4 (2005): 397-415.

Dittmar, Linda, and Gene Michaud (editors), *From Hanoi to Hollywood: The Vietnam War in American Film*, New Brunswick: Rutgers University Press, 1990.

Dyer, Richard, *Stars*, London: British Film Institute, 1979.

Dyer, Richard, *White: Essays on Race and Culture*, London and New York: Routledge, 1997.

Dyer, Richard, *Heavenly Bodies: Films Stars and Society*, second edition, London and New York: Routledge, 2002.

Dyer, Richard, *Only Entertainment*, second edition, New York and London: Routledge, 2002.

Dyer, Richard, *Pastiche*, London and New York: Routledge, 2007.

Dyson, Michael Eric, *Reflecting Black: African-American Cultural Criticism*, Minneapolis: University of Minnesota Press, 1993.

Elsaesser, Thomas, *European Cinema: Face to Face with Hollywood*, Amsterdam: Amsterdam University Press, 2005.

Eco, Umberto, *Travels in Hyperreality: Essays*, translated by William Weaver, San Diego, New York, and London: Harcourt, Brace & Company, 1986.

Farr, Cecilia Konchar, *Reading Oprah: How Oprah's Book Club Changed the Way America Reads*, Albany: State University of New York Press, 2004.

Feldman, Allen, "On Cultural Anesthesia: From Desert Storm to Rodney King," *American Ethnologist* 21:2 (May 1994): 404-418.

Fluck, Winfried, "California Blue: Americanization as Self-Americanization," in Alexander Stephan (editor), *Americanization and Anti-Americanism: The German Encounter with American Culture after 1945*, New York and Oxford: Berghahn Books, 221-237.

Frascina, Francis A., "Advertisements for Itself: *The New York Times*, Norman Rockwell, and the New Patriotism," in Dana Heller (editor), *The Selling of 9/11: How a National Tragedy Became a Commodity*, New York: Palgrave Macmillan, 2005, 75-96.

Fuchs, Cynthia, "Michael Jackson's Penis," in Sue-Ellen Case, Philip Brett, and Susan Leigh Foster (editors), *Cruising the Performative: Interventions into the Representation of Ethnicity, Nationality, and Sexuality*, Bloomington and Indianapolis: Indiana University Press, 1995, 13-33.

Gabler, Neal, *Life: The Movie: How Entertainment Conquered Reality*, New York: Vintage Books, 1998.

Gamson, Joshua, *Freaks Talk Back: Tabloid Talk Shows and Sexual Nonconformity*, Chicago: University of Chicago Press, 1998.

Garman, Bryan K., *Race of Singers: Whitman's Working Class Hero from Guthrie to Springsteen*, Chapel Hill: University of North Carolina Press, 2000.

Garofalo, Reebee, "Who Is the World?: Reflections on Music and Politics Twenty Years after Live Aid," *Journal of Popular Music Studies* 17:3 (December 2005), 324-344.

Gillan, Jennifer, "From Ozzie Nelson to Ozzy Osbourne: The Genesis and Development of the Reality (Star) Sitcom," in Su Holmes and Deborah Jermyn (editors), *Understanding Reality Television*, London and New York: Routledge, 2004, 54-70.

Gledhill, Christine (editor), *Stardom: Industry of Desire*, London and New York: Routledge, 1991.

Goodwin, Andrew, *Dancing in the Distraction Factory: Music Television and Popular Culture*, London: Routledge, 1993.

Hadleigh, Boze, *The Vinyl Closet: Gays in the Music World*, San Diego: Los Hombres Press, 1991.

Hall, Stuart, "The Local and the Global: Globalization and Ethnicity" (1989), in Anthony D. King, *Culture, Globalization and the World-System: Contemporary Conditions for the Representation of Identity*, Minneapolis: University of Minnesota Press, 1997, 19-39.

Halpern, Richard, *Norman Rockwell: The Underside of Innocence*, Chicago and London: University of Chicago Press, 2006.

Harper, Philip Brian, *Are We Not Men? Masculine Anxiety and the Problem of African-American Identity*, New York: Oxford University Press, 1996.

Hart, William, "The Country Connection: Country Music, 9/11, and the War on Terrorism," in Dana Heller (editor), *The Selling of 9/11: How a National Tragedy Became a Commodity*, New York: Palgrave Macmillan, 2005, 155-173.

Hartley, John, and Roberta E. Pearson (editors), *American Cultural Studies: A Reader*, Oxford: Oxford University Press, 2000.

Hauerwas, Stanley, and Frank Lentricchia (editors), *Dissent From the Homeland: Essays after September 11*, Durham and London: Duke University Press, 2003.

Heller, Dana (editor), *The Selling of 9/11: How a National Tragedy Became a Commodity*, New York: Palgrave Macmillan, 2005.

Hermes, Joke, *Re-Reading Popular Culture*, London: Blackwell, 2005.

Higson, Andrew, "The Limiting Imagination of National Cinema," in Mette Hjort and Scott MacKenzie (editors), *Cinema and Nation*, London and New York: Routledge, 2000, 63-74.

Holleran, Andrew, "The Face of Atta," *The Gay & Lesbian Review Worldwide* 8:6 (1 January 2002): 8-10.

Illouz, Eva, *Oprah Winfrey and the Glamour of Misery: An Essay on Popular Culture*, New York: Columbia University Press, 2003.

Illouz, Eva, "From the Lisbon Disaster to Oprah Winfrey: Suffering as Identity in the Era of Globalization," in Ulrich Beck, Natan Sznaider, and Rainer Winter (editors), *Global America? The Cultural Consequences of Globalization*, Liverpool: Liverpool University Press, 2003, 189-205.

Kamioka, Nobuo, "Support Our Troops: The U.S. Media and the Narrative of the Persian Gulf War," *The Japanese Journal of American Studies* 12 (2001): 65-81.

Kellner, Douglas, *Media* Spectacle, London and New York: Routledge, 2003.

Keulemans, Chris, *De Amerikaan die ik nooit geweest ben*, Amsterdam: Augustus, 2004.

Knol, Meta, and Pauline Terreehorst (editors), *This is America: Visies op de Amerikaanse droom*, Amsterdam: Meulenhoff, 2006.

Kompare, Derek, "Extraordinarily Ordinary: *The Osbournes* as 'An American Family'," in Susan Murray and Laurie Ouellette (editors), *Reality TV: Remaking Television Culture*, New York and London: New York University Press, 2004, 97-116.

Kooijman, Jaap, "From Elegance to Extravaganza: The Supremes on *The Ed Sullivan Show* as a Presentation of Beauty," *The Velvet Light Trap* 49 (Spring 2002): 4-17.

Kooijman, Jaap, "Bombs Bursting in Air: The Gulf War, 9/11, and the Super Bowl Performances of 'The Star-Spangled Banner' by Whitney Houston and Mariah Carey," in Ruud Janssens and Rob Kroes (editors), *Post-Cold War Europe, Post-Cold War America*, Amsterdam: VU University Press, 2004.

Kooijman, Jaap, "'Ain't No Mountain High Enough': Diana Ross as American Pop-Cultural Icon of the 1960s," in Avital Bloch and Lauri Umansky (editors), *Impossible to Hold: Women and Culture in the 1960s*, New York: New York University Press, 2005: 152-173.

Kooijman, Jaap, "Let's Make Things Better: Hyper-Americanness in Dutch Pop Culture," in Kate Delaney and Ruud Janssens, *Over (T)here: Transatlantic Essays in Honor of Rob Kroes*, Amsterdam: VU University Press, 2005, 82-95.

Kooijman, Jaap, "Michael Jackson: *Motown 25*, Pasadena Civic Auditorium, March 25, 1983," in Ian Inglis (editor), *Performance and Popular Music: History, Place and Time*, Aldershot: Ashgate, 2006, 119-127.

Kroes, Rob, *If You've Seen One, You've Seen the Mall: Europeans and American Mass Culture*, Urbana and Chicago: University of Illinois Press, 1996.

Kroes, Rob, "Advertising: the commodification of American icons," in Anne-moon van Hemel, Hans Mommaas, and Cas Smithuijsen (editors), *Trading Culture: GATT, European cultural policies and the transatlantic market*, Amsterdam: Boekman Foundation, 1996, 137-147.

Kroes, Rob, "European Anti-Americanism: What's New?," *The Journal of American History* 93:2 (September 2006): 417-431.

Kumar, Deepa, "War Propaganda and the (Ab)uses of Women: Media Constructions of the Jessica Lynch Story," *Feminist Media Studies* 4:3 (November, 2004): 297-313.

Lipset, Seymour Martin, *American Exceptionalism: A Double-Edged Sword*, New York: W.W. Norton & Company, 1996.

Lotz, Amanda D., *Redesigning Women: Television after the Network Era*, Chicago: University of Illinois Press, 2006.

Marcus, Greil, *In The Fascist Bathroom*, New York: Harvard University Press, 1993.

Mariscal, George, "In the Wake of the Gulf War: Untying the Yellow Ribbon," *Cultural Critique* 19 (Fall 1991): 97-117.

McCarthy, Anna, "Ellen: Making Queer Television History," *GLQ: A Journal of Lesbian and Gay Studies* 7:4 (2001): 593-620.

McCarthy, Kate, "Deliver Me from Nowhere: Bruce Springsteen and the Myth of the American Promised Land," in Eric Michael Mazur and Kate McCarthy (editors), *God in the Details: American Religion in Popular Culture*, New York and London: Routledge, 2001, 23-45.

McDonald, Paul, *The Star System: Hollywood and the Production of Popular Identities*, London: Wallflower Press, 2000.

Mercer, Kobena, *Welcome to the Jungle: New Positions in Black Cultural Studies*, New York and London: Routledge, 1994.

Merck, Mandy (editor), *America First: Naming the Nation in US Film*, London and New York: Routledge, 2007.

Merrin, William, *Baudrillard and the Media: A Critical Introduction*, Cambridge: Polity Press, 2005.

Miller, Toby, *Sportsex*, Philadelphia: Temple University Press, 2001.

Murdock, Graham, "Talk Shows: Democratic Debates and Tabloid Tales," in Jan Wieten, Graham Murdock, and Peter Dahlgren (editors), *Television across Europe: A Comparative Introduction*, London: Sage, 2000: 198-220.

Nantais, Cynthia, and Martha F. Lee, "Women in the United States Military: Protectors or Protected? The Case of Prisoner of War Melissa Rathbun-Nealy," *Journal of Gender Studies* 8:2 (1999): 181-191.

Norris, Christopher, *Uncritical Theory: Postmodernism, Intellectuals, and the Gulf War*, Amherst: University of Massachusetts Press, 1992.

Oldenziel, Ruth, "America made in Europe: De triomf van het Amerikaanse consumentisme," in Meta Knol and Pauline Terreehorst (editors), *This is America: Visies op de Amerikaanse droom*, Amsterdam: Meulenhoff, 2006, 107-115.

Osgerby, Bill, *Playboys in Paradise: Masculinity, Youth, and Leisure-style in Modern America*, New York: Berg Publishers, 2001.

Ouellette, Laurie, and Justin Lewis, "Moving Beyond the 'Vast Wasteland': Cultural Policy and Television in the United States," in Robert C. Allen and Annette Hill (editors), *The Television Studies Reader*, London and New York: Routledge, 2004, 52-65.

Palmer, Gareth, "Bruce Springsteen and Masculinity," in Sheila Whitely (editor), *Sexing the Groove: Popular Music and Gender*, London and New York: Routledge, 1997, 100-117.

Parry-Giles, Trevor, and Shawn J. Parry-Giles, *The Prime-Time Presidency: The West Wing and U.S. Nationalism*, Urbana and Chicago: University of Illinois Press, 2006.

Patton, Tracey Owens, "Ally McBeal and Her Homies: The Reification of White Stereotypes of the Other" *Journal of Black Studies* 32:2 (November 2001): 229-260.

Pells, Richard, *Not Like Us: How Europeans Have Loved, Hated, and Transformed American Culture Since World War II*, New York: Basic Books, 1997.

Pendergrast, Mark, *For God, Country, and Coca-Cola: The Definitive History of the Great American Soft Drink and the Company That Makes It*, second edition, New York: Basic Books, 2000.

Pfeil, Fred, *White Guys: Studies in Postmodern Domination and Difference*, New York: Verso, 1995.

Price, Sally, *Primitive Art in Civilized Places*, second edition, Chicago and London: University of Chicago Press, 2001.

Puar, Jasbir K., and Amit S. Rai, "Monster, Terrorist, Fag: The War on Terrorism and the Production of Docile Patriots," *Social Text* 72, 20:3 (Fall 2002): 117-148.

Rabinovitz, Lauren, "Soap Opera Woes: Genre, Gender, and the Persian Gulf War," in Susan Jeffords and Lauren Rabinovitz (editors), *Seeing Through the Media: The Persian Gulf War*, New Brunswick, New Jersey: Rutgers University Press, 1994, 190-201.

Ramet, Sabrina P., and Gordana P. Crnković (editors), *KAZAAAM! SPLAT! PLOOF! The American Impact on European Popular Culture since 1945*, Lanham and New York: Rowman & Littlefield, 2003.

Ritzer, George, *The McDonaldization of Society: Revised New Century Edition*, Thousand Oaks, London, and New Delhi: Pine Forge Press, 2004.

Ritzer, George, and Michael Ryan, "Americanisation, McDonaldisation and Globalisation," in Neil Campbell, Jude Davies, and George McKay (editors), *Issues in Americanisation and Culture*, Edinburgh: Edinburgh University Press, 2004, 41-60.

Rollins, Peter C., and John E. O'Connor (editors), *The West Wing: The American Presidency as Television Drama*, Syracuse: Syracuse University Press, 2003.

Rose, Tricia, *Black Noise: Rap Music and Black Culture in Contemporary America*, Middletown: Wesleyan University Press, 1994.

Rowe, John Carlos, "Culture, US Imperialism, and Globalization," *American Literary History* 16:4 (Winter 2004): 575-595.

Scheffer, Paul, *Het land van aankomst*, Amsterdam: De Bezige Bij, 2007.

Shattuc, Jane M., "The Oprahification of America: Talk Shows and the Public Sphere," in Mary Beth Haralovich and Lauren Rabinovitz (editors), *Television, History, and American Culture: Feminist Critical Essays*, Durham/London: Duke University Press, 1999: 168-180.

Shohat, Ella, and Robert Stam, *Unthinking Eurocentrism: Multiculturalism and the Media*, London and New York, Routledge, 1994.

Shuker, Roy, *Understanding Popular Music*, second edition, London and New York: Routledge, 2001.

Spigel, Lynn, "Entertainment Wars: Television Culture after 9/11," *American Quarterly* 56:2 (June 2004): 235-270.

Stam, Robert, "Mobilizing Fictions: The Gulf War, the Media, and the Recruitment of the Spectator," *Public Culture* 4:2 (Spring 1992): 101-126.

Swofford, Anthony, *Jarhead: A Soldier's Story of Modern War*, London: Scribner, 2003.

Tate, Greg, *Flyboy in the Buttermilk: Essays on Contemporary America*, New York: Simon & Schuster, 1992.

Tate, Greg (editor), *Everything But the Burden: What White People Are Taking from Black Culture*, New York: Harlem Moon, 2003.

Tomlinson, John, *Globalization and Culture*, Chicago: University of Chicago Press, 1999.

Veer, Peter van der, "Pim Fortuyn, Theo van Gogh, and the Politics of Tolerance in the Netherlands," *Public Culture* 18:1 (Winter 2006): 111-124.

Verhagen, Frans, *The American Way: Wat wij kunnen leren van het meest succesvolle immigratieland*, Amsterdam: Nieuw Amsterdam, 2006.

Vink, Maarten P., "Dutch 'Multiculturalism' Beyond the Pillarisation Myth," *Political Studies Review* 5 (September 2007): 337-350.

Wagnleitner, Reinhold, *Coca-Colonization and the Cold War: The Cultural Mission of the United States in Austria after the Second World War*, translated by Diana M. Wolf, Chapel Hill: University of North Carolina Press, 1994.

Wallace, Michelle, *Invisibility Blues: From Pop to Theory*, London and New York: Verso, 1990.

Weber, Cynthia, *Imagining America at War: Morality, Politics, and Film*, London and New York: Routledge, 2006.

Wenders, Wim, *Emotion Pictures*, London: Faber and Faber, 1986.

Wenner, Lawrence, "The Super Bowl Pregame Show: Cultural Fantasies and Political Subtext," in Lawrence Wenner (editor), *Media, Sports, and Society*, Newbury Park: Sage, 1989, 157-179.

Wermuth, Mir, "Rap in the Low Countries: Global Dichotomies on a National Scale," in Toni Mitchell (editor), *Global Noise: Rap and Hip-Hop Outside the USA*, Middletown: Wesleyan University Press, 2002, 149-170.

Willis, Susan, "Old Glory," in Stanley Hauerwas and Frank Lentricchia (editors), *Dissent From the Homeland: Essays after September 11*, Durham and London: Duke University Press, 2003, 121-130.

Wilson, Sherryl, *Oprah, Celebrity and Formations of Self*, New York: Palgrave McMillan, 2003.

Žižek, Slavoj, *Welcome to the Desert of the Real!: Five Essays on September 11 and Related Dates*, London and New York: Verso, 2002.

Žižek, Slavoj, "Welcome to the Desert of the Real!," in Stanley Hauerwas and Frank Lentricchia (editors), *Dissent From the Homeland: Essays after September 11*, Durham and London: Duke University Press, 2003, 131-135.

Zwagerman, Joost, "Met de vrije slag: Van 'This is not America' tot 'I'm an American'," in Meta Knol and Pauline Terreehorst (editors), *This is America: Visies op de Amerikaanse droom*, Amsterdam: Meulenhoff, 2006, 83-90.

Index

06/05 124, 126, 140
50 Cent 115, 130
7th Heaven 66
9/11-9, 15-17, 19, 41-67, 76-83, 89-90, 94,
  96, 119-124, 127, 132-136, 139, 143-
  144, 147-148, 152-153, 155-157, 160

A
Absolute fake, the 10, 16-17, 19, 94, 98-100,
  144
Abu Ghraib 93
AC/DC 86
Adam's Family 104, 107, 110
Addams Family, the 107
Adorno, Theodor 11
Adrenaline 108
Advertising 12, 15, 22, 32-34, 39-40, 70,
  76-77, 83, 141-142
AIDS 65
Akon 113
Ali, Muhammad 95
Ali B 16, 94, 100, 112-116, 123, 132, 160
Allach, Mohammad 133
All Stars 109
Ally McBeal 15, 41-42, 46, 53, 58-62, 66,
  153-155
"Always on My Mind" 93
"America the Beautiful" 77
American Beauty 142
American Dream 24, 26-27, 30, 32, 40, 44,
  48, 52, 71, 88, 90, 95, 100-102, 104-111,
  114-116, 132-133, 140-143
American exceptionalism 43, 45, 51-52, 58,
  66, 158
American Family 22, 66, 159
American flag 31, 45, 49, 69, 75-83, 119,
  150
American foreign policy 19, 50, 63, 77
American ideology 28, 37, 45, 48

American Idol 19, 27, 73
American I never was, the 16, 94, 96, 100,
  101, 116, 143, 145
Americanization 10-18, 20-22, 35, 39, 47,
  99-101, 119, 122, 128, 139, 141, 143-
  144, 149, 151, 159
American Music Awards 22
American President, the 53
American Psycho 142
"America the Beautiful" 38
Anderson, Benedict 15, 41-43, 120, 122,
  152-153
Andrew Sisters, the 104
Ang, Ien 47, 154
Angelou, Maya 39
Ansary, Tamim 55, 154
Anti-Americanism 62-63, 94, 95, 100, 151,
  153, 156, 158-159
Antonia 97, 158-159
Apocalypse Now 86
Arnoldussen, Paul 19, 148
Arsenio Hall Show, the 39
Artforum magazine 32
Asgedom, Mawi 52
Ashford & Simpson 38
Atta, Mohammed 135, 161
"At Your Service" 125-126
Avant Garde magazine 106

B
Bacharach, Burt 126
Bal, Mieke 17, 148
Balkenende, Jan Peter 112
Bananarama 23
Band Aid 22, 23, 24, 25, 37, 40, 149
Barend & Van Dorp 104
Barr, Roseanne 67, 73
Barthes, Roland 15, 68-70, 74, 83, 155
Barthesian myth 68, 71, 74, 80, 82, 143

Baseball 31, 44, 67
Batman and Robin 95
Battle, Kathleen 38
Baudrillard, Jean 15, 17-18, 68, 70-72, 76, 84-90, 93, 98-100, 142-144, 148, 155-159, 162
Bauers, de 107
Baywatch 105
Beach Boys, the 86
Beacon of Freedom and Democracy 66, 101, 143
Beacon of Freedom and Opportunity 51
"Beat It" 26, 31
Beatrix, Queen 103, 104, 115
Beau Monde magazine 106
Beetje Verliefd, 'n 123, 138
Benjamin, Daniel 63, 64
Bennett, Tony 101
Berlant, Lauren 57
Berlin, Irvin 44
Berlusconi, Silvio 125
Big Brother 13
Billboard's charts 76, 77
bin Laden, Osama 44, 135
Black Hawk Down 83
Blue jeans 14, 31
BNN Family 110
Bokma, Pierre 110
Bolton, Michael 38
Bombardment of signs 17, 142
Bon Jovi, Jon 106
Bono (U2) 23, 65, 143
Boonstra, Cor 141
Boorstin, David 70
"Born in the USA" 26, 31
Born in the USA 26, 30, 105, 150
Borsato, Marco 115
Boston Public 66
Boy George 23
Bradaz 123
Brainpower 123
"Break on Through" 86
Breitz, Candice 95
Breskin, David 29, 150, 151
Brown, James 95

Bryman, Alan 14, 148
Burger King 14
Burleson, Stanley 133
Buruma, Ian 125, 161
Buscemi, Steve 111
Bush, George H.W. 67, 70, 85
Bush, George W. 19, 31, 44-46, 48-49, 54, 62, 66-68, 78, 80, 93-94, 119, 129, 143, 151, 155, 160
Bush, Laura 49

C
Caldicott, Helen 64
"Candle in the Wind" 126
"Can't Do Nuttin' for Ya Man" 87
Capitalism 12, 35
Carey, Mariah 15, 19, 67, 77-79, 82-83, 90, 148
Carousel 103
Centraal Museum Utrecht 95
Charles, Ray 22, 26, 33, 38, 150
Cher 73, 106
Christmas 22-24, 26, 40, 58-62
Civil rights movement 38
Clash of civilizations 119, 136
Clay, Tom 126
Clinton, Bill 38, 39, 54, 101, 104, 152
Clooney, George 84, 85
CNN (Cable News Network) 34, 155
Coca-Cola 21, 22, 33-36, 39, 95, 98, 151-152
Coca-Colonization 32, 34, 35, 151
Cold War 19, 35, 148, 151
Collins, Joan 132
Colombani, Jean-Marie 43
Communism 35, 152
Consumerism 22, 40, 48-49, 76, 77, 136
Coppola, Francis Ford 86
Costa! 108, 109
Courage under Fire 83
Crash 137
Cultural appropriation 10-13, 16, 18, 36, 93, 94, 99-101, 116-117, 123, 128, 134, 141, 143-145, 157
Cultural imperialism 11-13, 18, 35, 100, 117, 122, 139

Curry, Adam 16, 94, 100, 104-108, 116

D
Davies, Jude 85, 147, 157
Degeneres, Ellen 45, 153
Delivery, the 108, 159
Democracy 18, 21, 35-37, 40, 44-46, 50,
    55-58, 66, 85, 125
Democratic National Convention 73
Denotation / connotation 68
Desert of the real, the 89
Desperate Housewives 131
Diamond, Neil 101
Diana, Princess 125-126
Dion 126
Dion, Celine 44
Dirty Dancing 105, 109
Disney 22, 95, 105, 149
Disneyfication 14
Disneyland / Disney World 14, 98
Dixie Chicks, the 15, 67, 77, 80-83, 90
Docile patriot 57, 66
Domestic Disturbance 51
Do Not Disturb 108
Doors, the 86
"Do They Know It's Christmas? (Feed the
    World)" 22-26, 40
Douglas, Michael 53, 156
Down / The Shaft 108
Dr. Dre. 130
Dr. Phil 46-47, 49, 51, 153
Duck, Donald 119
Dunya & Desie 123
Dutch Dream 16, 114-115, 120, 131-134,
    139-140
Dutchness 94, 116, 121-122, 124, 129, 139
Dyer, Richard 11, 18, 27, 100, 107, 147-149,
    159, 161
Dylan, Bob 22, 26
Dynasty 107, 132

E
E-Life 102
Ebony magazine 29
Eco, Umberto 10, 16-19, 94, 98-99, 143-
    144, 147-148, 159, 162

Edin, Salah 130-131, 139-140, 161
Education of Max Bickford, the 66
Ellis, Bret Easton 111
Ellis in Glamourland 131
Elsaesser, Thomas 16, 18, 25, 40, 42-43, 94,
    96-97, 100, 108, 123-124, 135, 144, 148-
    149, 152, 153, 158, 159, 161, 162
Emmy Awards 45
Engine of global hegemony 18, 21, 40
Entertainment 11-12, 17-19, 24, 29, 42, 47-
    49, 54, 70, 83, 96, 111, 138, 150
Expedition Robinson 13

F
Fahrenheit 9/11 90
Federal Communication Commission
    (FCC) 82
Feliciano, José 73
"Fight the Power" 87, 112
Filmkrant, de 110, 159, 162
Finest Hour, the 83
Firefighters (heroes of 9/11) 49, 51, 53,
    60-61, 80, 90
Fleetwood Mac 39
Flockhart, Calista 58
Fluck, Winfried 98, 159
Focus 130
"Fok de Macht" 112
Fonda, Jane 34, 150
Fortuyn, Pim 16-17, 120, 122-127, 129-
    130, 132-133, 139-140, 144, 160-161
Four Freedoms 9, 44
Fox News Network 44, 78, 79
Franklin, Aretha 38, 73, 107
Franklin, Thomas 80
Freedom 9, 18, 21-22, 35-37, 40, 44-46,
    50-53, 55-58, 66, 81, 83-85, 119, 127,
    129-130, 143
Frith, Simon 25, 149
Fuchs, Cynthia 85, 150, 157
"Fuck tha Police" 112

G
Gable, Clark 105
Gabler, Neil 70, 155

Gangsta rap 113, 115-116, 130, 139
Garman, Bryan 30, 149, 150
Gaye, Marvin 73
Geldof, Bob 23, 24, 37
Gerges, Fawaz 63
Get Rich or Die Tryin' 115
"Ghetto" 113
Gibson, Debbie 38
Globalization 11-15, 21-22, 34, 40
Global pop culture 12-13, 21, 35, 40, 142, 143, 145
"God Bless America" 38, 44, 75
"God Bless the USA" 87
Goede Tijden, Slechte Tijden 110
Gogh, Theo van 16-17, 110, 119-120, 122-124, 126, 129-133, 137, 139-140, 144, 160-162
Gooische Vrouwen 131
Gore, Al 48
Gorris, Marleen 97
Graceland 101, 106
Grammy Awards 32
Grease 109
Greenwood, Lee 87
Grey, Jennifer 109
Griffith, Laetitia 133, 134
Groban, Josh 155
Groene Amsterdammer, de 19, 148, 159
Ground Zero 51, 53, 76, 80, 156
Guantànamo Bay 46, 130, 143
Guardian 71, 162
Guerrilla Girls, the 95
Gulf War, the 15-17, 19, 67-68, 70-74, 76, 82-91, 96, 148, 155-157

H

Hadley, Tony (Spandau Ballet) 23
Hall, Stuart 12, 39, 148, 152
Haoud, Touriya 133
Harris, Sam 46
Hart, William 44, 153, 157
Hasselhoff, David 105
Hasted Hunt Gallery 9
Heerdt, Albert ter 16, 109, 112, 120, 123, 134, 137, 162

Heineken 142
Heller, Dana 43, 76, 147, 152-153, 156-157
Hendrix, Jimi 73, 86
Heterogeneity, global 12, 26
"Het Land Van..." 129-131, 140
Highbrow culture 11, 95, 97, 111
Highway of Death 85
Higson, Andrew 13, 148
Hill, Faith 73
"Hilltop" Coca-Cola commercial 33, 34
Hind 133
Hip-hop 11, 21, 98, 102, 112-116, 119-120, 123, 127-131, 139-140
Hollywood 10-11, 13, 15, 18, 21-22, 24-25, 27-28, 36, 40, 43, 44, 51, 56, 68-70, 72, 83, 85, 87, 89, 90, 95-97, 105, 108-111, 116, 120, 123-125, 132, 135-140, 142-143, 148-149, 153, 157-158, 161
Homogeneity, global 12, 22, 25, 26
Horkheimer, Max 11
Horn, Trevor 23
Houston, Whitney 15, 19, 67, 73-79, 81-83, 90, 102, 148, 156
Human universalism 22-23, 25, 27, 32-35, 37-40, 45, 50-51, 140
Huntington, Samuel 119
Hurt, William 108
Hussein, Saddam 64
Hyper-Americanness 16, 94, 99-102, 116-117, 141, 144
Hyperreality 10, 15-18, 68, 70-72, 86-89, 98-99, 143-144

I

Ice Cube 84
Idols 27, 120, 121, 124, 133, 139
Ieperen, Ab van 97, 159
"I'd Like to Teach the World to Sing" 33, 151
Illouz, Eva 48, 50, 153, 154
Imagined America 10, 12, 15, 17, 27, 33, 38, 42-45, 51, 66, 68, 87, 90, 95, 99, 105-106, 119, 124, 127, 134, 139, 143-144
Imagined community 15, 41-43, 45-46, 65, 120, 122, 124, 139, 143
Indianapolis 500 73

Individualism 28, 30, 33, 37, 53
Infantile citizenship 57, 66
Ingram, James 26, 38
Interview 110-111
Irangate 96
Iraq War 41-42, 46, 50, 62-65, 67-70, 81,
    83-85, 88, 94, 96, 104, 155
"Isaac and Ishmael" 54-57, 62
Islam 46, 49, 55, 63, 122, 125, 127, 136,
    139, 162
Iwo Jima monument 79-80

J

J-Lo (Jennifer Lopez) 112
Jackson, Janet 73
Jackson, Michael 22, 26-32, 38, 82, 88,
    149-150, 157
Jackson 5, the 29
Jacott, Ruth 133
Jarhead 15, 68, 72, 83-87, 90, 157
Jarreau, Al 29
Jazz 11
JFK 124-126
JK 121
Joel, Billy 22-24, 32, 73, 151
John, Elton 126, 149
Johnson, Ken 9, 147
Joling, Gerard 125-127, 139, 140
Jones, Quincy 22, 29, 33, 38
Jonze, Spike 84

K

Karaoke Americanism 16, 19, 94, 100, 116-
    117, 120-122, 124, 127, 139, 144
Keeley, Yvonne 105
Keitel, Harvey 90
Keith, Toby 44, 126
Kelder, Jort 134
Kellner, Douglas 78, 156
Kennedy, John F. 120, 124-127, 139, 161
Kennedy, Robert 126
Kerry, John 19, 150
Keulemans, Chris 16, 94-96, 148, 158
Kevin Masters 102
Kicks 120, 137-139

King, Jr., Martin Luther 126
KLM Royal Dutch Airlines 142
Knowles, Beyoncé 15, 68, 77, 80-83, 90
Kool & the Gang 23
Koolhoven, Martin 109, 115, 123, 138
Kopspijkers 93
Kroes, Rob 11, 13, 18, 77, 94-96, 99, 142,
    147-148, 151, 153, 156, 158-162
Kroon, Hans 97, 159
Kubrick, Stanley 86
"Kutmarokkanen??!" 127-128, 131
Kyoto Protocol 93

L

Land of Freedom and Opportunity, the 45
Lange Frans & Baas B 123, 129, 131, 139-
    140
Las Vegas 98, 101-103, 116
Late Show with David Letterman 102
Lauper, Cyndi 22, 32
Law & Order 53
LBJ Library 98
Lek 109
Lewinsky, Monica 54
Lewis, Huey 26
Libération 71
Life magazine 29
LINDA. magazine 16, 114, 120, 131-134,
    139-140, 161
Live Aid 37, 152
Loggins, Kenny 29
Los Angeles riots of 1992 88
Lotz, Amanda 66, 154, 155
Lowbrow culture 11, 97, 111
Lowe, Rob 83
Luyn, Thomas van 93
Lynch, Jessica 69-70, 91, 155

M

Màxima, Princess 103
Maas, Dick 108-109
Madame Tussauds 80, 112
Madonna 27, 105-106
Manhattan Purchase Act, the 98
Manifest Destiny 43

Marcus, Greil 22, 32-34, 151
Martini 62
Marx, Karl 30
Marx, Richard 61
Matrix, the 89, 157
McDonald's 14, 98
McDonaldization 14, 148
Mecca-Cola 36, 152
Mercer, Kobena 30, 150
Mergen, Bernard 19, 148
Meritocracy 27-28, 32, 40, 52-53, 108, 114, 133
Michael, George (Wham!) 23
Mik, Aernout 95
Miller, Judith 50
Miller, Sienna 111
Miller, Toby 73
Minority Report 83
Mohammed B. 119, 129-131
Mol, Linda de 114-115, 131-134
Moloney, Janel 54
Monde, le 43, 94, 159
Monroe, Marilyn 27, 105, 110-111, 126
Moore, Michael 63, 90
Motown 24, 29, 121, 126, 149
MTV (Music Television Channel) 26, 104-109, 112, 131, 160
Multicultural drama, the 122-123, 138
Multiculturalism 16, 23, 26, 34, 37-38, 40, 51, 114, 116, 120, 122-123, 132, 134, 136, 138-140
Murdock, Graham 47, 154
Music video 15-16, 22-24, 26-28, 38, 61, 94, 100, 112-114, 128-130, 142
Muslim fundamentalism 50, 55, 57, 62, 122

N
N.W.A. (Niggaz with Attitude) 112
Naidu, Ajay 55
Najib en Julia 123
Nation-state USA 10, 15-17, 24, 30, 38, 42-45, 56, 58, 65-66, 68, 76-77, 80, 83, 85, 87, 90, 95, 96, 119, 124, 139, 142-144
Nationalism 73, 76
National soccer team, Dutch 103, 121, 129

Nelson, Willie 22, 24
New Seekers, the 33, 151
Newsweek magazine 69
New Yorker, the 123, 161
New York Fire Department 60, 61, 80
New York Police Department 60, 61
New York Times, the 9, 50, 137, 147, 153, 162
NFL (National Football League) 78, 82
"Nine One One" 58-59, 62
Noonan, Peggy 64-65
No Planes, No Trains 110
Norris, Christopher 72, 156
NYDP Blue 53

O
O'Neill, John P. 90
Oaïssa, Mimoun 133, 135-137, 162
Oerlemans, Reinout 121
Oesters van Nam Kee 110
Olaf, Erwin 9-10, 142-143, 147
Olivier, Laurence 110
Olympic Games 34, 73, 103
O magazine 132
"One Moment in Time" 102, 103
Operation Desert Storm 67, 71, 84
Opposites, the 112
Oprah.com website 52, 63
Oprahification 41, 47, 65
Oprah's Book Club 41, 48, 154
Oprah Winfrey Show, the 15, 41-42, 46-58, 62-66, 81, 153-154
Osbournes, the 107, 159
Otazu, Rodrigo 133
Oudkerk, Rob 127
Ouellette, Laurie 47, 154, 159
Oval Office. the 98

P
Paay, Patricia 16, 94, 100, 104-108, 110, 116, 159
Pace, Peter 81
Palmer, Gareth 30, 149
Paris Match 68-69, 74
Pastiche 9, 43, 101, 122, 147

Path to 9/11, the 90
Patriot Act, the 45, 143
Patriotism 30, 49, 51, 66-68, 73-78, 80, 82-83, 87, 103-104, 120, 142
Patty's Posse 107, 110
Pauw & Witteman 113
Pearl Harbor 83
Pells, Richard 18, 35-36, 147-148, 152
Pentagon 70
People magazine 69
Pepsi 21, 32-34, 37, 40, 152
Peterson, Tobias 77, 156
Phileine zegt Sorry 109
Philips 141-142
Pitt, Brad 135
Playboy magazine 77, 105, 110, 159
Pollack, Kenneth 63, 64
Pop Idol 27
PopMatters website 18
Postman 123
Postman, Neil 70
Powell, Michael 82
"Power", the 87
Presley, Elvis 27, 87-88, 93, 101-102, 106
Presley, Lisa Marie 88
Price, Sally 34-35, 151
Puar, Jasbir 44, 57, 153-154
Public Enemy 87, 112

R
Racial profiling 55-57, 135
Racism 48, 52, 88, 112-113, 130, 131
Rai, Amit 44, 57, 153-154
Rain 9, 147, 154
Rambo 27, 30
Rap Around the World 112, 160
Rathbun-Nealy, Melissa 91, 158
Raymann, Jörgen 132
Raymzter 123, 127-129, 131, 135, 139, 161
Reagan, Ronald 27, 30-32, 37, 64, 125, 150-152
Redding, Otis 102
Reiné, Roel 108-109
Rhodes, Tom 102, 159
Rice, Condoleezza 63

Richie, Lionel 22, 28, 32
"Ride of the Valkyries" 86
Ritzer, George 12, 14, 147-148
Robertson, Roland 12
Rock 'n' roll 11, 128
Rockwell, Norman 9-10, 44, 147, 153
Rodney King video 87, 88, 157
Rogers, Kenny 24, 38
Rolling Stone magazine 32
Ronse, Tom 97, 159
Roos, Govert de 106
Roosevelt, Franlin D. 9, 44
Rosenthal, Joe 80
Ross, Diana 22, 28-30, 38, 44, 73, 150
Rowe, John Carlos 69-70, 155
Rules of Attraction, the 111
Ruyter, Michiel de 113, 121

S
Sachs, Tom 95
Salon.com website 55
Saturday Evening Post, the 9, 147
Saving Jessica Lynch 69
Saving Private Ryan 69
Scheffer, Paul 122, 160
Schnitzelparadijs, het 109, 115-116, 123, 138
Schuurman, Katja 16, 94, 100, 108-112, 116
Schuurmans, Daan 109
Schwarzenegger, Arnold 27, 125
Sedaka, Neil 105
Sesame Street 133
Shales, Tom 56
Shattuc, Jane 47, 153
Shell 142
Shields, Brooke 91, 154
Shohat, Ella 72, 156
Shouf Shouf 123, 138
Shouf Shouf Barakka! 137
Shouf Shouf Habibi! 16, 109, 112, 120, 123, 133-134, 136-140
Shut Up & Sing 80
Simon, Paul 24
Simons, Sylvana 132, 133
Simulacrum 17, 70, 71, 99

Sinatra, Frank 101
Sitcom (situation comedy) 67, 138
Snap! 87
Sorkin, Aaron 53, 54, 154
Sparks, Jordin 73
Spigel, Lynn 41, 45-46, 56-57, 66, 152-155
Sports 34, 72-78, 82-83, 103, 107, 132, 156
Springsteen, Bruce 22, 24, 26-33, 38, 95,
    149, 150
Stallone, Sylvester 27, 91
Stam, Robert 72, 156
Starbucks 14
Star myth 27-28, 31-32, 40, 48, 100-101,
    105, 107, 109-113, 115-116, 132, 134,
    143
Starship Troopers 83
Star Sisters, the 104
"Star-Spangled Banner", the (American
    national anthem) 15, 19, 44, 67, 73-77,
    80-83, 90, 103, 156
Sting 23
Stone, Oliver 32, 86, 90, 124-125, 151, 158
Super Bowl 15, 19, 67, 72-73, 75-80, 82, 90,
    103, 148, 156
Supremes, the 29, 150
Swayze, Patrick 109
Swofford, Anthony 68, 83-84, 86, 157

T
Taghmaoui, Saïd 88
Taliban 45, 49, 51, 56, 154
Talk show 15, 41, 47-50, 52-53, 65, 102,
    104, 113, 132, 153
Tan, Humberto 132-133
Tate, Greg 88, 150, 157, 161
Taxi Driver 95
Telegraaf, de 128
Television 10-15, 19, 21-22, 26-27, 32, 37,
    41-49, 53-58, 62, 64-72, 75, 77, 81-82,
    86-90, 93-95, 100-112, 117, 120-128,
    131-132, 136-138, 143, 153-154
Terrorism 46, 55-57, 62, 79, 130
Third Watch 53-54
Three Kings 15, 68, 72, 83-88, 90, 157
Thriller 26, 150

Thugmarokkaan (thug Moroccan) 113,
    115-116
Timberlake, Justin 73, 82
Time magazine 127
TMF (The Music Factory) 131
Top Gun 72
Top of the Pop Awards 104
Towers, Lee 16, 94, 100-103, 106, 116, 135,
    159, 161
Traïdia, Hakim 133
Travolta, John 51
Truman Show, the 89
Truth or Dare 105
Turner, Ted 34
Turner, Tina 22-24, 102, 148, 151, 155, 158,
    162
Turtles, the 107
Twin Towers 41, 55, 59, 90, 127, 135
Tyler, Steven (Aerosmith) 73

U
United 93 90
Universal logo 115
Ure, Midge 23
USA for Africa 15, 21-40, 95, 126, 142-143,
    149-150

V
Vanessa (Connie Breukhoven) 104, 107,
    126-127, 139
Vanity Fair 132
Veer, Peter van der 122, 125, 160
Verbaan, Georgina 109
Vet Hard 109
Vietnam War 31, 68, 83, 86, 157
Village Voice 88, 150, 157

W
Wagner, Richard 86
Wag the Dog 69, 70
Wahlberg, Mark 84, 88
Warhol, Andy 12
Warner Brothers 110
War on Terror, the 19, 42, 46, 94, 119, 129,
    143

FABRICATING THE ABSOLUTE FAKE

War Spin 70
Warwick, Dionne 24
Washington, Denzel 83
Washington Post, the 56
Watley, Jody 23
Watts, Naomi 108
Wayne, John 44, 87
"We Are the World" 15, 21-40, 66, 127,
    142-143
Weber, Cynthia 83, 157
*Welcome Home Heroes with Whitney
    Houston* 77
Wenders, Wim 65, 155
Wermuth, Mir 115, 160
West Side Story 95, 109
West Wing, the 15, 41-42, 46, 53-54, 57-58,
    62, 64, 66, 153-154
We Were Soldiers 83
"What the World Needs Now Is Love" 126
"When You Say Nothing At All" 126
White House 31, 53-55, 57, 150, 153-155
Willem Alexander, Crown Prince 103
Williams, Jody 64
Willis, Susan 76, 80, 156
Winfrey, Oprah 42, 46-53, 56, 58, 62-63,
    65, 132, 134, 143, 153-155, 161
Wonder, Stevie 21-24, 29-30, 33, 38
World Series 73
World Trade Center 90

Y
Yes-R 113, 138
Yorin FM 126
"You'll Never Walk Alone" 46, 101, 103
Young, Paul 23

Z
"Zinloos" 129
Žižek, Slavoj 89-90, 157
Zucker, Jeff 54, 154
Zwagerman, Joost 95, 158